Solutions for the New Millennium

Race, Class, and Gender

Vernon McClean
William Paterson College

KENDALL/HUNT PUBLISHING COMPANY
4050 Westmark Drive   Dubuque, Iowa 52002

Dedication

for Freda Isaacs McClean

Contents

Introduction

Problems of race, class, and gender—undeniable social ills long entrenched in North American life—have inimical consequences for minorities, economically depressed groups, and women. It is therefore not surprising that, as we enter the twenty-first century, colleges and universities throughout the United States now require courses dealing with these problems.

Although there are several fine anthologies which examine race, class, and gender issues, few have focused on a discussion of *solutions* to such problems. This collection of essays and studies, *Solutions for the New Millennium*, is an attempt to fill the apparent void in this field's scholarship.

In North American society, it is often believed that African-Americans and other people of color are innately inferior to whites, women are naturally subordinate to men, and homosexuals are below both people of color and women. These are just three attitudinal problems related to issues of race, class, and gender. The reasons underlying these and other wrongminded attitudes are as numerous as they are diverse.

Likewise, there are many approaches which can be taken toward *neutralizing* socially pernicious attitudes and *rooting out* their destructive effects on human lives. In other words, there is no single solution to any given problem involving disharmonious ethnic interaction, socio-economic stratification, or asymmetrical relationships between the sexes.

Long-standing problems resulting from racism, classism (class inequality) and sexism cannot be eliminated merely by applying quick and easy remedies. Consequently, the articles in this anthology do not claim to offer facile and painless cure-alls to problems that are so deeply ingrained in our social fabric. Nor is this anthology analogous to a fix-it, a do-it-yourself, or a popular self-help manual.

Nevertheless, many readings contained herein do identify problems and detail specific ways of resolving (or at least mitigating) some of the most glaring inequities in the spheres of race, class, and gender relations. The articles have thus been selected with an eye toward presenting a variety of clear and direct steps that may be useful in attacking the triple evils of racism, classism, and sexism.

Solutions for the New Millennium is primarily for use by college undergraduates. The objectives of this anthology are to provide students with:

- An exposure to current theories proffered by academics, policymakers, and social commentators regarding issues of race, class, and gender, and how they intersect in contemporary American life;
- An opportunity to develop an awareness of race, class, and gender as factors that shape, and that are in turn shaped by, political economy, health care, education, religion, communication, the arts, and the family.
- A chance both to envision broad-based social change, and to assess how such change might ameliorate the problems of race, class, and gender inequities in America.

Acknowledgments

I wish to thank Lois Lyles of San Francisco State University, with whom I co-edited a previous volume on race, class, and gender. I also appreciate the support of the members of the Race and Gender Project at the William Paterson University of New Jersey who have engaged me in a long-running and rewarding dialogue about solutions for the new millennium on problems of race, class and gender.

I thank all of Kendall/Hunt, who has agreed to put our solutions into print. I also acknowledge the contributions of Freda Isaacs McClean (to whom this book is dedicated) and my brother, Arthur Raymond Moore, Jr. I am also indebted to University of the Virgin Islands librarian Cynthia Richards, who went out of her way to provide me with articles for use in this anthology; and to Provost Chernoh Sesay and Associate Vice President Nina Jemmott at William Paterson University in Wayne, New Jersey for their critical encouragement and support. This includes the many members of the faculty, staff, and students at William Paterson University who provided photographs for the cover; especially Julie Barrier, Dennis Santillo, and Mary Shine.

Finally, I must acknowledge the generosity of the publishers and scholars who have graciously permitted me to reprint their works in this volume. These articles are among the best analyses in their field and some, therefore, may have been reprinted elsewhere. (However, for the convenience of students interested in the intersection of race, class and gender, this is the first time that these articles are collected together in a single volume dealing specifically with *solutions* to such problems.)

Vernon McClean
William Paterson University
Wayne, New Jersey

There is brutality
against Blacks,
vandalism against Jews,
battering against Asians
and bashing
against Gays.
And if it...happens
to one group,
the others seem to sit
on their hands,
not realizing that
the cruelties against one
are the cruelties
against all.
And we all pay.

—Maya Angelou

Part I

Race, Class, and Gender—
Envisioning the New Millennium

In this section, the student will read about similarities (and differences) in the conceptual, theoretical, and ideological ways of grasping the issues of race, class, and gender. Moreover, the student will be presented with a brief introduction to general *solutions* for confronting the problematical issues in the new millennium.

A composite portrait of inferiorized people is first presented by analyzing the similarity of oppression between blacks, gays and Jews in "A Composite Portrait of Inferiorized People" and sexist quotes affecting women of all nationalities and religious groups, are presented in "Why we Burn: Sexism Exorcised." For example, the problem of heterosexuality is questioned in "The Heterosexual Questionnaire" as well as solutions for "Common Behavioral Patterns that Perpetuate Relations of Domination."

One unique element of this anthology is that, here, men are not depicted solely as oppressors. The anthology therefore documents the reality that problems of race, class, and gender do not simply affect people of color and women; rather, these ills afflict many men as well, including white males (a category of people often targeted as "the oppressor"—as if all white men uniformly possessed and exercised the same degree and kind of power.) This anthology attempts to integrate issues pertaining to men in their relationship with women, as well as in their relationship with each other. Hence, Part I includes "Some Effects of Sexism on Men," "Why Black Men Don't Join the Men's Movement," and "Angry White Guys for Affirmative Action."

The same fallacy about males as oppressors can be made about European-Americans, as if they can be oppressors. One butt of most jokes is Polish-americans. I therefore conclude this section with suggestions of inclusivity from "The Polish American Congress."

1

Jewish, black,
and gay people
face an alien image
purported to represent
themselves in the
wider culture.
The composite portrait
accommodatingly adjusts
in order to negatively
index the norms of
propriety, decency,
conventionality...

—Barry D. Adam

1

Composite Portrait of Inferiorized People

by Barry D. Adam

> The mythical portrait of the Jew paves the way for and adds the finishing touches to his actual oppression. It is the symbol of his oppression; its preliminaries and its crowning point: the myth justifies the oppression in advance and makes the consequences lawful.
>
> Memmi

Jewish, black, and gay people face an alien image purported to represent themselves in the wider culture. In comparing the stereotypes assigned to such outgroups as Jews in medieval Europe with blacks and gay people in America, each group seems, at first glance, uniquely characterized: lewd as greedy and rich, gay people as effeminate men or masculine women, blacks as shiftless and lustful. The complete incongruity of the stereotype to the real lives of the people to whom it is applied becomes evident with cursory observation.

The traits attributed to these groups reveal striking similarities upon closer examination. The interchangeable aspects of these images lead one to suspect the irrelevance of assigned traits to any characteristic peculiar to the people they purport to represent. In comparing stereotypes, a "portrait" of the inferiorized person draws into view. The coherence of "logic" of the stereotypes can be understood only as the artifact of the dominant majorities. The traits assigned in common to such diverse groups united only in their status as subordinated people, can be read only as symptomatic of the superordinate imagination. The common portrait retains the role of foil to ideals of health and the good. As these standards of "official reality" evolve, the composite portrait accommodatingly adjusts in order to negatively index the norms of propriety, decency, conventionality right. Official communications agents comply in propagating the product.

The composite portrait is founded on three axioms: the inferiorized are (1) a "problem," (2) all alike, and (3) recognizable as such without exception. This consistency and totality is postulated for the series of beliefs outlined in the following subsections.

They Are Animals

Inferiorization is accomplished with placement of people into subhuman categories. Medieval debates centered around the question of whether, like animals, Jews, sodomites, or savages could have souls. The sentiment is concretized in the charge: they smell! The primacy of smell

3

as a criterion of distinction from animals has been noted by Max Horkheimer and Theodor Adorno: "The multifarious nuances of the sense of smell embody the archetypal longing for the lower form of existence, for direct circumambient nature, with the earth and mud....Hence the sense of smell is considered a disgrace in civilization, the sign of lower social strata, lower races and base animals." Smell is repeatedly attributed to Jews in the Middle Ages through to the modern era. Hitler wrote in Mein Kampf of his "discovery" of Jewish smell following his reading of anti-Semitic pamphlets distributed in the streets of Vienna. References to the smell of blacks recurs frequently in North American literature.

"Brutishness" is claimed for the reputed instinctiveness and "horrific impassiveness towards suffering" in blacks. The higher passions are thought, therefore, to be excluded from their experience. Slaves were sold without regard for family ties because, it was argued, black sexuality could not include love. Psychiatric ideologies deny the possibility of love to gay people, echoing popular opinions that homosexuals are given to "mindless animal promiscuity." The subhumanity of homosexuals is imputed "scientifically" in terms of "immature," "regressive," or "atavistic" stages of development.

"Uncivilized" behavior is believed to be characteristic of all three groups. They are "unrefined, ill-mannered and unclean." They are unethical, unscrupulous, and deceitful." As perceived by white children, "Negro children are described as bad, ill-mannered, naughty, disobedient, dirty, careless, in sum everything that the white child struggles so hard not to be."

THEY ARE HYPERSEXUAL

Otto Fenichel remarks that in the ancient world, foreigners were considered sacer, a word signifying simultaneously holy and cursed. The outsiders contained by society represent a similar uneasy fusion for the majority. Minority members are suspected of special powers. The oppressor is convinced of their enormous hidden powers for vengeance. The symbol of the libidinal "underworld," the subordinated are never adequately repressed. In earlier times, witchcraft was "discovered" among them; in a secular age, these special powers become primarily sexual. The confining of sexuality to procreation and the family in "civilized" society manufactures the illusion of sexual liberation in its social foil. The subordinated are made to bear the social anxiety concerning sexual repression: "Society can conceive of no more powerful menace to its culture than would arise from the liberation of the sexual impulses." The socially privileged launch periodic campaigns against the symbols of sexuality as part of the general struggle against "vice," "lewdness," and other signs of sexuality not contained by social institutions. Yet as sexual symbols, black, Jewish, and gay people acquire an inordinate attractiveness: they are sacer as the personification of erotic ambivalence.

The early linkage of Jews with witchcraft accompanied popular mythologies of Jewish infanticide, sadism, and bloody rituals. Luther was convinced of the irresistible Jewish ability to corrupt and seduce Christians. Indeed, in medieval literature, the Jew:

> ...has monstrous sexual powers; and his sexual powers transform him into an ogre threatening the sexual life, the existence, and very soul of his helpless primordial son. Each—the Jew as much as the Devil—runs insanely about the countryside mutilating or castrating little boys and

4

leading Christian youths into vile debauchery. And each wantonly seduces or rapes beautiful Christian virgins.

Nazi ideology perpetuated the theme. The same sexual paranoia is evident in Hitler's images of Jewish "white slave traffic" and in this fantasy from Mein Kampf:

> For hours the black-haired Jew boy, diabolic joy in his face, waits in ambush for the unsuspecting girl whom he defiles with his blood and thus robs her from her people.

"Excessive sexuality" endures as a trait attributed to Jews by anti-Semites.

White fascination with black sexuality is well known. Early twentieth-century sociology generally argued that "Black" morality (read: Black sexual conduct) was hopelessly unrestrained." The fixation upon reputed black promiscuity continues with the social scientific essentialization of black problems in "family break down." Lynching was traditionally justified with the contention that "many Negroes were literally wild beasts with uncontrollable sexual passions and criminal natures stamped by heredity." The ideology of black hypersexuality was absorbed into American psychiatry. The belief materializes in the black penis, to which widespread conviction assigns a remarkable size.

Colonizers have thought colonized peoples to have a special propensity toward rape. Rape fantasies have been especially predominant in the racist ideology of the American South. The anxiety manifests itself in rape laws which prescribe death. In practice, the law is univalent. In Florida, for example, 54 percent of black men convicted of raping a white woman are executed, while no white man convicted of raping a black woman has been executed. The rape specter is summoned forth with the first signs of black restiveness. As the move to integrate public transit got under way with Martin Luther King, Jr., a leading Alabama politician charged that the main goal of the NAACP was "to open the bedroom doors of our white women to the Negro Man."

Anthropological evidence suggests that homosexual men have frequently been cast into the role of shaman or witchdoctor—a being with special powers including supernatural understanding." The high estimation of homosexual witchcraft among "primitives" is matched inversely by the pervasive fear of gay sexuality in the modern period. The assumed extraordinary sexual appetite of gay people is thought to require special prohibitory legislation in many jurisdictions. Without controls, the argument runs, the youth of the nation will be molested, if not "converted." Gay people were banned from employment in the United States' federal government in the McCarthy period, when one congressman described homosexual orgies and "palatial surroundings where these people worship at the fleshpots and cesspools of immoral sex demonstration." Eugene Levitt and Albert Klassen report that 59 percent of a nationwide United States survey agree that "homosexuals have unusually strong sex drives." "Thirty five percent agree strongly with the proposition that frustrated homosexuals seek out children for sexual purposes." Convinced that gay workers are sure to seduce fellow employees and schoolchildren, employers and school boards deny them the means to earn a living.

An axiom of psychoanthropological theory asserts that the existence of strong taboos against certain behavior implies a strong tendency or desire of a people to perform that behavior. The control measures taken to quell the hypersexuality imputed to the inferiorized conceal a symbolic countertrend. The dominated are secretly glamorized; forbidden sexuality

5

offers special "promesse de bonheur." The equation of uninhibited sensuality with blackness appears, for example, to enhance the image of black masculinity among certain male subcultures. The moral outrage which condemns gay sexuality as "too easy" or "promiscuous" conceals resentment of imputed sexual freedom.

The heightened attractiveness of black, Jewish, and gay people may be contained by a liberal, "sophisticated" society through the collective adoption of some of its members as "pets." As Hannah Arendt writes, observing turn-of-the-century French society: "They did not doubt that homosexuals were "criminals" or that Jews were "traitors"; they only revised their attitude toward crime and treason.... The role of the inverts was to show their abnormality, of the Jews to represent black magic ("necromancy"), of the artists to manifest another form of supranatural and superhuman contact.

THEY ARE HERETICS AND CONSPIRATORS

The role of Jews as heretics in Christian society is perhaps self evident. The possibility of "moral contamination" of those faithful to the established moral order provoked persistent anxiety in the medieval Church. Containment of the infidels to segregated areas of cities and close supervision of Jewish intercourse with the local population countered this threat to the "natural" order. As the fount of social evil, Jews found themselves, for example, held responsible for causing the Black Death by poisoning wells in the fourteenth century. In the secular age, heresy against the Church reemerges as heresy against the state, i.e., treason. It is no surprise that Dreyfus, the man who became the cause celebre of late nineteenth-century France, stood falsely accused of treason. The press did not hesitate to vilify all French Jews with the charge in the wake of his conviction. Treason became a stock indictment in the National Socialist barrage against the Jews. In the United States in 1950, a public survey asked people to "recognize" persons who had been accused of spying. "Scattered through the list were the names of six imaginary persons—three Jewish sounding (Max Finkelstein, Isaac Shapiro, Samuel Levinsky) and three others (Daniel Carpenter, William Brooks, Robert L. Phillips). The nonentities with non-Jewish names, taken together were remembered by 3 percent of the sample, those with Jewish names by 20 percent, or more than six times as often."

The charge of heresy, however, has been by no means the preserve of groups defined by religion. As early as 1240, an English law provided: "Those who have dealings with Jews of Jewesses, those who commit bestiality, and sodomists, are to be buried alive, after legal proof that they were taken in the act, and public conviction." Derrick Bailey speculates that the early Albigensian heresy, credited with sexual practices forbidden by the Church, established the link between heresy and sodomy. The Albigensians or "Bulgarians" became embodied in English law as "buggery." The term outlawed not only sexual relations between men (women were omitted) but included sexual relations between Christians and Jews. Sexual heretics, with other heretics, were to fall prey to the fires of the Inquisition. Modern exclusion of gay people from diplomatic service continues as a standard practice against their supposed susceptibility to treason, despite the absolute lack of evidence to support the belief. Fear of heretical influence can be detected in the modern opinion poll where

55 percent of the public agree, "Homosexuality is a social corruption that can cause the downfall of a civilization." The fear of "moral contamination" by sexual heretics is clear in this 1975 statement by Canada's largest newspaper rationalizing its censorship practices: "Advertising of homosexual organizations where the purpose of the advertising is to recruit or convert [sic], for example, promoting circulation subscriptions to periodicals which they may publish is not acceptable."

Special powers and heresy as qualities of outcast groups intersect psychologically in the fear of conspiracy. Hidden international conspiracies of Jews arise periodically in the anti-Semitic mind. Luther proclaimed: "They want to rule the world." French parliamentarians during the Dreyfus period demanded protection of French society against the takeover by an alien race. The notorious, fabricated Protocols of the Learned Elders of Zion were taken up by the Nazis to demonstrate conspiracies threatening "civilization."

Rumors of conspiracy circulated constantly among whites in Southern slave society. The rise of black militance in the United States provoked a rash of "conspiracy" trials, a charge familiar to the labor movement.

Conspiracies to subvert "culture" are attributed to the three groups. Jewish domination of the arts and press was a persistent Nazi theme. Homosexual conspiracies in the arts are "exposed" periodically. Rumors of an international conspiratorial "Homintern" circulated in the 1950s, an echo of the 1906–1908 scandal in Germany. The prejudiced person is convinced that black people are "taking over."

Dominators characterize their suppression of inferiorized groups as "defense." Paranoid hyperbolization of "secret" or mysterious "powers" and organizations summons forth the demons to be destroyed. Real people divested of even the limited powers assumed by members of privileged groups must face a formidable arsenal at the disposal of the privileged elite.

> An anti-Semite could not stand to see Jews tortured if he really saw them, if he perceived that suffering and agony in an individual life—but this is just the point: he does not see Jews suffering; he is blinded by the myth of the Jew; he tortures and murders the Jew through these concrete beings; he struggles with dream figures, and his blows strike living faces.

THEY ARE OVERVISIBLE

All three groups have a reputation for offensive flamboyance. Characterizations of these groups never fail to include claims about gregariousness and garrulousness. They are loud, pushy, aggressive, careless, extroverted. The charge is accepted by the inferiorized in an acute embarrassment which arises when they perceive their compatriots acting overvisibly. Black people report feeling uncomfortable in the presence of blacks who become "noisy and boisterous around white people." Gay men frequently practice a studied disassociation from "effeminate" men in a social setting with heterosexual onlookers. Memmi expresses the same anxiety in reference to Jews: "To dress in bright colors was Jewish. To speak too loudly, to call out, to gather in the streets was Jewish. The typified black and drag queen is "flashy" and rude. The public image insists on ugliness: the black man as gorilla, the Jew as vulture, the homosexual as "fairy" or "diesel dyke."

Stember found an overwhelming public tendency toward overestimation of the Jewish population in the United States. It is indicative of a syndrome of perceived overvisibility of the subordinated groups. Its very existence is interpreted as offensive, "too much," "obsessive," "loud," etc. Despite limited numbers, the "failure" to be totally invisible provokes the resentment of the larger society. The theme is preserved even in the legalization of homosexuality. The universal stipulation "in private" is prescribed by statutes stigmatizing visibility as "gross indecency" or "lewd and obscene conduct." The perception of the subordinated as overvisible is reminiscent of Hindu caste regulations which prescribed that an Untouchable could not raise his or her voice "because the sound of his voice falling on a caste Hindu's ear was deemed to be as polluting as his touch" or that he or she could in no way adorn himself or herself.

A final contradictory subtheme can be detected. Despite the imputation of special powers and conspiracy, of suspected megalomanic tendencies and pervasive ability to corrupt and contaminate, the inferiorized are subject to an opposing image complex in the composite portrait. They are, it seems, weak and incompetent, yet moronically cheerful. Scientific studies have repeatedly attempted to link low intelligence with inferiorized groups. Academic "proof" of Jewish stupidity was presented in 1925. The black IQ controversy rages to this day. Attempts to link homosexuality with imbecility persist. The association between male homosexuality and weakness, passivity, or incompetence pervades Western values. The social construction of homosexuality as failure is so extensive, that Lionel Ovesey identifies a "pseudohomosexual" syndrome among men who show no signs of homoeroticism, yet fear they must be homosexual. "The equation is the following: I am a failure = I am not a man = I am castrated = I am a woman = I am a homosexual." An experiment performed by T. Weissbach and G. Zagon in 1975, where a videotaped man was labeled "homosexual" to one group of viewers but not labeled to another, found that viewers indicated the "homosexual" subject to be more "weak, feminine, emotional, submissive, and unconventional."

Exclusion of the subordinated from the economic system leads to fantasies, on the one hand, of parasitism and laziness, and on the other, of cheerful carefreeness (the Sambo image).

The composite portrait of the inferiorized person functions dialectically to convince the majority of its own identity as the "good." In terms of the phenomenology of mind, "the unessential consciousness [the bondsman] is, for the master, the object which embodies the truth of his certainty of himself." Erik Erikson remarks in the same vein:

> Psychoanalysis shows that the unconscious evil identity (the composite of everything which arouses negative identification—i.e., the wish not to resemble it) consists of the images of the violated (castrated) body, the ethnic outgroup, and the exploited minority. Thus a pronounced he-man may, in his dreams and prejudices prove to be mortally afraid of ever displaying a woman's sentiments, a Negro's submissiveness, or a Jew's intellectuality.

The insight recurs to members of inferiorized groups pondering the genesis of their own identities and to their observers:

> If the Jew did not exist, then he would have to be invented. [Memmi]

The negro, then, is the white man's fear of himself. [Mannoni]

People invent categories in order to feel safe. White people invented black people to give white people identity…Straight cats invent faggots so they can sleep with them without becoming faggots themselves. [Baldwin]

Unlike [sic] other minorities, we [gay people] lie within the oppressor himself, and our very invisibility, the fact that we represent a human potential that has been realized, makes the need to draw the line against us that much sharper. [Altman]

POPULAR IDEOLOGIES

The systematic selection of negative and distorted images of inferiorized peoples by agents of cultural transmission clearly affects the wider population. Public opinion surveys reveal persistent stereotypes relatively stable both in content and over time. The image is almost universal. The study of anti-semitism by Bruno Bettelheim and Morris Janowitz found no statistically significant differences among stereotype-holders according to age, education, religious denomination, political affiliation, formal family composition, class or occupational status. Social distance scales developed from surveys in the present-day United States show residual anti-Semitism (exclusion from marriage but tolerance as neighbors or more distant social contacts); significant anitblack prejudice [exclusion from marriage or the status of "close friend" and tolerance of social contact in church and school); and great homophobia (exclusion from church, school, and neighborhood; tolerance only at community and nation level, with slightly greater tolerance of lesbians). In the latter case, "more than 80 percent prefer not to associate with them." Indeed, Levitt and Klassen found an "overwhelming objection to homosexuals' dancing with each other in public places—55 percent strongly object and nearly three-quarters have at least some objection. Nearly one half (46 percent) do not agree that homosexuals should be allowed to organize for social and recreational purposes (31 percent object strongly), and 43 percent would not permit bars serving homosexuals (27 percent feel this strongly)."

In interpersonal relations, these social distance statistics translate into a hierarchy of deference, whereby the standards of conduct of the dominant group prevail even when as few as one representative is present in a social gathering of inferiorized members. Deference expressed in demeanor and forms of address is required of the black toward the white. The presence of heterosexuals in a group of gay people tends to constrain all to observe dominant norms of linguistic and personal interaction. This resembles the linguistic stratification of Canada, where, until recently, the presence of English-speakers in a Francophone group prompted the use of English.

Hierarchy itself nurtures oppressive ideologies. Inferiority ipso facto becomes read as its own justification. "In the United States a relatively illiterate, criminal, diseased, base, poor, and prostituted colored people serves by comparison as proof to the world that Negroes do not deserve the social opportunities available to whites. The dominant ideology offers everyone a set of "rationalizations" to "explain" his or her own inferior status in terms of personal inadequacy plus "compensation" in form of symbolic superiority over some other group. Robert Lane found that among members of the working class, status tends to be accounted for in terms of "failure to continue one's education due to lack of family pressure (they should have made me), or youthful indiscretion, or the demands of the family for money, or the depression of the thirties. He speculates that "lower status people generally find it less punishing to think of themselves as correctly placed by a just society than to think of themselves as exploited, or victimized by an unjust society." Each consoles himself or herself with his or her even minimal status superiority over some other. Racism presents symbolic status to the degraded by identifying a more degraded group than one's own. Memmi delineates the psychological ground of racism of the Dominated Man: "Racism offers everyone the solution that suits him best; he need only find someone smaller, more humiliated than himself, and there he has his victim, the target for his scorn and prejudice. Racism is a pleasure within everyone's reach." This "poor man's snobbery" channels discontent away from the larger structure of oppression, toward the more oppressed. "The racist instinctively chooses the oppressed, heaping more misfortune on the unfortunate."

The modern Prince ranges his subjects upon a status hierarchy with numerous gradations to distribute subtle or symbolic values according to rank. Seeing themselves only in comparison to others in their immediate world, the subjects do not occupy themselves with the larger relations between subjects and Prince. The frustrated, the resentful, the dominated themselves fall prey to the logic of status differentiation.

The socially produced "fact" of inferiority comes to a life of its own. Inferiorized status collects devalued attributes which reinforce and legitimize the initial inequality. The salutary language of religion and medicine "assures" the victim of his or her essential depravity in the name of his or her "own good." The dominator "does not punish his victim because his victim deserves to be punished; he calls him guilty because he is already punished or, at best, because he, the accuser, is preparing to punish him."

Every act of the dominated person falls under suspicion. His virtues, if he has any, turn to vices by reason of the fact that they are his; work coming from his hands necessarily bears his stigma." The logic of oppression draws a protective cloak about itself; the dominated become locked in their very being, into the constraint structure.

**Blessed art thou,
O Lord our God
and King
of the universe,
that thou did not
create me
a woman.**

—Orthodox Jewish male

2

Why We Burn: Sexism Exorcised

by Meg Bowman

What did famous men throughout history really think of women?

One hundred women are not worth a single testicle.

Confucius (551–479 BCE)

The five worst infirmities that afflict the female are indocility, discontent, slander, jealousy, and silliness.

...Such is the stupidity of woman's character, that it is incumbent upon her, in every particular, to distrust herself and to obey her husband.

The Confucian Marriage Manual

A proper wife should be as obedient as a slave.

The female is a female by virtue of a certain lack of qualities—a natural defectiveness.

Aristotle (384–322 BCE)

In childhood a woman must be subject to her father; in youth to her husband; when her husband is dead; to her sons. A woman must *never* be free of subjugation.

If a wife has no children after eight years of marriage, she shall be banished; if all of her children are dead, she can be dismissed after ten years; and, if she produces only girls she shall be repudiated after eleven years.

The Hindu Code of Manu (c. 100 Ct.)

Among all savage beasts, none is found so harmful as woman.

St. John Chrysostom (345–407 Ct.)

Any woman who acts in such a way that she cannot give birth to as many children as she is capable of, makes herself guilty of many murders.

St. Augustine (354–430 Ct.)

Do you know that each of your women is an Eve? The sentence of God—on this sex of yours—lives in this age; the guilt must necessarily live, too. You are the gate of Hell, you are the temptress of the forbidden tree; you are the first deserter of the divine law.

Tertullian in 22 CE

Woman in her greatest perfection was made to serve and obey man, *not* rule and command him.

John Knox (1505–1572)

The souls of women are so small that some believe they've none at all.

Samuel Butler (1612–1680)

What a misfortune to be a woman! And yet, the worst misfortune is not to understand what a misfortune it is.

Kierkegaard (1813–1855)

Woman is ontologically subordinate to man.

Karl Barth

The pains that, since original sin, a mother has to suffer to give birth to her child only draw tighter the bonds that bind them, she loves it the more, the more pain it has cost her.

Pope Pius XII in 1941

It seems to me that nearly every woman I know wants a man who knows how to love with authority. Women are simple souls who like simple things, and one of the simplest is one of the simplest to give....Our family airedale will come clear across the yard for one pat on the head. The average wife is like that. She will come across town, across the house, across the room, across to your point of view, and across almost anything to give you her love if you offer her yours with some honest approval.

Dr. C.W. Shedd, Presbyterian Minister in Houston, TX since 1955 wrote this advice "Letters on How to Treat a Woman" (1968).

You must lean and adapt yourselves to your husbands. The husband is the head of the wife.

St. Paul

Let a woman learn in silence with all submissiveness. I permit no woman to teach or to have authority over men; she is to keep silent...Yet women will be saved through bearing children....

I Timothy 2:11–15

Let us set our women folk on the road to goodness by teaching them…to display…submissiveness…Every woman should be overwhelmed with shame at the thought that she is a woman.

St. Clement of Alexandria in 96 C. E.

In the year 584, in Lyons, France, forth-three Catholic bishops and twenty men representing other bishops, held a most peculiar debate: "Are Women Human?" After many lengthy arguments, a vote was taken. The results were: thirty-two, yes; thirty-one, no. Women were declared human by *one vote!*

Council of Macon

Men are superior to women.

The Koran (c. 650 CE)

Blessed art thou, O Lord our God and King of the universe, that thou didst not create me a woman.

Daily prayer, still used today, of the Orthodox Jewish male

If…the tokens of virginity are not found in the young woman, then they shall bring out the young woman to the door of her father's house, and the men of her city shall stone her to death with stones because she has wrought folly…so you shall purge the evil from the midst of you.

Deuteronymy 22:20–21

To the woman he said, I will greatly multiply your pain in childbearing; in pain you shall bring forth children, yet your desire shall be for your husband, and he shall rule over you.

Genesis 3:16. In 1847, a scandal resulted when British obstetrician, Dr. Simpson, used chloroform as an anesthetic in delivering a baby. The holy men of the Church of England prohibited the use of anesthetic in childbirth, citing this quote.

Women should remain at home, sit still, keep house, and bear and bring up children.

If a woman grows weary and, at last, dies from childbearing, it matters not. Let her die from bearing; she is there to do it.

Martin Luther (1483–1546)

Why do you insist on flaunting your heterosexuality? Can't you just be who you are and keep it quiet?

—M. Rochlin

3

The Heterosexual Questionnaire

by M. Rochlin

1. What do you think caused your heterosexuality?

2. When and how did you decide you were a heterosexual?

3. Is it possible that your heterosexuality is just a phase you may grow out of?

4. Is it possible that your heterosexuality stems from a neurotic fear of others of the same sex?

5. If you have never slept with a person of the same sex is it possible that all you need is a good Gay lover?

6. Do your parents know that you are straight? Do your friends and/or roommates know? How did they react?

7. Why do you insist on flaunting your heterosexuality? Can't you just be who you are and keep it quiet?

8. Why do heterosexuals place so much emphasis on sex?

9. Why do heterosexuals feel compelled to seduce others into their lifestyle?

10. A disproportionate majority of child molesters are heterosexual. Do you consider it safe to expose children to heterosexual teachers?

11. Just what do men and women do in bed together? How can they truly know how to please each other being so anatomically different?

12. With all the societal support marriage receives the divorce rate is spiraling. Why are there so few stable relationships among heterosexuals?

13. Statistics show that lesbians have the lowest incidence of sexually transmitted diseases. Is it really safe for a woman to maintain a heterosexual lifestyle and run the risk of disease and pregnancy?

14. How can you become a whole person if you limit yourself to compulsive, exclusive heterosexuality?

15. Considering the menace of overpopulation how could the human race survive if everyone were heterosexual?

16. Could you trust a heterosexual therapist to be objective? Don't you feel s/he might be inclined to influence you in the direction of her/his own leanings?

17. There seem to be very few happy heterosexuals. Techniques have been developed that might enable you to change if you really want to. Have you considered trying aversion therapy?

18. Would you want your child to be heterosexual, knowing the problems that s/he would face?

**Power differences
are expressed
in institutional
and cultural contexts
which form the basis
of interpersonal
relationships.**

—Margo Adair & Sharon Howell

4

Common Behavioral Patterns that Perpetuate Relations of Domination

by Margo Adair & Sharon Howell

Power is the ability to do—the more access to resources one has, the more options one has. Power differences are expressed in institutional and cultural contexts which form the basis of our interpersonal relationships. The following patterns are common ways people learn to interact in order to protect themselves in a hierarchical society. To not conform to expected behavior risks social ostracism or one's survival. (These are relational patterns and are to be read horizontally.)

an individual from the...

an individual from the...

DOMINANT GROUP

Defines parameters, judges what is appropriate, patronizes.

Is seen as, and feels, capable of making constructive changes.

Assumes responsibility for keeping system on course. Acts unilaterally.

Self-image of superiority, competence, in control, entitled, correct.

Presumptuous, does not listen, interrupts, raises voice, bullies, threatens violence, becomes violent.

Seeks to stand out as special.

OPPRESSED GROUP

Feels inappropriate, awkward, doesn't trust own perception, looks to expert for definition.

Is seen as, and feels, disruptive.

Blames self for not having capacity to change situation.

Self-image of inferiority, incompetent, being controlled, not entitled, low self-esteem.

Finds it difficult to speak up, timid, tries to please. Holds back anger, resentment, and rage.

Feels secure in background, feels vulnerable when singled out.

Assumes anything is possible, can do whatever one wants, assumes everyone else can too. Does not acknowledge constraints in current situations.	Feels confined by circumstances, limits aspirations. Sees current situations in terms of past constraints.
Initiates, manages, plans, projects.	Lacks initiative, responds, deals, copes, survives.
Sees problems and situations in personal terms.	Sees problems in social context, results of system, "them."
Sees experiences and feelings as unique, feels disconnected, often needs to verbalize feelings.	Sees experiences and feelings as collectively understood and shared. No point in talking about them.
Sees solutions to problems as promoting better feelings.	Sees solutions to problems in actions that change conditions.
Thinks own view of reality is only one, obvious to all, assumes everyone agrees with their view. Disagreements are result of lack of information, misunderstandings, and/or personalities.	Always aware of at least two views of reality, their own and that of the dominant group.
Views self as logical, rational. Sees others as too emotional, out of control.	Often thinks own feelings are inappropriate, a sign of inadequacy.
Believes certain kinds of work below their dignity.	Believes certain kinds of work beyond their ability.
Does not believe or trust ability of others to provide leadership.	Does not believe has capacity for leading.
Unaware of hypocrisy, contradictions.	Sees contradictions, irony, hypocrisy.
Fears losing control, public embarrassment.	Laughs at self and others. Sees humor as way of dealing with hypocrisy.
Regards own culture as civilized, regards other's as underdeveloped, disadvantaged. Turns to other's culture to enrich humanity while invalidating it by calling it exotic.	Feels own culture devalued. Uses cultural forms to influence situation. Humor, music, poetry, etc. to celebrate collective experience and community. Sees these forms as being stolen.

Men hurt themselves and other men through: competition...scorn or embarrassment towards other men, working too hard... not seeking support.

—Robert Heasley

5

Some Effects of Sexism on Men

by Robert Heasley

Internalized oppression: Men hurt themselves and other men through: competition, attacking male leaders, scorn or embarrassment towards other men, working too hard (and allowing others to insist we work too hard); drugs; going off by ourselves when we feel bad, not seeking support; etc.

Isolation: Tendency to live with notion that help isn't possible or even desirable; dismiss as "sissy" those who seek help, talk about feelings, express concern for others.

Despair: Men have given up on the notion that we matter by virtue of just being; in order to be accepted, some "performance" must occur, some external acknowledgement of success, some form of recognition; too often men feel that what they accomplish is not enough and must do more at the expense of inner peace and quality in their relationships.

Desperation: Men's isolation can lead to feeling a sense of urgency about relationships, when we get a glimpse that things could be less isolated, we act in desperation—"I finally found her!" "I've got to have her" etc. and out of the extremes of that desperation, men rape, batter, assault (both women and other men) when their desperate expectations aren't met.

Numbness: As a result of not having our feelings paid attention to as young ones, or having been encouraged to keep doing (playing harder, working harder) when we really needed to express our feelings, we've become numb. We separate from our feelings so that we can continue to function, and in the process we lose the ability to hear other's feelings except as signs of other's weakness and our need to "rescue" or to "run".

Inability to think well about ourselves: Expectations to perform, to earn a living, to support others, force us into situations where we ourselves are not necessarily doing what we really want, what is good for us, etc. We don't take good care of our health, often don't eat well, etc.

Vulnerability to addictions: We are often numb, but when we are in touch with our feelings, we often don't have access to expressing them, and so turn to drugs, food and activity in addictive ways as a means of further numbing ourselves.

Pretense: It rarely feels safe to level about our feelings. Also, fear of criticism or rejection will often lead us to hide how difficult certain things are. We are reticent to own mistakes in work, relationships, etc., for fear that if we fail, we are failures all the way through.

Fear of Intimacy: While we desperately want closeness, we are also afraid to show how terrible it sometimes feels, for fear of rejection, or fear that someone will have power over us because they know our needs. So we hold back, don't communicate, appear to "have it all together."

Competition: One consequence of the competition we are raised with is an urge to always seek to be the best, and see relationships and activities as opportunities for competition, for winning or losing, and miss the awareness of satisfaction that relationships built of cooperation, love, mutuality, etc. can have.

Attacking leadership: While this is common to any group that experiences any form of oppression, it is particularly likely to come up between men because of male socialization. Men are disappointed easily (many of us experience this in our relationship with our fathers and male friends, where living up to their standards can sometimes seem impossible—and often is!). we can become even more critical when someone comes close to offering what we desperately want—it is partly our hope in someone that directs our disappointment at him.

Fear of Change: Fear of change is common to all humans, but for men in American society who have been raised where men generally are granted privilege over women, simply for being men, it can be extremely difficult to look at life through other people's eyes, and to imagine that change is desirable, or that change will be safe. Males are raised more rigidly in our society, raised to not change, not be different from the idealized way to be masculine, thus, when confronted with the need and opportunity to change, men are more likely to resist, find fault with leaders, look for ways to argue against change, etc., when though such arguments are not rational.

Acting out Against Others: To assume others to be enemies; to pursue relationships as opportunities for conquest, sexual, financial, status, etc.; to develop the perception that manipulation is the basis of relationships.

**Without ranking level
or degree
of oppression,
we must admit
that as black men
we are more oppressed
because we are *black*
rather than because
we are *men.*

—Vernon McClean

6

Why Black Men Don't Join the Men's Movement

by Vernon McClean

As W.E.B. DuBois pointed out, the black man in America is constantly confronted by a conflict between his two parts: to be an American and yet to be African, to be white and yet to be black. Men of color seem to be at war with themselves wanting to be both American and African, both white and black, both men of color and men of pale face. When I attend men's gatherings, it is quite usual for mine to be the only black face in the room (although I will occasionally be joined by Jesse, another black member of NOMAS). Moreover, the absence of Hispanic faces, as well as Asian, Native American, and Arabic ones, is equally striking.

Because of the existence of racism, black women went through the same problem when joining the feminist movements. Women like Belle Hooks were always in the minority, and the man of color today finds himself in the same predicament. The question is: Why do men of color not join predominantly white male organizations?

Without ranking level or degree of oppression, we must admit that as black men we are more oppressed because we are *black* rather than because we are *men*. This, I believe, is also true of other men of color. Therefore, most of our energies are spent fighting racism, rather than combatting the oppressive conditions of being male in American society. Moreover, much of male oppression is imposed not so much by society as by individuals; many times this oppression is by white men toward men of color.

So a second reason why so few men of color join NOMAS and other white, male-oriented (and male-dominated) groups is that justly, legitimately, we view the white man as our *enemy* and not our *brother*. And since most of the enemies of people of color are in fact white males, there is a third reason why few of us are members of NOMAS: the hard facts of economic reality. If one looks around the room at the annual conference on Men and Masculinity, the vast majority of the men there not only are white, but also do not share the socio-economic status of most men of color in this country. Hence, beyond the commonality of a penis, we have little to talk about.

Yet another reason for the absence of men of color is due to the warped sense of masculinity of many men of color and many white men of a lower socio-economic status. White working class males, when asked, repeatedly respond that if they have a problem they retreat to the neighborhood bar, share a drink with their "buddies," and rap about the difficulty. They claim that they need neither a men's group nor a male support group. Men of color, and white working class males, because of our economic oppression, place a lot of emphasis on masculinity, "being macho." It is "macho" to suffer in silence, and die six years before one's wife or lover, but at least we are men, we are "masculine."

Related to this obsolete and outdated definition of masculinity is a final reason for the absence of men of color: homophobia, or lack of touching between men. Except when we touch each other on the behind at athletic events, men of color are not supposed to touch, ever! The only time it is permitted to touch others is when we have sex or when we fight. We men of color are also not suppose to show emotion, since if we do we might be called gay. However, what we men of color often fail to realize is that non-Western cultures do encourage touching beyond a cold handshake, even beyond expressing brotherhood with a hug and a kiss on the cheek.

An organization like NOMAS, which is pro-feminist and gay-affirmative will always have difficulty reaching out to men of color who make up the majority of the economic underclass in the USA. All that men of color have left to define ourselves is our penis. And since this is all we have, we have to be sure to use it in the right way, with the "right sex" lest even this symbol of our masculinity be taken away. How many black parents have wished their child dead after they found out the kid was gay? To be even more concrete, consider the slow response to AIDS by most of the black community, many of whose members said that AIDS was caused only by homosexuals, and that homosexuality, in turn, was caused by the white man.

Fortunately, men of color are now forming our own organizations. Now when we join organizations like NOMAS, it will be as equals, and not as former slaves seeking comradely empathy from our former masters. At the same time, we men of color are intelligent enough to know that our former and present masters are also our former and present slaves. You too are oppressed by racism when you deprive us of a thorough and efficient education, and you spent your money building jails to keep us in, as well as apartments to keep *yourselves* in, with multiple locks on yours doors. You too are oppressed by racism, because you have to lie to yourself about your education, your religion, your economics, and your politics.

We men of color will take advantage of NOMAS to speak out against racism, and we ask those of you in the white majority to help us by giving suggestions for the elimination of racism, both over and covert, both intentional and unintentional.

It takes years
to train children
to believe the lies
and to pass on
violence to
people of
other colors...
There must also
be safety for
white people.

—Allan Creighton and Paul Kivel

7

An Exercise In Unlearning Racism

by Allan Creighton & Paul Kivel

WHITES STAND UP

The devastation that racism produces for people of color must be clearly understood by whites. Whites must also understand the social and institutional nature of racism in order to move beyond self-guilt or the blaming of other whites. Although changing personal views and behaviors is useful, acting to change social practice is where real community building will happen.

Racism is damaging to whites, too. Whites' early experiences of learning about racism are hurtful, often coming from people they trust or love who are passing on their own hurt. Racism also operates to deny the different ethnic heritages of white people, persuading whites they have no cultural heritage, but instead a bland monoculture. Or it assigns different status to different white ethnic groups, based upon hierarchies or structures of domination inherited from European culture: Eastern European, Mediterranean and Irish people are often "one down" within white society. Racism falsifies their view of the world. It saddles them with resentfulness, unawareness, fear, guilt or hate when the subject of racism is brought up. All of these are affecting white people—adults and children—now.

The following exercise for white people can help demonstrate how racist training takes place and what the costs are for whites. White participants are asked to stand up if a statement applies to them. They are to notice who else is standing, and to notice their feelings. Everyone has the right not to stand, but they are asked to pay attention to how they feel if that is what they choose.

Please Stand Up Silently If:

You don't know exactly what your European/American heritage is, what your great-grandparents' names are, or what regions or cities your ancestors came from.

You have ever been told, or believe, you are a 'Heinz 57' or a 'mutt.'

You grew up in a household where you heard derogatory racial terms or racial jokes.

You grew up in a household where you heard that racism was bad, so you were never to notice out loud or comment on racial differences.

(For example, people told you, 'It doesn't matter if you're purple or green, we're all equal, so don't notice a person's color.')

You grew up in a household where you heard that racism was bad, that some or all white people were racist, and that you would always have to fight against it.

You grew up, lived, or live in a neighborhood, or went to a school or a camp which, as far as you knew, was exclusively white.

You grew up with people of color who were servants, maids, gardeners or babysitters in your house.

33

You were ever told not to play with children of a non-white ethnicity when you were a child.

For this next question, remain standing if the next item applies to you:

You ever saw pictures or images in magazines, film or television, or heard in music or on radio, of:

- Mexicans depicted as drunk, lazy or illiterate.
- Asians depicted as exotic, cruel or mysterious.
- Asian Indians depicted as excitable or 'silly.'
- Arabs depicted as swarthy, ravishing or 'crazed.'
- Black people depicted as violent or criminal.
- Pacific Islanders depicted as fun-loving or lazy.
- American Indians depicted as drunk, savage or 'noble.'
- Character-roles from non-white cultures acted by white actors.

You did not meet people of color in person, or socially, before you were well into your teens.

You ever find yourself trying to pretend 'not to notice' the ethnicity or race or skin color of people of color.

You ever felt like 'white' culture was 'wonderbread' culture—empty, boring—or that another racial group had more rhythm, more athletic ability, were better with their hands, better at math and technology, better at trade or handling money, or had more musical or artistic creativity than you.

You ever felt that people of another racial group were more spiritual than white people.

You have ever been sexually attracted to a person from another racial group because it seemed exotic, exciting or challenging.

You ever learned to fear or distrust people of a non-white racial group.

You ever felt yourself being nervous, fearful or stiffening up when encountering people of color in a neutral public situation (e.g., in an elevator or on the street).

You ever worked in a place where all the people of color had more menial jobs, were paid less or were otherwise harassed or discriminated against.

You ever ate in a public place where all the customers were white, and the people of color who were present were service workers.

You have ever been in an organization, work group, meeting or event that people of color protested as racist, or that you knew or suspected to be racist.

You ever felt racial tension in a situation and were afraid to say anything about it.

You ever had degrading jokes, comments or put-downs about people of color made in your presence and felt powerless to protest.

You ever witnessed people of color being mistreated in any way be white people.

You ever saw people of color being put down or attacked verbally or physically and did not intervene.

You ever felt guilty or powerless to do anything about racism.

You ever felt embarrassed by, separate from, superior to, or more tolerant than other white friends or family members.

You have ever been in a close friendship or relationship with another white person where that relationship was damaged or lost because of a disagreement about racism.

You have ever been in a close friendship or relationship with a person of color where that relationship was affected, endangered or lost because of racism between you or from others.

You are not in a close significant relationship with any people of color in your life right now.

The exercise ends with participants discussing in pairs how they felt during the exercise and how they feel now. A whole group discussion can then follow.

Someone may ask, "Are you saying that all white people are racist?" Let's be clear: no one is born a racist, and no one is born inferior. It takes years to train children to believe the lies and to pass on violence to people of other colors. Young white people resist these lies as best as they can, but with an entire culture training them, many end up believing and passing on the lies.

Young people of color also resist the lies and violence as best they can. But the oppression takes its toll, and many end up internalizing it. It takes years to train people of color that they are less able than white people.

The situation is not hopeless. Every day we can resist and challenge—and see others resisting and challenging—the realities of racism. It is particularly crucial for adults who work with children who are white, Jewish and of color—often in the same classroom or group—to be com-

34

pletely clear about what racism is, what anti-Semitism is, and how they operate to divide us from one another. In fact, it is doubly important, because adult society elsewhere is actively feeding these children lies and confusions about racism. To strengthen ourselves in this struggle, there are many things we can do. We can learn to identify how racism operates and affects *us* day to day, looking at our own ethnic heritages, our early memories of learning about other groups, and areas where we might get stuck when the issues are brought out into the open—in the classroom and elsewhere. We can prepare ourselves to initiate frank and open dialog about racism. This particularly contradicts young people's experience where adults often pretend racism doesn't exist or have great ambivalence about discussing it. The various oppressions are an interlocking system. One will not be lessened while others, with their own sets of abuses and despairs, are left in place. *This means making racial issues a part of all our work.*

We must ensure that cultural diversity is represented in our actual numbers—that whites and people of color are all working together and modeling cooperative relationships, especially within the white-dominated institutions in which so many of us work.

We can acknowledge the strong and powerful things we and others are doing to end racism. We need not blame ourselves for racism, or for times when we failed to do more. Blame isn't useful for us, and it's absolutely useless for young people. Nothing is quite as useless to women as guilty men, as useless to people of color as guilty whites, or as useless to children as guilty adults.

We can make mistakes, fix them, take responsibility for our actions, analyze and learn from them, and go forward. We can assume that no one wants to participate in this racist system. *Everyone is doing the best they can with the lies and the ignorance they were given.*

We can recognize that we all come from cultural and ethnic traditions. By taking pride in our own, we are less likely to fear and attack others'.

We can examine how we learned about racial difference and discrimination through early experiences and impressions, and give healing attention to what was hurtful.

Since we experience and learn racism in groups, as well as from and with those around us, it is particularly powerful to *unlearn* it with others. Working in multiracial groups to end racism is perhaps the most effective way of all to counteract our training.

But like sexism, issues of racism have great emotional pain attached to them. *Feeling safe ourselves and creating emotional safety among people with whom we work has to be of prime importance.*

There must be safety for people of color so that they: do not become targets of further abuse; do not become isolated from the group; are not set up to be spokespeople for their race or ethnic identity; and can do their personal work of healing and becoming more powerful.

There must also be safety for white people so that they: can get in touch with and heal from the lies of the early painful "learning" process they had; are not faulted for what they have been told and can honestly bring up doubts, confusion, anger and other painful emotions; can listen attentively and supportively to people of color speaking out; and can support and challenge each other to continue working on this issue.

Finally, safety comes for all groups when adults are clear and the information presented is direct, basic and consistent. If we can create safety for the process, each person will become clearer, stronger and closer to others. The group itself will take on safety, interest and strength to end racism within the group and within the larger society.

**A generation
of Americans
of Polish ancestry
has been virtually
left, unwittingly,
to the assimilative
structure of
the melting pot,
without any
knowledge about
their heritage.**

—Polish American Congress

8

Polish American Congress Convention Resolution Committee Report

Conceived during a devastating war, the Polish American Congress was organized in 1944 to unite and solidify the patriotic, political and social conscience of Americans of Polish descent or birth.

Poland had already been victimized by Nazi German brutality and bondage. The potential of Soviet oppression in the post World War II era was evident. Poland's geographical, historical and very cultural identity was threatened with extinction.

The establishment of the Polish American Congress as a strong, central force in the United States created a platform upon which Polish Americans could defend and advance Poland's right to freedom and independence as a sovereign nation. The Congress provided a ray of hope and rejuvenation to Polish Americans, inspired a renewed awareness of their ethnic heritage and aroused in them a renewed desire to elevate their status in the American mosaic of pluralism.

The emergence of the Polish American Congress as a unifying umbrella laid a firm base for the defense of the interests of Poland. It created the avenue for Polish Americans and encouraged visions of positive achievements that would be the driving force following the Second World War serving to elevate the good name and prestige of Poland, the Polish people and Americans of Polish heritage.

More than 2,600 delegates representing organizations from 26 states participated in our founding convention. Negative world events that ensued after World War II led to the eventual absorption of Poland into the Soviet Union orbit with Allied consent and the threat of Soviet inspired Communist domination of the world, including the United States. This development made the cause of Poland and struggle against fascism and communism the dominant issues on the Polish American Congress agenda.

Its people's tragic fate under Soviet domination caused the Congress to focus its energies on the work to free Poland.

As the years passed, generations of Americans of Polish descent lost interest in the Polish American Congress because of the lack of programs about their concerns. They became the invisible Polonia of largely assimilated citizens with Polish surnames, who knew little if anything about their ancestral roots.

We recognize the complexities of the dilemma that confronts and hurts Americans who trace their heritage to Poland. We are also aware that 383 years of Polish presence in America has fostered and evolved with a redefined heritage—the Polish American Heritage. The unfortunate fact is that Americans of Polish ancestry, especially the present younger generations, have had and continue to have very limited exposure to learning and knowing about the great accomplishments of Poles who immigrated here and Americans of Polish descent who have made contributions at the highest levels to the progress of the United States. Curriculums in schools do not focus on Poland and the Polish American heritage. Our many once Polish oriented parochial schools no longer emphasize any curriculum on Polish heritage, arts, music, etc. The Polish language in most cases was eliminated decades ago. There are very few qualified texts on Polish American heritage for primary and secondary schools.

We continue to have a very deep affinity and sympathy for Poland, her struggle and needs. Poland is free, but not totally secure. The latter has been a problem over centuries. The collapse of the Soviet Union, disintegration of Communist governments in Eastern Europe and the emergence of new free republics in the former Soviet Union may have led to overstated optimism. Former Soviet republics, whose politics are unpredictable, have access to or control of nuclear and conventional weapons. There is a rise in right-wing extremist attacks on ethnic immigrants in Germany. Most notable are the recent reports and investigation of "ethnic cleansing" and genocide in the former Yugoslavia, a grim reminder of the Nazi rise to power in the 1930s. Nonetheless, the Polish American Congress has attained one of its primary goals. Poland is free. The Polish American Congress Charitable Foundation is continuing its outstanding assistance. That effort is ongoing and highly successful. It should be encouraged and supported.

This is a historic convention because it is the first Polish American Congress convention held in a time of elation over a free Poland. It is a critical convention because Poland's emergence as a free nation places the Polish American Congress at the crossroads. The Congress played a lead role in the struggle for Poland's freedom and defeat of Communism in Europe. Ironically, it has yet to focus equivalent vigor and resources in meeting the challenges of domestic Polish American problems. During the years of actions for Poland's freedom, the issues affecting the esteem and quality of status of Polish Americans may have become the inadvertent casualties of that commitment and dedication.

A generation of Americans of Polish ancestry has been virtually left, unwittingly, to the assimilative structure of the melting pot, without any knowledge about their heritage, and, perhaps, feeling left out of its own ethnicity and regarded as second class.

There are very few Polish Americans in the highest levels of political, business, educational and governmental hierarchies. Polish Americans are out of the inner circle of power and influence. Compared to other ethnic groups, there are very few Polish Americans ascending to those lofty positions. Our successes have been unnoticed or, to be blunt, almost non-existent or very short termed.

Over the years, the Polish American Congress has built an effective lobby for Poland at the highest levels of influence. However, that influence has not translated into effective programs to help Americans of Polish ancestry to advance in politics, government, business, and other endeavors.

We have often heard the phrase: "Let Poland be Poland". Now is the time to put this into practice. Poland is a free and independent sovereignty. It has a duly elected government. Neither the Polish American Congress or any other private group is the government of Poland. Our current responsibility is to respect that sovereign status which the Polish American Congress helped attain, continue the caring humanitarian work of the Charitable Foundation, offer counsel when requested and encourage American government aid. Above all, we must place faith in the resolve and capability of the Polish people to succeed in their newly discovered free enterprise and remain vigilant to all ill-intended obstacles.

It is imperative that the Polish American Congress broaden its priorities toward a vigorous program that addresses and pursues solutions to the domestic concerns of Polish Americans. Dedicated people have given years of devotion to Poland's freedom. The same type of concerted energies must now be exercised in creating and implementing positive actions for the benefit of Americans of Polish ancestry.

Consequently, having considered and thoroughly reviewed the record of the Polish American Congress and looking to the future, we, the delegates to the Polish American Congress Convention, assembled in Washington, D.C., do hereby recommend and resolve, with firm conviction, the following proposals for consideration by the National Council of Directors:

1. We recommend that the conduct of Polish American Congress affairs be pursued from a broad domestic concept which includes all efforts of Polish Americans or permanent residents of the United States in acting on behalf of our own ethnic community and Poland.

2. Our Polish American fraternal organizations, mainly the Polish National Alliance, the Polish Roman Catholic Union, the Polish Women's Alliance, and the Polish Falcons of America have been the resource lifelines of the Polish American Congress. Considering their financial and human resource commitments to maintain the work of the Polish American Congress on the national and international levels, we express our appreciation and commend their contributions.

3. One of the very serious and chronic problems facing the organization is its lack of sufficient funding. It is amazing that so much has been accomplished, almost unnoticed, on a very frugal budget. We recommend with urgency that the executive leadership and Nation Council of Directors appoint a qualified committee of individuals to address the PAC funding needs. We also recommend that this special committee include a review and consideration of suggestions made at the American Agenda Workshop on October 13, 1992, prior to the convention sessions.

4. We recognize the absence of Polish Americans in the hierarchy of political parties and actions. We recommend the establishment of a national political network to develop and enhance the progress of Polish Americans toward the highest levels of all major parties and government. The network should include all Polish American elected federal, state and local officials, regardless of political party affiliation.

5. We need effective initiatives and organized efforts to respond quickly and accurately to defamation and bigotry against Poland, the Polish people and Polish Americans. An organized network throughout the Polish American Congress districts should provide a united effort to respond and prevent such attacks.
6. One of the major problems in building an effective organization is communication. We urge the National Council of Directors to appoint a qualified editor for the Polish American Congress Newsletter and ensure regular issuance of the publication on a quarterly basis. The newsletter costs can be covered by adding a publication fee to membership dues. The final responsibility for content would rest with the leadership of the Polish American Congress, the publisher.
7. Today, many Polish Americans have only a limited knowledge of their heritage. To help deal with this problem we recommend to the National Council of Directors that we consider pursuing the following course:

  A. A close alliance is needed between the Polish American Congress and educators, and educational, historical and cultural organizations. We call upon the Polish American Congress state divisions to work with colleges and universities in their areas to create and promote workshops, courses and lectures on the Polish experience.
  B. Establish a national network to promote and promulgate the inclusion of a Polish and East Central European studies curriculum either independently or as part of existing courses, in social studies, American history and multicultural studies at the public and parochial schools, so that children of Polish and other backgrounds are not "educated away" from their respective ethnic values, customs and heritage and can build esteem and pride from the accomplishments of their forefathers.
  C. Organize national and regional conferences of primary and secondary educators to develop appropriate materials for a Polish and East Central Europe curriculum.
  D. Encourage Polish American authors by promoting their publications among publishers and other communication outlets.
  E. Utilize the capabilities and expertise of Polish Americans who are involved in higher education at the college and university level through existing qualified organizations such as the Polish Institute of Arts and Sciences and Polish American Historical Association. These resources, including the Kosciuszko Foundation and similar established groups, can be very productive and positive sources for addressing the problems Polish Americans face in getting a college or university education. Regarding higher education, we recommend creation of a national scholarship resource information bank utilizing appropriate professional expertise to help Polish American students attain grants and scholarships. The resource bank could be effectively organized with assistance of some well known groups already operating in our community.

F.   We appreciate and commend the educational work of Polish Language Schools. We recognize the effort to teach immigrants English. Given today's societal structure and economic needs, we encourage bilingualism on the part of our people.

8.   We encourage the creation of Polish American Centers for Culture and Heritage in local communities, and development of a cooperative spirit that assures their survival and growth. Such centers can be vital arms to the Polish American Congress in matters dealing with heritage, folklore, music, history and arts. They can be a vary influential force in putting the younger generation in practical touch with the Polish American Heritage.

9.   We recommend that the National Council of Directors utilize the spiritual leadership of the Polish American clergy to develop a program for strengthening the Polish American family. In these times of various concepts of family life, it is important that the traditional units of the Polish American Family be focused toward the values of unity and understanding.

10.   On the occasion of the 14th anniversary of his elevation to the Papacy, we recommend that a communication be sent to Pope John Paul II wishing him well and expressing our happiness that he has recovered from his recent illness and continues his spiritual crusade for world peace and for the less fortunate who live in poverty and starvation conditions.

11.   We commend and appreciate the President of the United States, the Congress, all other government agencies, and the private sector for their assistance to Poland during her ordeal under Communism and after her emergence as a free nation, and we urge its continuance in the future.

12.   We are grateful to the United States Government for the revered care and respect provided for a half century to the memory of Ignacy Jan Paderewski, Polish Statesman, and for the honors bestowed during the ceremonies transferring his remains to Poland.

13.   We acknowledge, with appreciation, that a delegation of Polish Americans participated in the historic Conference of World Polonias, the first held since prior to World War II. The conclave, sponsored by "Spolnota Polska", was held in Krakow, Poland, August 13–23, 1992.

We honor those who contributed toward the eventual freedom of Poland and the demise of Communist domination in Eastern Europe. We especially pay tribute to the memory of those who gave their lives on the battlefields, leaders and activists of the Polish American Congress who dedicated their lives to Poland's cause and who did not live to experience the joys of triumph.

We congratulate and appreciate the organizers of this convention for their hospitality and excellent arrangements.

This had been a crossroads meeting of diverse groups and individuals; the representation spans different ideas and concepts based on generational experience. It is evident that the Polish American Congress needs a healing process to bring itself together and a deeper

41

understanding of its own diversity and organizational personality, and the broad generational constituency it represents. This convention can be the body that creates the moving force for a united community. Let us begin.

Long live the United States of America
Long live a fully Free Poland
Long live the ideals of the Polish American Congress.

Resolutions Committee

Hilary Czaplicki, Chairman
Donald Pienkos, Vice Chairman and Secretary
Frank Milewski
John Olko
Ewa Gierat

Discussion Questions
Part I: Race, Class, and Gender
Envisioning the New Millennium

1. Discuss five commonalities of oppression. Highlight the pages in the text which relate to your answers.

   _____

   _____

   _____

   _____

   _____

   _____

   _____

2. Based on your readings in Part One, how does sexism affect both women and men?

   _____

   _____

   _____

   _____

   _____

   _____

   _____

"But of all the women
I've had the chance
to meet, I've probably
learned the most
from those you've
never heard of—
women who have never
written a book,
appeared on television
or been the subject
of a newspaper article."

—Hillary Rodham Clinton

Part II

(En)Gendering: Sex, Roles, and Family Life

In addition to women, this section presents stories from people you have never heard of. For example, "No More Jewels in the Crown," discusses a game allegedly played by black men who earn a prize for having children out of wedlock. "Sex and Violence," offers a unique perspective of looking at pornography, as well as "Eleven Things not to Say to Survivors of Sexual Assault (and What to Say Instead)."

According to FBI statistics, one of every three women will be the victim of attempted or actual rape at some point in her lifetime. A rape is committed once every two-and-a-half minutes in America. One-third of all rapes are committed by more than one man. More than 60 percent of rapes are committed by someone the victim knows: a friend, date or relative. The statistics go on....

With an emphasis on solutions, this section includes "Sex and Violence: A Perspective," "Eleven Things Not to Say to Survivors of Sexual assault," and "Resources for Maintaining Non-Violence."

Solutions to problems of race, class, and gender affects, "Black Fathers, and Forefathers," and "The Rite of Work: The Economic Man."

No More 'Jewels'
"Jewels in the Crown"
—a game in which
young black males
compete to see
who can father
the most children
out of wedlock.

—Vernon McClean

1

No More
'Jewels in the Crown':
Young Black Men Need
a New Definition
of Masculinity

by Vernon McClean

When Governor Whitman made her now famous remark about the "jewels in the crown"—a game in which young black males compete to see who can father the most children out of wedlock—it was greeted with outrage by many African-American leaders.

As black man and a father, I had hoped the Governor's comment would also inspire a widespread discussion of the larger issue of black masculinity in our state. We have a lot to talk about, and it goes to the heart of our future as a community.

Yes, boys of every color define their maleness in sexual terms — the number of girls they have "scored" with. But too many black youths are particularly susceptible to this and a whole raft of mistaken, dangerous notions about masculinity. More than others, they find their role models in sports heroes. More than others, they equate maleness with a detached, macho "toughness." More than others, they sneer at education and nurturing as "effeminate."

This has not always been true. Historically, black men have been tender and loving with their families. They have yearned for schooling, too often in vain through no fault of their own. And today, many black men have got past the ugly vision of masculinity that predominates in parts of the cities.

Every month, I meet with a group called the Concerned African-American Men of New Jersey. We take turns gathering in each other's homes and talking over chicken suppers. Most were born in Newark, with few advantages; they have become successful, and not just financially.

Unlike the image of black males put forward by the Governor and the media, the members take family values, morality and education very seriously. There are building contractors who regularly volunteer their time and materials to putting up homes for the needy. There are doctors, lawyers and teachers who work with addicts and intervene with gangs, or belong to groups fighting the oppression of black women.

Yet too many black youths ignore such role models in their wrenching ambivalence about their masculinity. Of course there are reasons, and I have seen them working on our youth.

Start with the fact that so many whites still refuse to acknowledge that blacks are capable of intelligent achievement (witness the controversy over "The Bell Curve"). In that environment, young blacks doubt their intellectual capacity and leave school, ridiculing the idea of academic success and turning to macho swaggering, sexual score-keeping and an unhealthy fixation on sports.

My 13 year-old son, for example, was doing poorly in the Montclair schools, and nothing I did seemed to help. Then he went out for football, but the coach told him he could not be on the team unless his grades improved. Within a matter of weeks, his grades rocketed from failing to above average.

I was pleased, of course, at his progress. But it saddened me, as a father and a black man, that I had less influence with my son than a stranger who happens to be a football coach.

My son and other black boys, whether they live in inner-city projects or in suburbs like Montclair, cannot escape the fact that the black community worships its athletes, not its doctors and business leaders and, yes, its professors. Yet so often—and I am thinking in particular of Mike Tyson—these athletes' lives simply reflect and reinforce the macho sexual stereotypes of the streets.

How can we change this vicious circle? It's a topic that comes up again and again at the meetings of our Newark-based group. We see young black males wrestling with the conflict inherent in the conditions of their lives—the struggle for an education that can lead to success in the outer world versus the urge to gain peer approval within their community of the streets. They usually conclude that these goals are not compatible.

It seems to us that the adults of the black community must prove to these boys that they are wrong. We must come together, organizing people and programs that directly reach our boys and make them understand one essential fact: our community appreciates and rewards the values of education and responsible fatherhood.

**The crime of rape...
is defined around
penetration.
That seems to me
a very male
point of view on
what it means to be
sexually violated.**

—Catharine MacKinnon

2

Sex and Violence: A Perspective

by Catharine A. MacKinnon

I want to raise some questions about the concept of this panel's title, "Violence against Women," as a concept that may coopt us as we attempt to formulate our own truths. I want to speak specifically about four issues: rape, sexual harassment, pornography, and battery. I think one of the reasons we say that each of these issues is an example of violence against women is to reunify them. To say that aggression against women has this unity is to criticize the divisions that have been imposed on that aggression by the legal system. What I see to be the danger of the analysis, what makes it potentially cooptive, is formulating it—and it *is* formulated this way—these are issues of violence, *not* sex: Rape is a crime of violence, not sexuality; sexual harassment is an abuse of power, not sexuality; pornography is violence against women; it is not erotic. Although battering is not categorized so explicitly, it is usually treated as though there is nothing sexual about a man beating up a woman so long as it is with his fist. I'd like to raise some questions about that as well.

I hear in the formulation that these issues are violence against women, not sex, that we are in the shadow of Freud, intimidated at being called repressive Victorians. We're saying we're *op*pressed and they say we're *re*pressed. That is, when we say we're against rape, the immediate response is, "Does that mean you're against sex?" "Are you attempting to impose neo-Victorian prudery on sexual expression?" This comes up with sexual harassment as well. When we say we're against sexual harassment, the first thing people want to know is, "What's the difference between that and ordinary male-to-female sexual initiation?" That's a good question.... The same is also true of criticizing pornography. "You can't be against erotica?" It's the latest version of the accusation that feminists are antimale. To distinguish ourselves from this, and in reaction to it, we call these abuses violence. The attempt is to avoid the critique—we're not against sex—and at the same time retain our criticism of these practices. So we rename as violent those abuses that have been seen to be sexual, without saying that we have a very different perspective on violence and on sexuality and their relationship. I also think a reason we call these experiences violence is to avoid being called lesbians, which for some reason is equated with being against sex. In order to avoid that, yet retain our opposition to sexual violation, we put this neutral, objective, abstract word *violence* on it all.

To me this is an attempt to have our own perspective on these outrages without owning up to having one. To have our point of view but present it as *not* a particular point of view.

Our problem has been to label something as rape, as sexual harassment, as pornography in the face of a suspicion that it might be intercourse, it might be ordinary sexual initiation, it might be erotic. To say that these purportedly sexual events violate us, to be against them, we call them not sexual. But the attempt to be objective and neutral avoids owning up to the fact that women do have a specific point of view on these events. It avoids saying that from women's point of view, intercourse, sex roles, and eroticism can be and at times are violent to us as women.

My approach would claim our perspective; we are not attempting to be objective about it, we're attempting to represent the point of view of women. The point of view of men up to this time, called objective, has been to distinguish sharply between rape on the one hand and intercourse on the other; sexual harassment on the one hand and normal, ordinary sexual initiation on the other; pornography or obscenity on the one hand and eroticism on the other. The male point of view defines them by distinction. What women experience does not so clearly distinguish the normal, everyday things from those abuses from which they have been defined by distinction. Not just "Now we're going to take what *you* say is rape and call it violence"; "Now we're going to take what *you* say is sexual harassment and call it violence"; "Now we're going to take what *you* say is pornography and call it violence." We have a deeper critique of what has been done to women's sexuality and who controls access to it. What we are saying is that sexuality in exactly these normal forms often *does* violate us. So long as we say that those things are abuses of violence, not sex, we fail to criticize what has been made of *sex,* what has been done to us *through* sex, because we leave the line between rape and intercourse, sexual harassment and sex roles, pornography and eroticism, right where it is.

I think it is useful to inquire how women and men (I don't use the term *persons,* I guess, because I haven't seen many lately) live through the meaning of their experience with these issues. When we ask whether rape, sexual harassment, and pornography are questions of violence or questions of sexuality, it helps to ask, to whom? What is the perspective of those who are involved, whose experience it is—to rape or to have been raped, to consume pornography or to be consumed through it. As to what these things *mean* socially, it is important whether they are about sexuality to women and men or whether they are instead about "violence"—or whether violence and sexuality can be distinguished in that way, as they are lived out.

The crime of rape—this is a legal and observed, not a subjective, individual, or feminist definition—is defined around penetration. That seems to me a very male point of view on what it means to be sexually violated. And it is exactly what heterosexuality as a social institution is fixated around, the penetration of the penis into the vagina. Rape is defined according to what men think violates women, and that is the same as what they think of as the sine qua non of sex. What women experience as degrading and defiling when we are raped includes as much that is distinctive to us as is our experience of sex. Someone once termed penetration a "peculiarly resented aspect" of rape—I don't know whether that meant it was peculiar that it was resented or that it was resented with heightened peculiarity. Women who have been raped often do resent having been penetrated. But that is not all there is to what was intrusive or expropriative of a woman's sexual wholeness.

I do think the crime of rape focuses more centrally on what men define as sexuality than on women's experience of our sexual being, hence its violation. A common experience of rape victims is to be unable to feel good about anything heterosexual thereafter—or anything sexual at all, or men at all. The minute they start to have sexual feeling or feel sexually touched by a man, or even a woman, they start to relive the rape. I had a client who came in with her husband. She was a rape victim, a woman we had represented as a witness. Her husband sat the whole time and sobbed. They couldn't have sex anymore because every time he started to touch her, she would flash to the rape scene and see his face change into the face of the man who had raped her. That, to me, is sexual. When a woman has been raped, and it is sex that she then cannot experience without connecting it to that, it was her sexuality that was violated.

Similarly, men who are in prison for rape think it's the dumbest thing that ever happened....."It isn't just a miscarriage of justice; they were put in jail for something very little different from what most men do most of the time and call it sex. The only difference is they got caught. That view is nonremorseful and not rehabilitative. It may also be true. It seems to me we have here a convergence between the rapist's view of what he has done and the victim's perspective on what was done to her. That is, for both, their ordinary experiences of heterosexual intercourse and the act of rape have something in common. Now this gets us into intense trouble, because that's exactly how judges and juries see it who refuse to convict men accused of rape. A rape victim has to prove that it was not intercourse. She has to show that there was force and she resisted, because if there was sex, consent is inferred. Finders of fact look for "more force than usual during the preliminaries." Rape is defined by distinction from intercourse—not the preliminaries." Rape is defined by distinction from intercourse—not nonviolence, intercourse. They ask, does this event look more like fucking or like rape? But what is their standard for sex, and is this question asked from the *woman's point of view?* The level of force is not adjudicated at her point of violation; it is adjudicated at the standard of the normal level of force. Who sets this standard?

In the criminal law, we can't put everybody in jail who does an ordinary act, right? Crime is supposed to be deviant, not normal. Women continue not to report rape, and a reason is that they believe, and they are right, that the legal system will not see it from their point of view. We get very low conviction rates for rape.[1] We also get many women who believe they have never been raped, although a lot of force was involved. They mean that they were not raped in a way that is legally provable. In other words, in all these situations, there was not *enough* violence against them to take it beyond the category of "sex"; they were not coerced enough. Maybe they were forced-fucked for years and put up with it, maybe they tried to get it over with, maybe they were coerced by something other than battery, something like economics, maybe even something like love.

What I am saying is that unless you make the point that there is much violence in intercourse, as a usual matter, none of that is changed. Also we continue to stigmatize the women who claim rape as having experienced a deviant violation and allow the rest of us to go through life feeling violated but thinking we've never been raped, when there were a great many times when we, too, have had sex and didn't want it. What this critique does that is different from the "violence, not sex" critique is ask a series of questions about normal, heterosexual intercourse and attempt to move the line between heterosexuality on the one hand—intercourse—and rape on the other, rather than allow it to stay where it is.

Having done that so extensively with rape, I can consider sexual harassment more briefly. The way the analysis of sexual harassment is sometimes expressed now (and it bothers me) is that it is an abuse of power, not sexuality. That does not allow us to pursue whether sexuality, as socially constructed in our society through gender roles, is *itself* a power structure. If you look at sexual harassment as power, not as sex, what is power supposed to be? Power is employer/employee, not because courts are marxist but because this is a recognized hierarchy. Among men. Power is teacher/student, because courts recognize a hierarchy there. Power is on one side and sexuality on the other. Sexuality is ordinary affection, everyday flirtation. Only when ordinary, everyday affection and flirtation and "I was just trying to be friendly" come into the context of *another* hierarchy is it considered potentially an abuse of power. What is not considered to be hierarchy is women and men—men on top and women on the bottom. That is not considered to be a question of power or social hierarchy, legally or politically. A feminist perspective suggests that it is.

When we have examples of coequal sexual harassment (within these other hierarchies), worker to worker on the same level, involving women and men, we have a lot of very interesting, difficult questions about sex discrimination, which is supposed to be about gender difference, but does not conceive of gender as a social hierarchy. I think that implicit in race discrimination cases for a brief moment of light was the notion that there is a social hierarchy between blacks and whites. So that presumptively it's an exercise of power for a white person to do something egregious to a black person or for a white institution to do something egregious systematically to many black people. Situations of coequal power—among coworkers or students or teachers—are difficult to see as examples of sexual harassment unless you have a notion of male power. I think we lie to women when we call it not power when a woman is come onto by a man who is not her employer, not her teacher. What do we labor under, what do we feel, when a man—any man—comes and hits on us? I think we require women to feel fine about turning down male-initiated sex so long as the man doesn't have some *other* form of power over us. Whenever—every and any time—a woman feels conflicted and wonders what's wrong with her that she can't decline although she has no inclination, and she feels open to male accusations, whether they come from women or men, of "Why didn't you just tell him to buzz off?" we have sold her out, not named her experience. We are taught that we exist for men. We should be flattered or at least act as if we are—be careful about a man's ego because you never know what he can do to you. To flat out say to him, "You?" or "I don't want to" is not *in* most women's sex-role learning. To say it is, is bravado. And that's because he's a man, not just because you never know what he can do to you because he's your boss (that's two things—he's a man and he's the boss) or your teacher or in some other hierarchy. It seems to me that we haven't talked very much about gender *as* a hierarchy, as a division of power, in the way that's expressed and acted out, primarily I think sexually. And therefore we haven't expanded the definition according to women's experience of sexuality, including our own sexual intimidation, of what things are

54

sexual in this world. So men have also defined what can be called sexual about us. They say, "I was just trying to be affectionate, flirtatious, and friendly," and we were just all felt up. We criticize the idea that rape comes down to her word against his—but it really *is* her perspective against his perspective, and the law has been written from *his* perspective. If he didn't mean it to be sexual, it's not sexual. If he didn't see it as forced, it wasn't forced. Which is to say, only male sexual violations, that is, only male ideas of what sexually violates us as women, are illegal. We buy into this when we say our sexual violations are abuses of power, not sex.

Just as rape is supposed to have nothing against intercourse, just as sexual harassment is supposed to have nothing against normal sexual initiation (men initiate, women consent—that's mutual?), the idea that pornography is violence against women, not sex, seems to distinguish artistic creation on the one hand from what is degrading to women on the other. It is candid and true but not enough to say of pornography, as Justice Stewart said, "I know it when I see it."[1] *He* knows what he thinks it is when he sees it—but is that what *I* know? Is that the same "it"? Is he going to know what I know when I see it? I think pretty much not, given what's on the newsstand, given what is not considered hard-core pornography. Sometimes I think what is obscene is what does *not* turn on the Supreme Court—or what revolts them more. Which is uncommon, since revulsion is eroticized. We have to admit that pornography is not erotic. When we say it is violence, not sex, we are saying, there is this degrading to women, over here, and this erotic, over there, without saying to whom. It is overwhelmingly disproportionately men to whom pornography is erotic. It is women, on the whole, to whom it is violent, among other things. And this is not just a matter of perspective, but a matter of reality.

Pornography turns primarily men on. Certainly they are getting something out of it. They pay incredible amounts of money for it; it's one of the largest industries in the country. If women got as much out of it as men do, we would buy it instead of cosmetics. It's a massive industry, cosmetics. We are poor but we have *some* money; we are some market. We spend our money to set ourselves up as the objects that emulate those images that are sold as erotic to men. What pornography says about us is that we enjoy degradation, that we are sexually turned on by being degraded. For me that obliterates the line, as a line at all, between pornography on one hand and erotica on the other, if what turns men on, what men find beautiful is what degrades women. It is pervasively present in art, also, and advertising. But it is definitely present in eroticism, if that is what it is. It makes me think that women's sexuality as such is a stigma. We also sometimes have an experience of sexuality authentic somehow in all this. We are not allowed to have it; we are not allowed to talk about it; we are not allowed to speak of it or image it as from our own point of view. And, to the extent we try to assert that we are beings equal with men, we have to be either asexual or virgins.

To worry about cooptation is to realize that lies make bad politics. It is ironic that cooptation often results from an attempt to be "credible," to be strategically smart, to be

---

[1]Jacobellis v. Ohio, 378 U.S. 184, 197 (1964) (Stewart, J., concurring).

"effective" on existing terms. Sometimes you become what you're fighting. Thinking about issues of sexual violation as issues of violence not sex could, if pursued legally, lead to opposing sexual harassment and pornography through morals legislation and obscenity laws. It is actually interesting that this theoretical stance has been widely embraced but these legal strategies have not been. Perhaps women realize that these legal approaches would not address the subordination of women to men, specifically and substantively. These approaches are legally as abstract as the "violence not sex" critique is politically abstract. They are both not enough and too much of the wrong thing. They deflect us from criticizing everyday behavior that is pervasive and normal and concrete and fuses sexuality with gender in violation and it is not amenable to existing legal approaches. I think we need to think more radically in our legal work here.

Battering is called violence, rather than something sex-specific: This is done to women. I also think it is sexually done to women. Not only in where it is done—over half of the incidents are in the bedroom.[2] Or the surrounding events—precipitating sexual jealousy. But when violence against women is eroticized as it is in this culture, it very difficult to say that there is a major distinction in the level of sex involved between being assaulted by a penis and being assaulted by a fist, especially when the perpetrator is a man. If women as gender female are defined as sexual beings, and violence is eroticized, then men violating women has a sexual component. I think men rape women because they get off on it in a way that fuses dominance with sexuality. (This is different in emphasis from what Susan Brownmiller says.[3]) I think that when men sexually harass women it expresses male control over sexual access to us. It doesn't mean they all want to fuck us, they just want to hurt us, dominate us, and control us, and that *is* fucking us. They want to be able to have that and to be able to say when they can have it, to *know* that. That is in itself erotic. The idea that opposing battering is about saving the family is, similarly, abstracted, gender-neutral. There are gender-neutral formulations of all these issues: law and order as opposed to depression, Victorian morality as opposed to permissiveness, obscenity as opposed to art and freedom of expression. Gender-neutral, objective formulations like these avoid asking *whose* expression, from whose point of view? Whose law and whose order? It's not just a question of who is free to express ourselves; it's not just that there is almost no, if any, self-respecting women's eroticism. The fact is that what we do see, what we are allowed to experience, even in our own suffering, even in what we are to complain about, is overwhelmingly constructed from the male point of view. Laws against sexual violation express what men see and do when they engage in sex with women; laws against obscenity center on the display of women's bodies in ways that men are turned on by viewing. To me, it not only makes us cooptable to define such abuses in gender-neutral terms like violence; when we fail to assert that we are fighting for the affirmative definition and control of our own sexuality, of our own lives as women, and that these experiences violate *that,* we have already been bought.

---

[2] R. Emerson Dobash and Russell Dobash, *Violence against Wives* (1979) at 14–21.

[3] Susan Brownmiller, *Against Our Will; Men, Women and Rape* (1975).

56

"More than 700,000 adult women in the U.S. are forcibly raped each year. That's one attack every 45 seconds."

—Jennifer Finnegan

3

Eleven Things Not to Say to Survivors of Sexual Assault (and what to say instead)

by Lawrence Cohen

1. **"Only crazy people need therapy."**
   Some experiences, like rape are traumatic for virtually anyone, no matter how well adjusted they are. Psychotherapy and rape crisis counseling can be very helpful for women with mild, moderate, or severe problems due to sexual assault.

2. **"I'll kill the guy who did this to you."**
   While anger is a natural reaction, it can be very harmful because the victim, who has faced one man whose anger was out of control, must now try to calm down another man, so that there won't be more violence.

3. **"It's better not to talk about it."**
   Studies have shown that talking about stressful events speeds up recovery, if people are allowed to talk at their own pace. Let her know you're willing to hear when she's ready to talk.

4. **"What are you afraid of me for? I didn't do it."**
   Rape and incest often make women fear men, or fear sex, at least for awhile. It also causes confusion about the relationship between sex and intimacy. Survivors may need to exert and feel more control in a relationship than they did prior to the assault.

5. **"It was my fault."**
   Victims often blame themselves. Many partners and family members also insist on blaming themselves. In fact, sexual assault is no one's fault except the perpetrator's.

6. **"Going to the police (or testifying in court) will just make things worse."**
   In fact, some studies show that reporting to police and testifying, though painful, actually help women recover. These actions also help get rapists off the street, and convey the message that our society does not condone violence against women.

7. **"Why can't you just forget about it?"**
   Forgetting may be impossible because the reminders are constant: sex, interactions with men, harassment on the street, being in vulnerable positions, and pornography are all possible reminders.

8. **"When you fall off a horse you have to jump right back on."**
   This saying may be true of some fears, but it does not apply to resuming sex after a sexual assault. Let her decide when she's ready to have sex (or ready to drive alone). Watch out for subtle pressures on her to have sex. If recovery time seems excessive, seek couples counseling.

9. **"What's the big deal?"**
   For many reasons sexual assault is a very big deal, even for sexually active women, even if it happened many years ago. An assault can totally upset a person's belief that the world is a safe place, that she is in control of her sexuality and her body, and that she knows who to trust. Rape is not sex, it is a life-threatening act. Incest is not sex, it is betrayal.

10. **"Why didn't you fight?"**
    Freezing, submitting, and fighting are all natural responses to being attacked. Since your partner survived, she did the right thing. Learning self-defense is recommended for all women, but untrained women must use their instincts to either fight or submit; neither one is wrong.

11. **"Nothing I can say (or do) will help."**
    Yes it can! Allow but don't force her to talk about it and express her feelings. Listen without criticism, judgment, or condemnation. Patience and love have healed many wounds.

I believe
that in no way
does my gender,
rank, position
or my inferior or
superior strength
convey to me
any permission,
right or obligation
to abuse anyone
ever.

—NOMAS

4

Resources for Maintaining Non-Violence

I believe abuse is any behavior that destroys self-esteem.

I believe that my abusive behavior is aimed at accomplishing my own purpose and that no one forces me to be abusive.

I believe that my abusive behavior is seriously damaging, intentional and plainly wrong.

I believe that no one deserves to be abused for any reason.

I believe that in no way does my gender, rank, position or my inferior or superior strength convey to me any permission, right or obligation to abuse anyone—ever.

I believe that my recovery means, first and foremost, freeing those that I have abused from harm by recognizing, stopping, admitting and becoming accountable for all my abusive behavior.

I believe that to grow in recovery, I must give up my need to control others and learn to control my own behavior.

I believe that the motivation for ending my abusive behavior should come from the internal recognition of my own maturity and any request for external reward, especially from those I have abused, is just another form of abuse.

I believe, as a recovering abuser, that I must play an active part in helping to build a society in which abuse between spouses, parents and children, friends, lovers, strangers, neighbors and nations is forever unacceptable.

POSITIVE SELF-TALK = PERSONAL POWER

Both research and experience show that when people with anger and abuse problems change what they say to themselves in tense situations, their anger de-escalates and they regain control of themselves. When you notice your cues escalating or start to feel angry, take a TIME OUT and read or say these statements to yourself.

- I don't need to prove myself in this situation. I can stay calm.
- As long as I keep my cool, I'm in control of myself.
- Time to relax and slow things down. Take a time out if I get uptight or start to notice my cues.
- My anger is a signal. Time to talk to myself and to relax.
- I don't need to feel threatened here. I can relax and stay cool.
- No matter what goes down, I WON'T HIT.
- Nothing says I have to be competent and strong all the time. It's okay to feel unsure or confused.
- It's impossible to control other people and situations. The ONLY thing I can control is myself and how I express my feelings.
- It's okay to be uncertain or insecure sometimes. I don't need to be in control of everything and everybody.
- If people criticize me, I can survive that. Nothing says that I have to be or can be perfect.
- People are going to act the way they want to, not the way I want.
- If this person wants to go off the wall, that's their thing. I don't need to respond to their anger with my anger or feel threatened.
- Most of the things we argue about are really small and insignificant. I can recognize that my anger comes from having old memories re-stimulated. It's okay to walk away from this fight, or to compromise for agreement.

Another Virginia slave...chopped off his left hand with a hatchet to prevent his being sold away from his child.

—Vernon McClean

5

Black Fathers, and Forefathers, Have an Important Role in the Family

by Vernon McClean

In the opening paragraph of Ralph Ellison's "Invisible Man," published in 1952, the male narrator says that he is invisible "simply because people refuse to see me." That is, "like the bodiless heads you see sometimes in circus sideshows, it as though I have been surrounded by mirrors of hard, distorted glass." And, "when they approach me they see only my surroundings, themselves, or figments of their imagination—indeed, everything and anything except me." This particular brand of invisibility generally characterizes the existence of black fathers in contemporary America.

The role of black father is one of the strongest and most important traditions in the black community. There is no question that in their earliest years in the New World enslaved African-Americans were concerned about their fathers. Moreover their loyalty to their fathers, and mothers, defied the efforts of their white slave-holders to sunder the family bond of their slaves.

Belle Hooks, in her "Ain't I a Woman: Black Women and Feminism," published in 1988, reminds us that "scholars have emphasized the impact of slavery on the black male consciousness, arguing that black men, more so than black women, were the 'real' victims of slavery." She documents the reality that "sexist historians and sociologists have provided the American public with a perspective on slavery in which the most cruel and de-humanizing impact of slavery on the lives of black people was that black men were stripped of their masculinity, which the psychologist and historians argue resulted in the dissolution and overall disruption of any black familial structure."

My argument, however, is that rather than being "stripped of our masculinity" and experiencing the "dissolution and overall disruption of any black familial structure," black fathers have served the black community well, including in the present.

Even during the many decades of slavery, black fathers performed what many have, often derisively, called "feminine tasks." Moreover, some psychologist and historians have mislabeled the carrying out of these tasks as constituting a form of "male castration" and have argued that performing these tasks—such as nurturing and caretaking—amounted to the "victimization" of black fathers.

My counter-argument, however, is supported by a careful assessment of the functions of fathers, especially those held in slavery, and draws upon slave narratives which clearly demonstrated male participation in such "feminine" roles as those of full-time fathers, nurturers, caretakers and single parents—roles which gave full scope to the sentimental abilities of African-American fathers.

A close reading of slave narratives reveals the emotive and caring nature of African-American fathers. For example, Eugene Genovese, in his "Roll, Jordan, Roll," published in 1978, relates the story of one George Payne of Virginia, who wept when his child was sold away from him. Similarly, Professor Genovese relates the story of another Virginia slave who chopped off his left hand with a hatchet to prevent his being sold away from his child.

These and many other instances point up the reality that for African-American fathers the traits of nurturance and devotion, or what sociologists have termed "positive behavioral characteristics" most definitely were present. It if appears to some that such traits were lacking, this is mainly because these traits have seldom been commented on in the media.

Regarding family and personal relationships, today's African-American males are no less sensitive than their forefathers. According to one black physician, "black men come to the psychiatrist's office in large numbers, in pain and genuinely seeking help. They have little or nothing to say about the statistics, myths and other sociological pronouncements so often made about them. Rather, they come in talking about depression, anxiety, frustration, fear, guilt, esteem issues and anger that are most often related to the close, ongoing relationships in their lives." This is taken from Henry E. Edward's "Black Families in Crisis: the Middle Class" published in 1988.

As a professor of African-American studies, in the courses which I teach, I emphasize solutions rather than problems. Thus, I cannot conclude this essay without advancing some suggestions for inclusion of black fathers in our communities on this Father's Day.

- Reach out to black fathers this Father's Day. If you know of a black father who is estranged from his children, you might call him to let him know you care and to encourage him to reconcile with his family.
- Take your husband or father to a church, synagogue or mosque. Religion/spirituality is a source of strength for all of us. Too often, because of a false sense of masculinity and machismo, black fathers do not want to acknowledge the need for a higher power. Encourage your clergyperson to use the occasion of Father's Day to speak positively about black fathers.
- If the black father has been abusive, use the occasion of Father's Day to discuss this situation. Again, acknowledging the role which sexism has played in our lives, it is moronically difficult for black men to express their emotions. Encourage him to be gentle and loving. Let him know you love him, even if he is not muscular like Mike Tyson or graceful like Michael Jordan.

- Boycott radio stations, newspapers and businesses which defame black fathers.
- Support an increase in the minimum wage and oppose further cutbacks in social service programs. Defend those programs and policies which will allow black fathers to earn the money necessary to provide for their families.
- Encourage your husband or father to join a black men's group, such as those organized in the wake of the Million Men March. Black men need the support of other black men in order to be a good father.
- Encourage teachers and professors to discuss the plight of the black father in their classes.

While these suggestions focus on what others can do to help black fathers, there are measures which we as black fathers can do to help ourselves. Black fathers are not entirely blameless in their own oppression. Too often, we are abusive toward black women—a black woman is 16 times more likely to be raped than a white woman. Moreover, we are too often absent as fathers in our families and communities.

Black fathers must therefore understand that black women are their equals. It is easy to blame the black woman for all pathologies in the black community, since many of us leave the raising of our children to mothers. And when children commit crimes, we blame the victims: black women and black children.

The positive examples cited in this essay without doubt debunk the opinion sometimes voiced by talk shows that black fathers do not care and have never cared about their children. Ironically, this view is sometimes echoed by some black women who assert that "there are no good black men left," and that "they, black men, take after their no-good fathers." Such sentiments, however, are not representatives of the majority of the black community. At the same time, this Father's Day, let us acknowledge that the majority of black men are still waiting to exhale. That is, we are still waiting for the media to acknowledge our presence and to write something good about us. Too long have we been invisible.

Will she turn away from me for not being black?

—Arnie Barnes-Schwartz

6

Black Daughter, White Father

by Arnie Barnes-Schwartz

This is Shara's story. Shara is an African American child whose biological mother died two months after Shara was born.

This is also my story. I am a white man of Hungarian Jewish ancestry, and Shara is now my daughter. Although my wife and I did not birth her, we helped give her life. As a foster family we were asked to consider taking a "border baby," a child who had never left the hospital since birth. We were told that every effort was being made to find someone in Shara's extended family to take her, but she desperately needed a home. We took her into our's.

Two-and-a-half years have passed since I was blessed with this beautiful child, and it is very likely that I will adopt her. I already have two other daughters—Elisabeth, 8½, and Becky, 20. After Becky's mother and I divorced, I assumed I would have only the one child, but when I remarried I found added joy with a second child, Elisabeth. And now Shara.

Shara's life will be one of struggle because of her physical conditions, race and gender. Shara was born 5½ weeks premature weighing 3½ pounds, with a condition known as fetal alcohol syndrome (FAS) because of her mother's addiction to alcohol. The legacy of FAS may always plague her. Currently she shows little visible signs of this syndrome. There are delays in many aspects of her development but so far no gaps. She is in an early intervention program with other children with learning delays, and these services will continue throughout most of her school years.

A FATHER'S CONCERNS

Equally important are my concerns over raising an African American child in a white family. I noticed the stares when she and I enter a store or restaurant. I get incensed when someone says, "Who's child is this?" I worry if her hair is fixed "right" when I encounter people of color. How do I say "thank you" to the strangers who tell me how to do her hair? And when I do try to do her hair the "right" way, Shara reminds me how miserable she feels having me pull at her tender hair just for the sake of others. I worry whether the African American community will expect her to behave differently from other kids?

With my first two girls, the bias was more: does this man know how to change diapers or cook a good meal? With my first two girls, it was always "Daddy" that one heard in my home in the middle of the night when one of them needed nurturing. Most of the time when I'm with Shara, the experience is the same as with the other two. For example, bath time and bed-time are fun, safe and comforting times with Dad as they were with my other daughters. But there is always a little voice ready to remind me that, overall, Shara's experience is not the same.

Being adopted certainly raises its own issues for any child. Shara will realize her status much sooner than a child in a non-interracial family. When she asks about her biological mother and father, how will she feel knowing her mother died and her father is not known? Beyond that, will she long to be with people of her "own kind?" Will she turn away from me for not being black? How will she relate to her black brothers and sisters in the community? Will she feel isolated?

I need to tell Shara that some people will look at us strangely. Some will want to know why "those people" have her. They will want to know what we are trying to "prove." Shara will hear rude, yet well-intentioned people commend us for adopting an African American child with FAS. They will say that we're "great to do this for a child nobody wants." They will say how "liberal" we are. Some will be happy we are doing something they couldn't. In some way I should feel complimented and proud. But Shara won't feel the compliment. Shara will be asking if I pity her or feel sorry for her.

In truth, I love Shara as my daughter and for who she is. I don't feel sorry for her. I have Shara because someone had to help and I felt it was mine to do. What's the big deal? It is true that she came into my life differently than the first two, but I love all three of my daughters equally, and my heart never gave me the choice whether I should or should not keep her.

Many years ago I read that children choose their parents. As children we choose the families we want to help us work through some of our karma. I believe this, along with the idea that our life on earth is an opportunity to reach a more spiritual level through the lessons we learn while we are alive. With that as a basis for being her parent, I feel that I don't have the right to reject or deny my daughter. Those who don't understand this say I'm crazy to look at life that way, but that's the way I see things. It is also my answer to many of my questions.

INSTITUTIONALIZED WHITE PRIVILEGE

Is not the desire of loving fathers to want to make a better world for their children? One way I can show Shara that I share this goal for her is to actively challenge racism. Racism is something I became aware of while in college in the 60s. I was affected deeply by the Civil Rights movement. Martin Luther King, Jr. and other leaders opened my eyes to the discrimination and hatred faced by African Americans, and I felt empathy with the struggles of other minorities. I was hurt by seeing how cruel whites were to black people. In the non-violent demonstrations I was enraged to see the beatings, the hoses, the disrespect for human life. With King's assassination and more hatred for people of color as their rage poured out into the streets, the contrast to the leadership of Malcom X—so poorly understood and so badly misrepresented by the media—fed the doubts and myths in many white's minds and intensified their racism.

Growing up in an orthodox Jewish home, I was clear about the anti-Semitic attitudes that were out there. I felt the spears of prejudice. I never hid the fact that I was part of a minority in this country. Shara can't either. While Shara will go to a school that reflects the broad cultural diversity of the community we live in, and our religious community invites inclusiveness, she will face racism in her life nonetheless. Having an African American sister already has made the issue of prejudice more keen for both of Shara's sisters, as it has for me. It is becoming a common occurrence for the girls to examine how they handle the bias they encounter.

Now, 30 years after the civil rights movement, I realize how much more needs to be done to challenge *institutionalized racism.* Institutionalized white privilege is the issue I need to look at. It was not enough for some of us to help carry the banner for the civil rights movement. It's not enough to be in support of affirmative action. It's not enough to be a consciousness "razor" to those who need to be educated. What I need to do is to take responsibility for my part in the system and structures of racism. I am part of the solution because I am part of the problem. It is important for whites to recognize their attitudes and undo their racism. We need to address our feelings with all people of color, and when we see discrepancies in our schools, for example, in the way children are treated or grouped, we need to demand not balance, but fairness. Speaking out about racism is speaking out against a white power structure that has little interest in changing and even less in loosening its racist grip on our lives.

SEXISM AND SELF

Each of my daughters faces sexism everyday of their lives. I know they feel the bias and deal with it the best they can. I also know how they can easily be part of the game of "playing up" to men in their lives, for example, by "acting feminine" and "looking pretty," since that's the way girls are socialized in the larger culture. I trust that as they grow up they will consider the anti-sexist values they were taught at home and act from their hearts.

I was raised in a home with two loving parents, a paternal grandmother and a sister two years older than me. The death of my father when I was 13 affected me greatly. A deep sense of loss stayed with me long after I graduated from college. Is it affecting my "job" now as a father by not affording me a male role model? How do I know I'm "doing right" by my daughters? Would I do it differently if they were boys? I know the pain I felt being "too gentle" as a boy. Perhaps I am helping to reverse that when I remind the girls to not take that stance towards boys they meet. Maybe my Dad could have helped me with these questions, and helped me accept who I was at an earlier age.

As a guidance counselor in the schools, I work with young people as a friend. But being a father is different. I have had to learn not to be a counselor to the girls, but a person who gives them unconditional love, a sense of discipline and the comfort of a secure home and a goodnight kiss.

At home I strive to be an "example." I want Shara to see and embrace my core values. She sees the way I treat women in the family and others in my life. She sees an equal partnership in the family dynamics. Whether I'm doing the dishes or the laundry, she sees me involved. I want to teach her humility, sincerity and to love humankind. And I want her to feel powerful, to know that she can make a difference in this world. I want her to mature into a woman who can be free to do what she truly wants, not what society dictates. I wish for her every opportunity to grow, to love and to be loved.

I also want to be able to father her responsibility as I get older. I know there are many men in their fifties who have children under the age of ten, but I still feel "old" knowing I'll be 65 when Shara is old enough to vote. I want to continue to be active and playful with her as she grows, and I hope she can understand that I may not be able to peddle the bike as fast as she can.

Responsible parenting will also require patience and an awareness of self. I know I never want to hit or hurt her, and I want to treat my entire family with all the love I can. As a child I was treated with respect, and I try to do the same for them. In school I see many different parenting styles, and when I meet the parents I see how misguided some are. Some children are very badly treated. In the writings of Alice Miller, I read how important it is for parents to understand their parenting styles. We easily repeat our own parents' mistakes and pass them on to our children. I find myself getting angry at one of the girls in a manner that, for example, can only reflect how I was treated. I was raised with high expectations placed on me. I always felt the pressure to be the "good little boy," though I don't remember ever not being good. I now realize I'm not the "perfect" father and my girls are not the "perfect" children—nor need we be.

So Shara's story is really my story as well. It's about a father who is looking at the lives he so dearly loves and cares for. This dad wants to make a difference, and will. Shara chose me as a father, in part, so I could examine myself. She has changed my life and is helping me grow.

It is my desire to return the gifts she is giving me.

Discussion Questions
Part II: Working out the Differences:
Sex, Gender Roles, and Family Life

1. Discuss the role that race, sex, and gender play in family life in the United States today.

_____

_____

_____

_____

_____

_____

_____

2. Discuss violence and sexual assault from the perspective of a female in the United States today.

_____

_____

_____

_____

_____

_____

_____

**Don't hesitate
to ask them for a
presentation that
will honor the
Polish American
taxpayers during
Polish American
Heritage Month. Invite
the entire Polonia to
attend as well as
the news media.**

Part III

Solutions for a Changing American Society: Economics and (Under) Development

Every April we are encouraged to take our daughters to work. A different perspective (and solutions) on this issue is discussed in "'Take Our Daughters'? Always Have." Economics is tied to citizenship in "Citizenship is everyone's Responsibility," as well as the contributions (and problems) of male equality in "The Rite of Work: The Economic Man."

Professional women also face problems of racial and sexual discrimination. "Pay Equity is a Necessary Remedy for Wage Discrimination," continues our discussions on such issues as what is today called "the glass ceiling," as well as "Federally Subsidized Housing in America," which affects the poor. Equal rights for all with regard of race, class, and gender and sexual orientation are included in "Myths about Gay men and Lesbians," "To Equalize Power Among Us," and "Things to do During National Polish American Heritage Month."

Black women have always taken their children to work. Of course, the lesson we learned going to work without mothers were not necessarily the lessons white feminists might have wanted us to learn.

—Vernon McClean

1

'Take Our Daughters'? Always Have

Blacks Need Opportunity, Not a Token Day at the Office

by Vernon McClean

In the Virgin Islands, my mother worked as a maid for Mr. Sebastian, the European proprietor of a white-owned store on Main Street. As a small boy, I'd come to work with her each day; I remember that she once slapped my face after I'd used his bathroom. (I later understood that I shouldn't have flushed: water was scarce on the island. But how was I to know? We blacks didn't have indoor plumbing at all.)

I think about Mr. Sebastian's house whenever I think about Take Our Daughters to Work Day, which is to be observed on Thursday. This is the fourth such observance; the day was started in 1993 by the Ms. Foundation for Women as a way for girls aged 9 to 15 to see what goes on in the working world.

But black women have *always* taken their children to work. Of course, the lessons we learned going to work with our mothers were not necessarily the lessons white feminists might have wanted us to learn. As a young boy, I learned that white people are powerful: they can make you abuse your children. I also learned that we were poor—which is why my mother, and like so many other black mothers, took her children to work. She had no day care, so she had no choice.

Which is not to say that I never learned anything of value. Another memory is that of my mother baking bread in Mr. Sebastian's oven. Through observation and with her guidance, I too learned how to bake bread. I helped her make the beds and wash the floor in Mr. Sebastian's home, so she could get home early. Decades before the word "sexism" was coined, she was a pioneer in non-sexist child rearing.

As I had children of my own, I too took them to work—partly out of economic necessity, and partly out of a paternal nurturing instinct. Why should I put my daughter in day care when I could lecture to a class at William Paterson College while she was sleeping in a box in the back of the classroom? And of course, my experience is not unique.

The experience of being with a parent at work, of learning the world of work, is far too important to be confined to a single day a year. That holds true for everyone, black, white, Latino or Asian. But there is a racial dimension to this issue that cannot be ignored, for the overall experience of work depends heavily on whether or not you are black. Consider the following:

- Despite affirmative action, according to a bipartisan Federal commission, white men make up only 29 percent of the work force but hold about 95 percent of all top management positions. The report by the Glass Ceiling Commission cited studies suggesting that "the glass ceiling exists because of the perception of many white males that as a group they are losing—losing the corporate game, losing control and losing opportunity."
- While an increasing number of white women have joined the work force in the past decade, the percentage who do so out of economic necessity is still far lower than the percentage for minority women. Where as white women's income may be supplemental, black women's income is required to maintain middle-income status.
- Finally, far too many black workers, and especially women, are confined to a sort of glass cellar. At William Paterson, for example, black women are still disproportionately represented among those cleaning the bathrooms. While the 325-member faculty has only 8 black women, the janitorial staff has many times that number.

As a whole, our parents—too many of them—still work in white people's homes, taking care of your daughters. Our daughters do not want to go to work in your home. They want other options. Black people want jobs for themselves and their mates. We want an education, and an end to race discrimination. We want programs of value to accomplish these aims, not one day a year exhorting us to "take our daughters to work."

If there is one message that I hope gets across it's that citizenship can't be dismissed as someone else's responsibility. Each of us has a role to play.

—Hillary Rodham Clinton

2

Citizenship Is Everyone's Responsibility

by Hillary R. Clinton

Every spring, I'm reminded of how hard it is to write and deliver a commencement address. Graduates are thinking much more about getting their diplomas than digesting sage advice from some wise and knowing elder. Those of us assigned the task of giving the speech inevitably find it a humbling experience—a bit like being parsley on a dinner plate.

Now I'm sure everyone who reads this column has a message of their own for graduates, and if you want to pass yours on to me, please do. I know I'll need some new ideas for next year.

In the meantime, I'd like to share some of what I said to graduates of the University of Arkansas, Drew University and the University of Maryland in commencement addresses earlier this month.

I talked about the importance of politics and government in a pluralistic democracy like ours, particularly at a time of such momentous change.

Just looking at the world around us, we see a new global economy taking shape, offering Americans the potential of greater prosperity but also the challenge of stiffer competition.

We also see how new technology is bringing the world closer together, changing the ways we communicate and do business but also reminding us that virtual reality will never substitute for human relationships.

Family dynamics are being transformed as most families send both parents—mothers and fathers alike—to work outside the home, posing the critical question of who is supposed to do what within our most intimate relationships.

And the world itself is changing. Communism has given way to capitalism, tyranny to democracy, closed markets to free trade, all of which is causing us to redefine the ideological labels and geographic boundaries that have framed our thinking for most of the last century.

At times like these, it's tempting to seize on easy answers, pat generalizations and stereotypes.

You know the stereotypes I'm talking about:

If you're under 25, you're an apathetic Generation X-er.

If you're over 40, you're a self-indulgent Baby Boomer.

If you're a liberal, you're a bleeding heart.

If you're a conservative, you have no heart.

If you're a Democratic President from Arkansas, you're all of those things, depending on what day it is.

And if you're the wife of a Democratic President from Arkansas, well, you just better make sure your hair is in place.

The truth is, there is no single label that applies to any of us. Our world is too complicated for that. So I urged the graduates I spoke to—and I urge all graduates—to stand up for the common values, ideals and traditions that have brought our country and our democracy this far.

And while I know it's not fashionable, I also urge them to get involved in politics and government. Politics, after all, is about more than pundits and pollsters, just as government is about more than building and bureaucrats.

Politics with a small "p" is the process that brings us together to work toward common ends peaceably. As I said to the graduates, when I talk about politics, I'm talking about you.

It's fine to bash those who believe government is the solution to every social ill. And it's fine to bash those who believe that every government power should be curbed. But one thing we can't do is reject politics and government in the process.

That's a cop-out.

Government and politics are not perfect. They may even be boring. Their achievements often seem minuscule in comparison to the issues we face.

But we are a better country today because generations before us paid the price to establish and maintain a stable, democratic government that protects our rights and expands opportunities that enable all of us to make the most of our lives.

My challenge to the Class of '96 is to go forth as active, committed citizens who believe that they have a stake in our government and our political system.

Now I can just see some of them rolling their eyes and saying to themselves, " Oh, c'mon, Mrs. Clinton. Really. I've go to pay off students loans. I need to find a job. I want to fall in love. I want to start a family. How am I going to find time for politics? You come from the Sixties. Your generation had higher hopes, bigger dreams. We're past that now."

My answer is: Give it your best shot. Work hard and love your spouses and your children. And make time for your neighbors, your communities and your government as well.

You may never run for office. You may never marry someone who runs for office. But go into the future thinking of yourselves as stewards of our democracy and as men and women who will keep the flame of freedom and justice alive.

If there is one message that I hope gets across it's that citizenship can't be dismissed as someone else's responsibility. Each of us has a role to play.

The only question then, is how much welfare benefits should be increased.

—Barbara Ehrenreich

3

Welfare is Not the Lap of Luxury

by Barbara Ehrenreich

I was not offended by the amount of money that Nancy Reagan reportedly spent for her inaugural wardrobe, $46,000, because I know that this sum would barely be enough to buy the pentagon a screwdriver. Since I can buy a screwdriver for $2.95 at the local hardware store, I appreciated the ingenuity Mrs. Reagan had shown in finding a way to cover herself, head to toe, at an equivalent price. What sets my teeth on edge is not the Administration's extravagance, but its apparent hostility to the female poor, who form a majority of the population known colloquially as "welfare cheats." The average family on welfare receives a good deal less than $4,600 a year, which, at official Washington prices, would not even finance a set of shoelaces-and even this sum is due for further cuts.

I used to think that the administration was stingy and mean-spirited, but the latest academic thinking on welfare is that it is positively unkind to shower the poor with largesse, even in the low four-figure range. Give an unemployed or bankrupt person a little help, according to the welfare critics George Gilder and Charles Murray, and he or she will lapse into the psychic slough known as demoralization-from which few ever venture forth again to seek honest employment at an hourly wage. The implication for public policy is that it would be much kinder to spare the poor the miser of demoralization, which is after all only a product of big government and other human errors, and let them experience the hunger that is natural to their condition.

There is someone I would like to introduce to the aforementioned gentlemen. She is a friend and former neighbor of mine, who will have to remain anonymous until public opinion takes a more generous turn. "Lori," let us call her, makes an excellent first impression. She is vivacious, smart, and although it shouldn't matter, disconcertingly pretty. She is also on welfare-and those who imagine the average welfare recipient as a slatternly mother of six or a young man apprenticing in street crime should know that Lori is a far more representative case: She is a single mother, as are close to 90 percent of recipients; she has only one child, which puts her among the 70 percent that have two or fewer; and, although this shouldn't matter either, she is white, as are a majority of welfare recipients.

Lori is no more demoralized by welfare than I am by an unexpected royalty check. True, she resents the days spent in the welfare office, the long waits, the interrogations about her limited inventory of household possessions. But she feels that she and her daughter have rights in the matter, like the right to a standard of living on some level exceeding vagrancy. She was not always, she will tell you, so assertive-certainly not in the two years when she was married to a man who routinely beat her and had once chased her around the house with a gun. Only welfare had made it possible to leave him, a move she says was like being born again, "as a human being this time."

In one way, though, Lori fits the worst stereotypes: She is a "cheat." That is to say, she has sources of income that she does not report to the welfare office. When she can find a friend to watch her daughter (welfare doesn't provide funds for child care), she rushes out to whatever job she can find: baby-sitting, waitressing, cleaning other people's houses, anything so long as it's off the books. I wouldn't want to sear to it in court, but she sometimes brings in close to $100 a week in this manner-not enough to enable her to get off welfare, but a useful supplement, along with the occasional house plant or pizza pie she accepts from an admirer.

If I was made of sterner stuff, if, for example, I was tough enough to disport myself in thousand-dollar-plus outfits while, only blocks away, my fellow citizens were warming themselves over bonfires in vacant lots, then I suppose I would turn Lori in. And if I were a welfare critic of the stature of Gilder or Murray, I suppose I would tell her I was doing it for her own good Instead, I merely sit back and reflect on what Lori's case reveals about welfare. The worst problem with it is not that it causes demoralization, atrophy of the work ethic, or craven dependency. The worst problem is that welfare doesn't pay enough.

This, I have realized, is the true cause of the demoralization critics are so concerned about: It is one thing to spend a day queueing up in a crowded stuffy room if the setting is OTB and you end up winning $50,000 in cash. But it is dispiriting to do the same thing for no greater reward than a $17 allowance for a child's winter jacket. And, as should be obvious, it is inadequate benefits, rather than depravity, that are the cause of cheating. Lori, for example, does not use her illicit income to build up a fleet of Cadillacs, but to buy little things that some pebble-hearted bureaucrat has determined are inessential to a welfare recipient's well-being: deodorant, hand lotion, an occasional commercial haircut.

The only question then, is how much welfare benefits should be increased. Bearing in mind that the primary purpose of welfare is to support mothers and young children, we might use an estimate offered in Newsweek's recent cover story on Yuppies, in which a young woman said she ordinarily required $200,000 to live on, but would of course need more if she were to have a baby. If $300,000 or so a year seems high, we might just go with the market value of the average mother's work: approximately $7 an hour, for both child and housekeeping, for what is minimally a 10-hour day, or about $26,000 a year.

Now, I can imagine the objections of the welfare critics, who will speak out manfully against this latest proposal to drive the poor beyond demoralization to outright despondency. Well, if they cannot understand that it feels better to have some money rather than none and more rather than less, I will base my argument on middle-class, self-interest: Welfare, as it is now, is degrading to the middle class. It makes us mean and petty, bad neighbors and worse citizens. In fact, the more miserly welfare is, the more anxious we feel, deep inside, about our own economic security. And the more anxious we feel, the more we are inclined to bluster about "not taking any handouts," and the nastier we get toward those who most need our understanding and support. It is a terrible cycle that we, the taxpayers and bread-winners have entered into, and perhaps far more debilitating in the long run than any "cycle of dependency" experience by the poor. Never mind the welfare recipients, we can't afford to go on like this.

Then there is the inevitable questions, asked by the well-meaning as well as the mean-willed, of where the money is supposed to come from. Awed as I am by the Federal deficit-and who cannot help but wonder when some international banking cabal will lose patience and set a collection agency loose on our nation's capital?—I have little patience for this question. Surely a nation that tolerates $46,000 wardrobes and equally overpriced screwdrivers can figure out how to support the poor at some level of dignity and comfort. Why, the President could hold a fund-raising dinner and invite a few dozen of his intimate friends and supporters. Or, as we say in the suburbs, the Pentagon could hold a garage sale.

One does not work to live; one lives to work.

—Max Weber

Have leisure and know that I am God.

—Psalm 65

4

The Rite of Work: The Economic Man

by Sam Keen

THE BOTTOM LINE—WORK AND WORTH

Preparations for the male ritual of work begin even before the age of schooling. Long before a boy child has a concept of the day after tomorrow, he will be asked by well-meaning but unconscious adults, "What do you want to be when you grow up?" It will not take him long to discover that "I want to be a horse" is not an answer that satisfies adults. They want to know what men plan to do, what job, profession, occupation we have decided to follow at five years of age! Boys are taught early that they are what they do. Later, as men, when we meet as strangers on the plane or at a cocktail party we break the ice by asking, "What do you do?"

Formal preparation for the rites of manhood in a secular society takes place first through the institution of schooling. Our indoctrination into the dominant myths, value system, and repertoire of heroic stories is homogenized into the educational process. My fifteen-year-old nephew put the matter more accurately than any social scientist. "Schools," he said, "are designed to teach you to take life sitting down. They prepare you to work in office buildings, to sit in rows or cubicles, to be on time, not to talk back, and to let somebody else grade you." From the first grade onward, schools teach us to define and measure ourselves against others. We learn that the world is composed of winners and losers, pass or fail.

The games that make up what we call physical education—football, basketball, and baseball—are minibattles that teach boys to compete in the game of life. Pregame pep talks, like salesmen's meetings, begin with the Vince Lombardi prayer: "Winning isn't the most important thing. It's the only thing." For many boys making the team, from Little League to college, provides the ritual form of combat that is central to male identity.

The first full-time job, like the first fight or first sex, is a rite of passage for men in our time. Boys have paper routes, but men have regular paychecks. Like primitive rites, work requires certain sacrifices and offers certain insignia of manhood. In return for agreeing to put aside childish dalliance and assume the responsibility for showing up from nine to five at some place of work, the initiate receives the power object—money—that allows him to participate in the adult life of the community.

Getting a credit card is more advanced rite of passage. The credit card is for the modern male what killing prey was to a hunter. To earn a credit rating a man must certify that he has

91

voluntarily cut himself off from childhood, that he has foregone the pleasure of languid mornings at the swimming hole, and has assumed the discipline of a regular job, a fixed address, and a predictable character. The Visa card (passport to the good life) is an insignia of membership, a sign that the system trusts you to spend what you have not yet earned because you have shown good faith by being regularly employed. In modern America going into debt is an important part of assuming the responsibilities of manhood. Debt, the willingness to live beyond our means, binds us to the economic system that requires both surplus work and surplus consumption. The popular bumper sticker, "I owe, I owe, so off to work I go" might well be the litany to express the commitment of the working man.

After accepting the disciplines of work and credit, a whole hierarchy of graduated symbolic initiations follows, from first to thirty-second degree. Mere employment entitles one to display the insignia of the Chevette. Acquiring the executive washroom key qualifies one for a Buick or Cadillac. Only those initiated into the inner sanctum of the boardroom may be borne in the regal Rolls-Royce. To the victors belong the marks of status and the repair bills. The right to wear eagle feathers or to sing certain sacred songs was recognized in American Indian tribes to signify the possession of a high degree of power and status, just as in contemporary society certain brand names and logos are tokens of class and rank. A man wears a Rolex not because it tells time more accurately than a $14.95 Timex but because, like a penis shield, it signifies an advanced degree of manhood. In a society where the marks of virtue are created by advertising, possession of stylish objects signifies power. For economic man a Ralph Lauren polo shirt says something very different than its Fruit of the Loom equivalent. The implicit message is that manhood can be purchased. And the expense of the luxury items we own marks our progress along the path of the good life as it is defined by a consumer society.

Within the last decade someone upped the ante on the tokens required for manhood. A generation ago providing for one's family was the only economic requirement. Nowadays, supplying the necessities entitles a man only to marginal respect. If your work allows you only to survive you are judged to be not much of a man. To be poor in a consumer society is to have failed the manhood test, or at least to have gotten a D–. The advertising industry reminds us at every turn that real men, successful men, powerful men, are big spenders. They have enough cash or credit to consume the best. Buying is status. "It's the cost of the toys that separates the men from the boys." The sort of man who reads *Playboy* or *The New Yorker* is dedicated to a life of voluntary complexity, conspicuous consumption, and adherence to the demanding discipline of style.

The rites of manhood in any society are those that are appropriate and congruent with the dominant myth. The horizon within which we live, the source of our value system, and the way we define "reality" are economic. The bottom line is the almighty dollar. Time is money, money is power, and power makes the world go round. In the same sense that the cathedral was the sacred center of the medieval city, the bank and other commercial buildings are the centers of the modern city.

Once upon a time work was considered a curse. As the result of Adam and Eve's sin we were driven from the Garden of Eden and forced to earn our bread by the sweat of our brows. Men labored because of necessity, but found the meaning and sweetness of life in free time.

According to the Greeks, only slaves and women were bound to the life of work. Free men discovered the joys and dignity of manhood in contemplation and in the cultivation of leisure. Until the time of the Protestant Reformation the world was divided between the realm of the secular, to which work and the common life belonged, and the realm of the sacred, which was the monopoly of the Church. Martin Luther changed all of this by declaring that every man and woman had a sacred vocation. The plowman and the housewife no less than the priest were called by God to express their piety in the common life of the community. Gradually the notion of the priesthood of all believers came to mean that every man and woman had a calling to meaningful secular work.

In the feudal era manhood involved being the lord of a manor, the head of a household, or at least a husbandman of the land. As the industrial revolution progressed men were increasingly pulled out of the context of nature, family, church, and community to find the meaning of their lives in trading, industry, the arts, and the professions, while women practiced their vocations by ministering to the needs of the home and practicing charity within the community. Gradually, getting and spending assumed the place of greatest importance, virtually replacing all of the old activities that previously defined manhood—hunting, growing, tending, celebrating, protesting, investigating. As "the bottom line" became our ultimate concern, and the Dow Jones the index of reality, man's world shrank. Men no longer found their place beneath the dome of stars, within the brotherhood of animals, by the fire of the hearth, or in the company of citizens. Economic man spends his days with colleagues, fellow workers, bosses, employees, suppliers, lawyers, customers, and other strangers. At night he returns to an apartment or house that has been empty throughout the day. More likely than not, if he is married with children, his wife has also been away at work throughout the day and his children have been tended and educated by another cadre of professionals. If he is successful his security (securus—"free from care") rests in his investments (from "vestment"—a religious garment) in stocks, bonds, and other commodities whose future value depends upon the whims of the market.

Nowadays only a fortunate minority are able to find harmony between vocation and occupation. Some artists, professionals, businessmen, and tradesmen find in their work a calling, a lifework, an arena within which they may express their creativity and care. But most men are shackled to the mercantile society in much the same way medieval serfs were imprisoned in the feudal system. All too often we work because we must, and we make the best of a bad job.

In the secular theology of economic man Work has replaced God as the source from whom all blessings flow. The escalating gross national product, or at least the rising Dow Jones index, is the outward and visible sign that we are progressing toward the kingdom of God; full employment is grace; unemployment is sin. The industrious, especially entrepreneurs with capital, are God's chosen people, but even laborers are sanctified because they participate in the productive economy.

As a form of secular piety Work now satisfies many of the functions once served by religion. In the words of Ayn Rand, whose popular philosophy romanticized capitalism and sanctified selfishness, "Your work is the process of achieving your values. Your body is a machine but your mind is its driver. Your work is the purpose of your life, and you must speed past any killer who assumes the right to stop you....Any value you might find outside your work, any other loyalty or love, can only be travelers going on their own power in the same direction."[1]

We don't work just to make a living. Increasingly, the world of work provides the meaning of our lives. It becomes an end in itself rather than a means. A decade ago, only twenty-eight percent of us enjoyed the work we did. And yet, according to a Yankelovich survey, eighty percent of us reported that we would go right on working even if we didn't need the money. By the 1980s this profile changed. We are just as attached to our work, but now we are demanding that the workplace provide an outlet for our creativity. Yankelovich reports in 1988 that fifty-two percent of Americans respond "I have an inner need to do the very best job I can, regardless of the pay" and sixty-one percent when asked what makes for the good life say "a job that is interesting."[2]

Something very strange has happened to work and leisure in the last generation. The great promise of emerging technology was that it would finally set men free from slavery and we could flower. As late as the 1960s philosophers, such as Herbert Marcuse, sociologists, and futurists were predicting a coming leisure revolution. We were just around the corner from a twenty-hour work week. Soon we would be preoccupied by arts, games, and erotic dalliance on leisurely afternoons. At worst we would have to learn to cope with "pleasure anxiety" and the threat of leisure.

Exactly the opposite happened. Work is swallowing leisure. The fast lane has become a way of life for young professionals who are giving their all to career. In the 1990s Americans may come more and more to resemble the Japanese—workaholics all, living to work rather than working to live, finding their identity as members of corporate tribes....

Part of the problem is that work, community, and family are getting mixed up and lumped together. Increasingly, Americans live in places where they are anonymous, and seek to find their community at work. Companies, with the help of organizational development consultants, are trying to make the workplace the new home, the new family. The new motto is: humanize the workplace, make it a community; let communication flourish on all levels. The best (or is it the worst?) of companies have become paternalistic or maternalistic, providing their employees with all the comforts and securities of home....

In short, the workplace is rapidly becoming its own culture that defines who we are. Like minisocieties, professions and corporations create their own ritual and mythology. Doctors share a common story, a history of disease and cure, a consensus about the means of healing with other doctors. Businessmen share the language of profit and loss with other businessmen and acknowledge the same tokens of success. As economic organizations have grown larger than governments, employees render them a type of loyalty previously reserved for God, country, or family.

To determine what happens to men within the economic world we need to look critically at its climate, its ruling mood, its ethos, its aims, and its method. We should no more accept

---

[1]Ayn Rand, *For the New Intellectual* (NY: Signet Books, 1961), p. 130. [Author's note]
[2]*American Health* (September 1988). [Author's note]

a profession's or a corporation's self-evaluation, its idealistic view of itself (we are a family, a "service" organization, dedicated to the highest ideals of quality, etc.) than we would accept the propaganda of any tribe or nation.

A recent critical study of the climate of corporate culture suggests it may be more like a tyrannical government than a kindly family. Earl Shorris, in a neglected and very important book, suggests that the modern corporation represents a historically new form of tyranny in which we are controlled by accepting the definitions of happiness that keep us in harness for a lifetime. Herewith, in short, his argument:

> The most insidious of the many kinds of power is the power to define happiness....
>
> The manager, like the nobleman of earlier times, serves as the exemplary merchant: since happiness cannot be defined, he approximates his definition through the display of symbols, such as expense account meals, an expensive house, stylish clothing, travel to desirable places, job security, interesting friends, membership in circles of powerful people, advantages for his children, and social positions for his entire family....
>
> In the modern world, a delusion about work and happiness enables people not only to endure oppression but to seek it and to believe that they are happier because of the very work that oppresses them. At the heart of the delusion lies the manager's definition of happiness: sweat and dirty hands signify oppression and a coat and tie signify happiness, freedom, and a good life.
>
> Blue-collar workers...resist symbolic oppression. One need only visit an assembly line and observe the styles of dress, speech, and action of the workers to realize the symbolic freedom they enjoy....They live where they please, socialize with whomever they please, and generally enjoy complete freedom outside the relatively few hours they spend at their jobs....No matter how much money a blue-collar worker earns, he is considered poor; no matter how much he enjoys his work, he is thought to be suffering. In that way, blue-collar wages are kept low and blue-collar workers suffer the indignity of low status.
>
> The corporation or the bureaucracy....becomes a place, the cultural authority, the moral home of a man. The rules of the corporation become the rules of society, the future replaces history, and the organization becomes the family of the floating man....By detaching him from the real world of place, the corporation becomes the world for him.
>
> Men abandoned the power to define happiness for themselves, and having once abandoned that power, do not attempt to regain it....[3]

The new rhetoric about the workplace as home and family needs to be balanced by an honest evaluation of the more destructive implications of the iron law of profit. Home and family are ends in themselves. They are, or should be, about sharing of love to no purpose. They file no quarterly reports. Business is an activity organized to make a profit. And any activity is shaped by the end it seeks. Certainly business these days wears a velvet glove, comporting itself with a new facade of politeness and enlightened personnel policies, but beneath the glove is the iron fist of competition and warfare.

---

[3]Earl Shorris, *The Oppressed Middle: Politics of Middle Management* (Garden City, NY: Doubleday, 1989). Now in print under a different title: *Scenes from Corporate Life* (NY: Penguin, 1990). [Author's note]

The recent spate of best-selling books about business that make use of military metaphors tell an important story about economic life and therefore about the climate within which most men spend their days. Listen to the metaphors, the poetry of business as set forth in David Rogers's *Waging Business Warfare* from the jacket copy:

> Become a master of strategy on today's corporate killing fields—and win the war for success....How to succeed in battle: believe it: if you're in business, you're at war. Your enemies—your competitors—intend to annihilate you. Just keeping your company alive on the battlefield is going to be a struggle. Winning may be impossible—unless you're a master of military strategy....You can be—if you'll follow the examples of the great tacticians of history. Because the same techniques that made Genghis Khan, Hannibal, and Napoleon the incomparable conquerors they were are still working for Chrysler's Lee Iacocca, Procter & Gamble's John Smale, Remington's Victor Kiam, and other super-strategists on today's corporate killing-fields....Join them at the command post! Mastermind the battle! Clobber the enemy! Win the war![4]

Or, maybe to succeed you need to know *The Leadership Secrets of Attila the Hun?* Or listen to the language of Wall Street: corporate raiders, hostile takeovers, white knights, wolf packs, industrial spies, the underground economy, head-hunting, shark-repellent, golden parachutes, poison pills, making a killing, etc.

When we organize our economic life around military metaphors and words such as *war, battle, strategy, tactics, struggle, contest, competition, winning, enemies, opponents, defenses, security, maneuver, objective, power, command, control, willpower, assault* we have gone a long way toward falling into a paranoid worldview. And when men live within a context where their major function is to do battle—economic or literal—they will be shaped by the logic of the warrior psyche.

THE HIGH PRICE OF SUCCESS

At the moment the world seems to be divided between those countries that are suffering from failed economies and those that are suffering from successful economies. After a half century of communism the USSR, Eastern Europe, and China are all looking to be saved from the results of stagnation by a change to market economies. Meanwhile, in the U.S., Germany, and Japan we are beginning to realize that our success has created an underclass of homeless and unemployed, and massive pollution of the environment. As the Dow rises to new heights everyone seems to have forgotten the one prophetic insight of Karl Marx: where the economy creates a class of winners it will also create a class of losers, where wealth gravitates easily into the hands of the haves, the fortunes of the have-nots become more desperate.

On the psychological level, the shadow of our success, the flip side of our affluence, is the increasing problem of stress and burnout. Lately, dealing with stress and burnout has become a growth industry. Corporations are losing many of their best men to the "disease" of stress.

---

[4]David J. Rogers, *Waging Business Warfare: Lessons from the Military Masters in Achieving Corporate Superiority* (New York: Scribner, 1987). [Author's note]

Every profession seems to have its crisis: physician burnout, teacher burnout, lawyer burnout. Experts in relaxation, nutrition, exercise, and meditation are doing a brisk business.

But finally, stress cannot be dealt with by psychological tricks, because for the most part it is a philosophical rather than a physiological problem, a matter of the wrong worldview. Perhaps the most common variety of stress can best be described as "rustout" rather than burnout. It is a product, not of an excess of fire but of a deficiency of passion. We, human beings, can survive so long as we "make a living," but we do not thrive without a sense of significance that we gain only by creating something we feel is of lasting value—a child, a better mousetrap, a computer, a space shuttle, a book, a farm. When we spend the majority of our time doing work that gives us a paycheck but no sense of meaning we inevitably get bored and depressed. When the requirements of our work do not match our creative potential we rust out. The second kind of burnout is really a type of combat fatigue that is the inevitable result of living for an extended period within an environment that is experienced as a battle zone. If the competition is always pressing you to produce more and faster, if life is a battle, if winning is the only thing, sooner or later you are going to come down with battle fatigue. Like combat veterans returning from Vietnam, businessmen who live for years within an atmosphere of low-intensity warfare begin to exhibit the personality traits of the warrior. They become disillusioned and numb to ethical issues, they think only of survival and grow insensitive to pain. You may relax, breathe deeply, take time for R and R, and remain a warrior. But ultimately the only cure for stress is to leave the battlefield.

The feminist revolution made us aware of how the economic order has discriminated against women, but not of how it cripples the male psyche. In ancient China the feet of upperclass women were broken, bent backwards, and bound to make them more "beautiful." Have the best and brightest men of our time had their souls broken and bent to make them "successful"?

Let's think about the relation between the wounds men suffer, our overidentification with work, and our captivity within the horizons of the economic myth.

Recently, a lament has gone out through the land that men are becoming too tame, if not limp. The poet Robert Bly, who is as near as we have these days to a traveling bard and shaman for men, says we have raised a whole generation of soft men—oh-so-sensitive, but lacking in thunder and lightning. He tells men they must sever the ties with mother, stop looking at themselves through the eyes of women, and recover the "wild man" within themselves.

I suspect that if men lack the lusty pride of self-affirmation, if we say "yes" too often but without passion, if we are burned out without ever having been on fire, it is mostly because we have allowed ourselves to be engulfed by a metabody, a masculine womb—The Corporation....

At what cost to the life of our body and spirit do we purchase corporate and professional success? What sacrifices are we required to make to these upstart economic gods?

Here are some of the secrets they didn't tell you at the Harvard Business School, some of the hidden, largely unconscious, tyrannical, unwritten rules that govern success in professional and corporate life:

Cleanliness is next to prosperity. Sweat is lower class, lower status. Those who shower before work and use deodorant make more than those who shower after work and smell human throughout the day. As a nation we are proud that only three percent of the population has to work on the land—get soiled, be earthy—to feed the other ninety-seven percent.

Look but don't touch. The less contact you have with real stuff—raw material, fertilizer, wood, steel, chemicals, making things that have moving parts—the more money you will make. Lately, as we have lost our edge in manufacturing and production, we have comforted ourselves with the promise that we can prosper by specializing in service and information industries. Oh, so clean.

Prefer abstractions. The further you move up toward the catbird seat, the penthouse, the office with the view of all Manhattan, the more you live among abstractions. In the brave new world of the market you may speculate in hog futures without ever having seen a pig, buy out an airline without knowing how to fly a plane, grow wealthy without having produced anything.

Specialize. The modern economy rewards experts, men and women who are willing to become focused, concentrated, tightly bound, efficient. Or to put the matter more poignantly, we succeed in our professions to the degree that we sacrifice wide-ranging curiosity and fascination with the world at large, and become departmental in our thinking. The professions, like medieval castles, are small kingdoms sealed off from the outer world by walls of jargon. Once initiated by the ritual of graduate school, MBAs, economists, lawyers, and physicians speak only to themselves and theologians speak only to God.

Sit Still and stay indoors. The world is run largely by urban, sedentary males. The symbol of power is the chair. The chairman of the board sits and manages. As a general rule those who stay indoors and move the least make the most money. Muscle doesn't pay. Worse yet, anybody who has to work in the sun and rain is likely to make the minimum wage. With the exception of quarterbacks, boxers, and race car drivers, whose bodies are broken for our entertainment, men don't get ahead by moving their bodies.

Live by the clock. Ignore your intimate body time, body rhythms, and conform to the demands of corporate time, work time, professional time. When "time is money," we bend our bodies and minds to the demands of EST (economic standard time). We interrupt our dreams when the alarm rings, report to work at nine, eat when the clock strikes twelve, return to our private lives at five, and retire at sixty-five—ready or not. As a reward we are allowed weekends and holidays for recreation. Conformity to the sacred routine, showing up on time, is more important than creativity. Instead of "taking our time" we respond to deadlines. Most successful men, and lately women, become Type A personalities, speed freaks, addicted to the rush of adrenaline, filled with a sense of urgency, hard driven, goal oriented, and stressed out. The most brutal example of this rule is the hundred-hour week required of physicians in their year of residency. This hazing ritual, like circumcision, drives home the deep mythic message that your body is no longer your own.

Wear the uniform. It wouldn't be so bad if those who earned success and power were proud enough in their manhood to peacock their colors. But no. Success makes drab. The higher you rise in the establishment the more colorless you become, the more you dress like an undertaker or a priest. Bankers, politicians, CEOs wear black, gray, or dark blue, with maybe a bold pinstripe or a daring "power tie." And the necktie? That ultimate symbol of the respectable man has obviously been demonically designed to exile the head from the body and restrain all deep and passionate breath. The more a corporation, institution, or profession requires the sacrifice of the individuality of its members, the more it requires uniform wear. The corp isn't really looking for a few good men. It's looking for a few dedicated Marines, and it knows exactly how to transform boys into uniform men. As monks and military men have known for centuries, once you get into the habit you follow the orders of the superior.

Keep your distance, stay in your place. The hierarchy of power and prestige that governs every profession and corporation establishes the proper distance between people. There are people above you, people below you, and people on your level, and you don't get too close to any of them. Nobody hugs the boss. What is lacking is friendship. I know of no more radical critique of economic life than the observation by Earl Shorris that nowhere in the vast literature of management is there a single chapter on friendship.

Desensitize yourself. Touch, taste, smell—the realm of the senses—receive little homage. What pays off is reason, will-power, planning, discipline, control. There has, of course, recently been a move afoot to bring in potted plants and tasteful art to make corporate environments more humane. But the point of these exercises in aesthetics, like the development of communication skills by practitioners of organizational development, is to increase production. The bottom line is still profit, not pleasure or persons.

Don't trouble yourself with large moral issues. The more the world is governed by experts, specialists, and professionals, the less anybody takes responsibility for the most troubling consequences of our success-failure. Television producers crank out endless cop and killing tales, but refuse to consider their contribution to the climate of violence. Lawyers concern themselves with what is legal, not what is just. Physicians devote themselves to kidneys or hearts of individual patients while the health delivery system leaves masses without medicine. Physicists invent new generations of genocidal weapons which they place in the eager arms of the military. The military hands the responsibility for their use over to politicians. Politicians plead that they have no choice—the enemy makes them do it. Professors publish esoterica while students perish from poor teaching. Foresters, in cahoots with timber companies, clear-cut or manage the forest for sustained yield, but nobody is in charge of oxygen regeneration. Psychologists heal psyches while communities fall apart. Codes of professional ethics are for the most part, like corporate advertisements, high sounding but self-serving.

When we live within the horizons of the economic myth, we begin to consider it honorable for a man to do whatever he must to make a living. Gradually we adopt what Erich Fromm called "a marketing orientation" toward our selves. We put aside our dreams, forget the green promise of our young selves, and begin to tailor our personalities to what the market requires. When we mold ourselves into commodities, practice smiling and charm so we will have "winning personalities," learn to sell ourselves, and practice the silly art of power dressing, we are certain to be haunted by a sense of emptiness.

Men, in our culture, have carried a special burden of unconsciousness, of ignorance of the self. The unexamined life has been worth quite a lot in economic terms. It has enabled us to increase the gross national product yearly. It may not be necessary to be a compulsive extrovert to be financially successful, but it helps. Especially for men, ours is an outer-directed culture that rewards us for remaining strangers to ourselves, unacquainted with feeling, intuition, or the subtleties of sensation and dreams.

Many of the personality characteristics that have traditionally been considered "masculine"—aggression, rationality—are not innate or biological components of maleness but are products of a historical era in which men have been socially assigned the chief roles in warfare and the economic order. As women increasingly enter the quasimilitary world of the economic system they are likely to find themselves governed by the logic of the system. Some feminists, who harbor a secret belief in the innate moral superiority of women, believe that women will change the rules of business and bring the balm of communication and human kindness into the boardroom. To date this has been a vain hope. Women executives have proven themselves the equal of men in every way—including callousness. The difference between the sexes is being eroded as both sexes become defined by work. It is often said that the public world of work is a man's place and that as women enter it they will become increasingly "masculine" and lose their "femininity." To think this way is to miss the most important factor of the economic world. Economic man, the creature who defines itself within the horizons of work and consumption, is not man in any full sense of the word, but a being who has been neutralized, degendered, rendered subservient to the laws of the market. The danger of economics is not that it turns women into men but that it destroys the fullness of both manhood and womanhood.

The entry of working women into the U.S. labor force is one of the most significant developments of the 20th century.

—Joy Anne Grune

5

Pay Equity Is a Necessary Remedy for Wage Discrimination

by Joy Ann Grune

INTRODUCTION

The entry of working women into the U.S. labor force is one of the most significant developments of the 20th century. Although most women work because they need to and many because they want to, the most powerful explanation for the extraordinary movement of women into the paid work force is the accelerated demand for their labor. The transformation of the U.S. economy, particularly since World War II, would not have been possible without women's response to the call for new workers, to fill new jobs, in growing industries. This is the terrain that gives birth to pay equity.

As a historical development, pay equity is a direct response to the societal importance—so often denied and ridiculed—of females and female-dominated jobs in today's economy. Women demand pay equity as they reject their trivialization as workers.

Culture, history, psychiatry, and social relations all have a role in wage discrimination, as they do in other legal rights issues. They contribute to the creation and maintenance of a gender-based division of labor in the market economy that is old, pronounced, and pays women less. But the focus of pay equity is on the translation of theory into practice, which occurs when an employer sets discriminatory wages for a job classification because of the sex, or race or ethnicity, of a predominant number of its occupants.

This paper defines pay equity as a matter of discrimination and shows why affirmative action is not a substitute. It examines five fallacies behind market-based arguments against pay equity and assesses the question of cost. Recent activities of Federal, State, and local government are described; the Federal Government's lack of enforcement of the 1964

Civil Rights Act is reviewed; and recommendations are offered for effective government involvement.

PAY EQUITY IS A NECESSARY REMEDY FOR WAGE DISCRIMINATION

The principle of pay equity requires the elimination of discrimination in pay within a firm that has operated to depress the wages of entire job classifications because of the sex of the overwhelming majority of occupants. The goal of pay equity is accomplished by raising the wages of predominantly female jobs in a workplace to match the wages of similarly valued male jobs.

The challenge of pay equity is deliberate and focuses directly on the wage-setting process. It does not rely on indirect or laissez faire overtures such as affirmative action programs or the market, which have shown themselves historically to be inadequate to the task of significantly reducing overall wage bias.

Pay equity is an essential remedy for wage discrimination based on sex. It is uniquely capable of reaching deeply structured patterns of wage discrimination associated with job segregation.

The majority of pay equity initiatives have been efforts to reach sex-based discrimination. When patterns of job segregation and wage depression in a workplace are associated with race or ethnicity, the principle of pay equity also can be applied. In New York State, for example, the pay equity job evaluation study now taking place is studying race and sex. U.S. House Resolution 239 introduced by Congresswoman Olympia Snowe (R-Me.) in 1984 calls for a pilot pay equity job evaluation study of the Federal sector that is not restricted to sex.

The U.S. Supreme Court, in Gunther v. County of Washington, has decided that wage discrimination involving jobs that are comparable, though not equal, is illegal. Such violations of Title VII of the Civil Rights Act must be stopped if women, and the men who work with them in predominantly female jobs, are to be released from employment discrimination.

The persistence of the wage gap and job segregation; the findings of virtually every pay equity job evaluation study showing that predominantly female jobs are paid less than male jobs of comparable worth; favorable court decisions in Gunther, Washington State, and IUE v. Washington; and growing research and understanding of how the labor market operates— all indicate that wage discrimination is at work in creating consistently low pay for female dominated jobs.

EQUAL PAY FOR EQUAL WORK AND
THE ELIMINATION OF DISCRIMINATION IN HIRING AND PROMOTION
ARE NOT SUBSTITUTES FOR PAY EQUITY

A comprehensive program to eliminate employment discrimination against women needs to include provisions for pay equity, equal pay for equal work, and the elimination of discrimination in hiring and promotion. These are complementary, but analytically distinct approaches to related, but different problems encountered in a workplace. All are required by law.

EQUAL PAY FOR EQUAL WORK

With few exceptions, equal pay for equal work is accepted by the public as a fundamental right of working people. The Equal Pay Act, passed by the U.S. Congress in 1963, mandates equal pay for equal work performed by men and women.

In 1962, 1 year before the Equal Pay Act was passed, full-time, year-round working women earned 59.5 cents for each dollar earned by their male counterparts. Today, the figure is 61 cents.[1]

The inability of the act to significantly reduce the wage gap should not be misconstrued. For example, 6 years ago Daniel Glisberg, then Assistant Secretary of Labor, reported in a speech to the Coalition of Labor Union Women that the Equal Pay Act "has obtained $164 million for some 272,000 employees, nearly all women. These figures do not include the $150 million settlement obtained for 13,000 employees of AT&T. In 1978 alone, we were able to restore income or other compensation to more than 15,000 workers for a total of $8.7 million."[2]

Enforcement of the Equal Pay Act has brought higher wages to many women. Stronger enforcement is still needed, particularly since greater numbers of women are slowly assuming jobs equal to men's.

Unfortunately, however, the vast number of employed women do not hold jobs equal to those held by men, and, therefore, the right to a nondiscriminatory wage afforded by the Equal Pay Act does not apply to their situation. In addition, the movement of women into nontraditional jobs over the last 20 years has been outpaced by the movement of women into the work force through low paying, mostly female jobs.

In 1982 over 50 percent of working women were found in 20 out of a total of 427 occupations.[3] It is estimated that two-thirds of all women and men would have to change jobs to achieve equality of distribution by sex.[4] The degree of occupational segregation by sex is as severe today as it was over 80 years ago.[5]

Women of all colors are concentrated in low paying, overwhelmingly female jobs. Although the employment distributions of different ethnic and racial groups of women are converging, there are still differences. For example, in 1979, clerical work employed more than 35 percent of all working women, including 35.9 percent of white women, 29 percent of black women, 31.1 percent of Mexican women, 38.4 percent of Puerto Rican women, and 31.2 percent of Cuban women.[6] Tow out of 12 occupational groups—service and clerical—employ about 60 percent of black women and 53 percent of white women.[7]

The Wage Gap: Myths and Facts (National Committee on Pay Equity, 1983).

[2]Joy Ann Grune, *Manual on Pay Equity: Raising Wages for Women's Work* (National Conference on Alternative State and Local Policies and National Committee on Pay Equity, 1980., p. 61.

[3]*The Wage Gap: Myths and Facts.*

[4]Heidi Hartmann, "The Case for Comparable Worth," *Equal Pay for Unequal Work* (Eagle Forum Education and Legal Defense Fund, 1984), p. 14.

[5]Ibid.

[6]*Women of Color and Pay Equity* (National Committee on Pay Equity, 1984).

[7]Ibid.

- Increasingly, women of color are moving into the same occupations as those in which White women work, so that:
- Clerical work now accounts for almost one-third of women workers in nearly every racial and ethnic group;
- Only Cuban, Chinese and Native American women have slightly higher percentages in operative, blue-collar work than in clerical;
- The jobs held by Black women have shifted significantly from blue-collar, operative work to white-collar work: clerical, professional, technical, managerial and sales;
- Mexican American and Puerto Rican women remain concentrated in operative occupations, although this occupational category is second for both of these populations to clerical work.[8]

The facts indicate that the vast majority—perhaps 80 percent—of women work in predominantly female jobs. The wage discrimination they experience is more often and more directly in reference to predominantly male jobs that are comparable, not equal. Thus, the Equal Pay Act is limited in its ability to help them.

THE ELIMINATION OF DISCRIMINATION IN HIRING AND PROMOTION

Women workers are moving into predominantly male, white-collar and blue-collar jobs. This movement has not seriously reduced the index of job segregation or the wage gap because simultaneously even more women have entered the work force through predominantly female jobs with low wages.

The entry of women into nontraditional jobs with nondiscriminatory wages is in large measure due to the Equal Pay Act, Civil Rights Act, and Executive Order 11246. If these laws had not been in place, it is likely that the degree of job segregation and the wage gap would have dramatically increased over the last 20 years because the entry of women into feminized jobs with low wages, particularly into the expanding clerical and service sectors, would have even more outpaced their movement into nontraditional work with higher wages.

The elimination of discriminatory obstacles that impede or prevent women from moving into jobs is required by law. It is one essential component of an antidiscrimination program that can allow women to operate as workers without being victimized by illegal acts. However, this approach is no substitute—legally or pragmatically—for requiring the elimination of sex-based wage discrimination.

First of all, the law is already clear in stating that wage discrimination is illegal and must be eliminated whether it occurs between jobs that are equal or between jobs that are comparable. The availability of an affirmative action program does not transform an illegal act of wage discrimination into a legal one. Similarly, a women's decision to enter or stay in a

---

[8]Ibid.

job—regardless of her reasons for so deciding—does not give the employer license to discriminate. This is the case in equal pay for equal work situations and in situations with comparable jobs. Finally, employer efforts to stop discrimination against women who try to move into male-dominated jobs do not, under any circumstances, permit the employer to reduce wages for other jobs because they are held by women.

A nurse has the right to an opportunity to be a doctor, and a secretary has the right to an opportunity to be an executive or a management analyst. To tell a nurse that she must be a doctor to escape discrimination in employment is to blame the victim and to turn antidiscrimination laws inside out.

Along similar lines, it has been suggested that pursuing job integration through affirmative action can take the place of pay equity. It is argued that if typists, nurses, secretaries, and librarians, for example, were to leave their fields and find jobs in higher paying, traditionally male jobs, the wage gap would close. This approach cannot legally substitute for pay equity, for the reasons offered above. It is an important complement, but has difficulties.

First, as indicated earlier, it is estimated that two thirds of men and women would have to change jobs for equality of occupational distribution to occur. Given these numbers, closing the wage gap through job integration and affirmative action would take a very long time, perhaps forever.

Second, this approach calls on women to forsake years or decades of experience and training. Some women may want to; many may not. But in any event, such an employment policy makes little sense because its success would depend on millions of skilled women deserting the service sector infrastructure of the economy.

Third, an employment policy whose goal is to place millions of women into industries and occupations that are male dominated presents the problem of training and attracting men to replace them. Finally, although the service sector has numerous predominantly female jobs and contains some of the fastest growing occupations, many traditionally male jobs, especially in basic industry, are suffering growing rates of unemployment. A wage gap reduction policy that tries to move growing numbers of women from high growth jobs to shrinking, predominantly male jobs is doomed to failure.

It is distinctly possible that the implementation of pay equity will do as much as or more than any other policy to promote job integration, affirmative action, and the elimination of discrimination in hiring and promotion:

- The empowerment of women, which is already a frequently visible accompaniment to pay equity, will result in more determined women seeking new types of work;
- There will be much less of an incentive to employers for maintaining sex-segregated jobs once pay equity is implemented;
- Affirmative action will be used by employers to integrate jobs so as to avoid financial and legal liability in pay equity cases; and
- Higher wages in predominantly female jobs will attract men.

THE FAILURE OF MARKET ARGUMENTS AGAINST PAY EQUITY

Great confusion is being created around pay equity and the market. It has been alleged that pay equity would destroy the market and is unnecessary and impossible because of the market. These arguments are not accurate and are based on five fallacies:

(a) The market is free and operates without interventions.
(b) The market will eliminate discrimination.
(c) Pay equity requires the setting of wages outside of a market economy and is an alternative to market-based wage determination.
(d) Employers currently respond directly and uniformly to market forces.
(e) Wages are currently set almost exclusively and directly on the basis of market wage rates.

THE MARKET IS FREE AND OPERATES WITHOUT INTERVENTIONS

There are few political tendencies today which claim that the market is or should be completely free. For the sake of employers, children, and adult workers, government has long intervened in the economy with legislation, Executive orders, appropriations, tax codes, etc. These steps are taken because of the belief that some principles take precedence over the right of a market to be free. Child labor laws, collective bargaining laws, antidiscrimination laws, health and safety laws, environmental laws, tax breaks, and targeted subsidies to ailing companies are examples of the belief in action.

In addition to government, companies have also intervened in market behavior. In the employment area, for example, 9 to 5: National Association of Working Women has claimed that "large employers in major cities form consortia to discuss wage rates and benefits. Working Women believes that such groups have been influential in holding down clerical salaries over the years."[9] Nine to 5 has specifically identified the Boston Survey Group, a group of large employers that has met for the purpose of setting clerical salaries.

THE MARKET WILL ELIMINATE DISCRIMINATION

The market has not eliminated discrimination, and there is nothing to indicate that it will. In fact, according to the National Academy of Sciences:
"market wages incorporate the effects of many institutional factors, including discrimination."[10]

When an employer sets wages directly on the basis of market rates for predominantly female jobs, it incorporates prior discrimination by other employers. Without efforts to remove bias from market rates, this type of reliance on the market becomes one of the most damaging transmitters of discrimination because it serves to carry discrimination from employer to employer to employer.

---

[9]Grune, *Manual on Pay Equity, p. 145.*
[10]Heidi Hartmann and Don Treiman, *Women, Work and Wages: Equal Pay for Jobs of Equal Value* (National Academy of Sciences, 1981), p.65.

PAY EQUITY REQUIRES THE SETTING OF WAGES OUTSIDE OF A MARKET ECONOMY AND IS AN ALTERNATIVE TO MARKET-BASED WAGE DETERMINATION

Pay equity does not mean the destruction of an external, market-based, salary-setting scheme that will be replaced by a purely internal one. The goal of pay equity is to eliminate bias and discrimination in wage setting. This bias may operate through market rates, through the way the employer responds to or relies on the market, through biased job evaluation systems, or through purely subjective judgments made by employers. The objective of pay equity is not to overturn the market, but merely to eliminate bias, whatever its sources.

> The Comparable Worth strategy can be seen as an attempt to bring wages of female-dominated jobs up to the going market wage rates for similar type work that is not female dominated. Wages for female-dominated jobs are seen to be artificially depressed by discrimination. In this view it is not Comparable Worth that interferes with a free market, but discrimination. Given that there is discrimination in the labor market, which depresses the wages of women's jobs, intervention is necessary to remove discrimination and its effects. It is therefore unnecessary to have an alternative to market wages; it is necessary only to adjust them. A variety of mechanisms, particularly job evaluation systems, exist that can be used to adjust wages to remove the effects of discrimination.[11]

It would be virtually impossible for firms to establish wages with no reliance on the market, and pay equity activists have not asked employers to do so. They usually suggest that wages for predominantly male jobs be derived from prevailing market rates and be used as the baseline. Under this approach, wages for predominantly female jobs are raised to match those of similarly valued, predominantly male jobs. This, for example, was the remedy that Judge Jack Tanner ordered in Washington State.

For all of these reasons, it is incorrect to characterize pay equity as necessarily a full substitute for or alternative to market-based wages. Pay equity requires a wage structure that is not consistently marred or dented by wage depressions that are tied to gender or race. On top of such an equitable structure, it is possible to build in contingencies that permit an employer to respond legitimately and fairly to real shortages, to seniority requirements, to employment needs of a labor pool. But in its essence, the structure needs to be nondiscriminatory and, therefore, cannot be entirely market dependent.

EMPLOYERS RESPOND AUTOMATICALLY AND UNIFORMLY TO MARKET FORCES

Pay equity advocates are beginning to believe that employers rely on and respond to market forces differently depending on the sex composition of the job for which wages are being set.

---

[11]Hartmann, "The Case for Comparable Worth," p.11.

In the area of supply and demand, an employer has choices in how to respond to a shortage of workers. The choices—relative to a shortage of nurses, for example—include temporarily absorbing the shortage, hiring temporary nurses, having the nurses who are employed work overtime, redesigning the workload, changing recruitment techniques, or possibly, raising wages. Pay equity advocates fear that the last choice—raising wages—is less likely to be used or will be used less quickly when the job is mostly female. They also fear that wages will be raised a smaller amount. The nurse shortage of several years ago was experienced by numerous metropolitan areas and led to a great variety of innovative recruitment techniques, including international forays to the Philippines and elsewhere. But wages did not increase as much or as quickly as might be expected.

The use of surveys to calculate prevailing wage rates is another example of how employers can incorporate bias into their reliance on the market. In West Virginia, for example, clerical workers are concerned that their large employer tends to survey lower paying firms in a smaller geographical area when the job in question is predominantly female or minority.

As pay equity activists begin to research seriously the wage-setting procedures in their places of employment, they are finding that employers have latitude in responding to and relying on the market and that it is too often exercised to the disadvantage of the predominantly female jobs.

WAGES ARE SET BY EMPLOYERS EXCLUSIVELY AND DIRECTLY ON THE BASIS OF PREVAILING WAGE RATES

Many employers use a combination of standards to determine wages. These include prevailing wage rates, job evaluation systems, and subjective judgments about the worth of a job. Some employers, such as Washington State, select a limited number of jobs whose wages are directly tied to the market. These are called benchmarks, and other jobs are then slotted into place. Slotting is sometimes accomplished formally through the use of a job evaluation system and sometimes informally through the personal judgments of those doing the slotting. The number of employers who tie every job classification directly to the market is probably a distinct minority.

It has been estimated that 60–65 percent of all public and private employers use job evaluation systems. They are standard management tools that permit the internal ranking of job classifications on the basis of worth for purposes of salary setting. They have been used by public and private employers to meet considerations of internal equity, to provide rationality and justification to the wage hierarchy, and to make it unnecessary to perform wage surveys for every job classification.

Some employers rely primarily on their own judgments concerning the value of a job. The judgments determine wages when there is no formal system, but sometimes the subjective judgment takes precedence over formal findings. In IUE v. Westinghouse, for example, the court ruled that Westinghouse had discriminated because it ignored the findings of its own point ratings and reduced wages for women's jobs, offering stereotypic judgments about women as justification.

THE COST OF IMPLEMENTING AND NOT IMPLEMENTING PAY EQUITY

There are no sound estimates of the overall implementation costs of pay equity in the United States. As individual employers begin to implement pay equity and to complete pay equity job evaluation studies, workplace by workplace costs and most estimates are becoming known.

In Minnesota, implementation will cost 0.3 per cent of the total biennial budget. It costs 4 percent of the State's annual payroll budget, and the State determined it could afford this at 1 percent a year for each of 4 years. In spring 1983, $21.8 million was appropriated for the first 2 years.

In Washington State, the implementation ordered by Judge Tanner will cost approximately 1 percent of the State's budget. However, on top of this will be the backpay award ordered by the court of approximately $500 million.

The primary reason for the cost difference between the two States is that Minnesota voluntarily identified discrimination in its civil service system and voluntarily decided to eliminate it. Washington State also voluntarily identified discrimination in its civil service system. This was first done in 1974. Unfortunately, despite several followup studies with the same findings of discrimination, the State refused to implement pay equity. It risked a lawsuit, lost, and was ordered to raise wages and provide backpay.

Given that wage discrimination is illegal, the most fiscally responsible route for an employer to take is voluntary compliance. This avoids long, expensive court battles and backpay awards. It allows an employer to stay in more control of the process and more effectively plan for orderly implementation.

It should be noted that because so little is known about the cost of implementing pay equity, the National Committee on Pay Equity is surveying all employers who have begun implementation and all employers who have estimates of cost based on completed pay equity job evaluation studies.

In 1982 full-time, year-round working women were paid 61 cents relative to every dollar of their male counterparts. In 1980 the equivalent figures were 56 cents in the private sector, 62.8 cents in the Federal sector, and 71.5 cents in State and local government.[12] In Table 1, these figures are broken down by race and ethnicity.

These statistics indicate that the greatest expense, on the average, will be in private firms, followed by the Federal Government and then by State and local governments. But cost will vary workplace by workplace. For example, according to the Communications Workers of America (CWA), AFL-CIO, women earned 78 cents for every man's dollar at AT&T—in the late 1970s. A Midwestern State preparing for a possible job evaluation study found that full-time, year-round women in State employment earn approximately 85 cents for every man's dollar.

The elimination of wage discrimination against women and men who work in predominantly female jobs will cost money. The single most important step an employer can take to

---

[12]*The Wage Gap: Myths and Facts.*

Table 1
Mean Earnings of Year-Round, Full-Time Workers by Work Experience, Sex, and Race as a Percentage of the Earnings of Men of All Races, 1980
Mean earnings as a percentage of the earnings of all men.

Work experience	All Men	White Men	Black Men	Hispanic Men	All Women	White Women	Black Women	Hispanic Women
Federal government	$24,050	103.1	80.8	90.7	62.8	63.1	62.2	N/A
State & local government	18,748	102.5	76.0	82.8	71.5	72.7	64.8	62.9
Private wage & salary	21,011	102.9	68.1	72.1	56.0	56.8	50.2	47.9

Source: *The Wage Gap: Myths and Facts,* National Committee on Pay Equity, 1983

contain costs is to act quickly and voluntarily. But in any case, to para phrase Winn Newman, the cost of correcting discrimination is no excuse or defense for breaking the law. Society makes regular judgments through the laws it makes about which corners may and may not be cut to save money. It has decided that money cannot be taken from the paychecks of women and used in other ways.

THE ROLE OF GOVERNMENT IN ELIMINATING WAGE DISCRIMINATION

FEDERAL GOVERNMENT ACTIVITIES

The Civil Rights Act forbids discrimination in compensation when the jobs in question are equal and when they are comparable. The law, which celebrates its 20th anniversary this year, is sufficient. No new Federal legislation of this sort is necessary.

Unfortunately, however, the Equal Employment Opportunity Commission (EEOC) is not adequately meeting its statutory obligation to enforce the law. Pay equity charges have been warehoused; no litigation is taking place in this area; and existing EEOC policy, first adopted in September 1981, which gives guidelines on how to investigate wage discrimination charges, is not being followed or enforced. The National Committee on Pay Equity has recommended that the EEOC take concrete steps in these directions. This document is in the appendix to this paper.

About the time of the congressional oversight hearings on the EEOC and pay equity that were held by Congressman Barney Frank (D-Mass.) in 1984, EEOC Chair Clarence Thomas announced that he had established a task force in headquarters that would review the backlog of charges, search for a litigation vehicle, and develop policy. The review of charges, assuming it is thorough and accurate, is long overdue, as are efforts to litigate in this important area. The development of new policy may be unnecessary, given that Commission policy already exists, and could easily become another excuse for postponing antidiscrimination actions.

These failures on the part of the executive branch of the Federal Government have provoked Congress, private citizens, and private organizations to take initiatives. Members of Congress have held hearings on the EEOC's role, introduced a resolution criticizing Federal enforcement agencies, and introduced legislation to give specific direction to enforcement agencies. Of particular note are House and Senate resolutions that call for a pilot pay equity job evaluation study of the Federal Government.

Private individuals and organizations are lobbying the EEOC and Congress for more enforcement. They are also assuming the expense of filing their own pay equity charges and lawsuits. Discrimination charges have been filed against Illinois, Hawaii, Los Angeles, Chicago, Philadelphia, Fairfax County (Va.), St. Louis Post-Dispatch, and elsewhere. Lawsuits have been filed against Michigan Bell And Nassau County (N.Y.).

STATE AND LOCAL GOVERNMENT ACTIVITIES

In large part because of the inaction of the Federal Government, the balance of pay equity activities shifted to State and local levels over the past 3 to 4 years. They have become the most productive areas. Well over 100 efforts have taken place in more than 30 States, with more now on the way.[13] The overwhelming majority of these apply only to the employers of the government taking action. They have occurred through collective bargaining, executive order, legislative action, and personnel department action. State, county, municipal, and school board government have:

- Held hearings and collected data on job segregation and the wage gap;
- Mandated and funded pay equity job evaluation studies;
- Amended civil service policies to require pay equity; and
- Enforced existing laws, such as equal and fair employment practice laws, to provide pay equity.

Pennsylvania is the only State seriously considering an amendment to State law specifically to forbid wage discrimination among comparable jobs in the private sector. This is still pending. Minnesota is the only State to pass legislation requiring that local governments move to pay equity. This passed in April 1984.

All of these victories have made pay equity activists determined to move more often and more quickly from pay equity policies and studies to implementation. Minnesota is the only State to adopt fully an implementation plan. New Mexico's legislation allocated $33 million to upgrade the 3,000 lowest paid jobs in the State government, 86 percent Washington State has been ordered to implement pay equity by a judge. Months before the trial, and 9 years after the first study, the Washington Legislature allocated $1.5 million to begin upgrading.

---

[13]*Who's Working for Working Women: A Survey of State and Local Government Initiatives* (National Committee on Pay Equity, 1984).

There are additional partial and full implementations that have taken place at the municipal level.

WHAT THE GOVERNMENT SHOULD DO

Many people may think that the most effective, fiscally sound, and least disruptive approach to eliminating discrimination is voluntary compliance. But if voluntary compliance is to work, the Federal Government must provide strict law enforcement.

A few public employers are now taking this route, but virtually no private employers appear to be. AT&T and CWA negotiated a joint labor-management committee that developed and field tested a job evaluation system in 1980–83. The 1983 contract calls for joint committees in all operating and other AT&T companies to develop systems. But no implementation of the plan or pay equity has yet occurred. Westinghouse, General Electric, and Charley Brothers have begun to implement pay equity because of lawsuits that they lost or that led to settlements. If private employers are engaging in voluntary compliance, they are keeping it a big secret. Employers have stated that voluntary compliance requires incentive and that the best incentive is strict enforcement of the law. Since this is not taking place, it should come as no surprise that there are so few private sector initiatives.

With the accumulation of preliminary victories in cities and States, activists will be turning to the EEOC directly and through their elected representatives for assistance, enforcement, and litigation. There are activists in every State, and their numbers, enthusiasm, and determination are growing. They see progress in virtually every tactical area, except the Federal Government's enforcement of law already on the books. The legal victories, particularly in Gunther and Washington State, have given people confidence that although pay equity is a moral, social, political, and personal right, it is also a legal right.

The Federal Government's role does not require it to develop a master job evaluation plan for all workplaces. This will take place workplace by workplace as it does now. Of course, it does not require establishing wage boards to determine wages. But the role of the Federal Government does not require an executive branch commitment to enforcing laws that Congress has passed and a previous President has signed into law.

CONCLUSION

Pay equity is one of the most fundamentally democratic women's issues to appear in the past 15 years. It will help the many, not the few, and the needy more than the privileged. It is also an issue at the intersection of economic and personal concerns; that is, it promises an end to unnecessarily low wages, but also expresses a new respect for much of the work that women do in this society.

The powerful sentiments that have carried pay equity this far will carry it further. But the elimination of this type of wage discrimination, which runs deep and deprives many, will be easier, faster, and less expensive if the Federal Government can be counted on as an ally in enforcing its own laws.

114

**Cubans encounter
the same economic
barriers and suffer
identical racial
discrimination in
everyday life
in the States.**

—Octavio de la Suaree

6

Cubans in the United States

by Octavio de la Suaree. Translated by Yvette Mato-March.

Cuban immigration in the United States is very similar to other Hispanic groups but, at the same time, is very different. In one sense, Cubans belong to the same ethnic minority groups as other Hispanic groups (Mexicans, Puerto Ricans, Argentineans, Salvadoreans, Colombians, etc.). Therefore, Cubans encounter the same economic barriers and suffer identical racial discrimination in every day life in the States. However, most other Hispanic groups came to the United States to improve their economic lot. For cubans, the story is slightly different. Most emigrated to the United States for political reasons: to escape Castro and his Communist takeover of the island in 1959.

Cubans are in fact victims of a double discrimination. Besides belonging to the above-mentioned ethnic minority, they are often marginalized in academic and intellectual circles, as well as by the media (television, newspapers, radio, etc.). They are all unjustly considered allies of the previous "Batista" regime. In other words, Cubans are paradoxically neither accepted as members of the majority nor as members of the minority in the United States.

Just as the U.S. Government should not be classifying the various Hispanic communities together under the all-encompassing term, "Hispanic" (since there are so many Hispanic groups), the same principle applies also to the various social strata one finds in the Cuban-American community. There are some Cubans who depend on welfare, but there also those (like the President of Coca Cola International) who are on a higher economical and social stratum.

When the United States Government opened up its doors in 1980 to more than 125,000 Cubans who were escaping Castro's "Communist Paradise" and risking their lives leaving the island through Mariel port, the well-known "Cuban economic miracle" in Miami was already firmly on its way to becoming a reality. Some commentators have said that this is the first time a generation of immigrants recently arrived in the States has managed to obtain in such a short time an average income level almost equal to that of the average American population.

Among the reasons which are offered as an explanation of this unique phenomenon we usually find the following: (1) the above mentioned political exile; (2) the fact that we are not dealing with an economic migration; (3) the fact that in Cuba these immigrants were used

117

to an economic level higher than the one offered to other minorities upon arriving here in the United States; and (4) the fact that these immigrants refused to accept that inferior social status offered to other minorities.

Cubans in the United States have succeeded in the professions, i.e., doctors, dentists, lawyers, educators, capitalists, etc. In this latter field, they show the highest index level per capita of business owners. Their establishment in two areas of the country (Dade County in Florida and Hudson County in New Jersey) has transformed these two down and out communities into two very vibrant and attractive centers with an international flavor.

The creative spirit of the Cuban immigrants and their independence are also observed in the arts. Caesar Romero and Desi Arnaz in the past generation and recently Celia Cruz, Gloria Estefan, Andy Garcia, Jon Secada, and others.

Among the most visible public figures are Congresswoman Ileana Ross-Letinien, Congressmen Lincoln Diaz-Balart and Roberto Menendez, as well as the controversial Jorge Mas Canosa (the late President of the Cuban-American National Foundation).

In 1959, when Cubans start abandoning their island in large numbers, most of them came to Miami. It is estimated that today there are between one million and a quarter million exiled Cubans in Metropolitan Dade County.

Many others moved up North into the New York-New Jersey area, where in the next millennium we find the second greatest concentration of Cubans in the United States, some 150,000 according to the 1990 Population Census.

Since the Cuban exile is essentially an urban phenomenon, concentrations of Cubans are found in practically any large city in the country, i.e., the Chicago-Cook county area and Los Angeles, California.

Other Cuban immigrants who have traveled into exile have gone wherever the opportunity presented itself: Puerto Rico the Dominican Republic, Spain, Mexico, Venezuela, Costa Rica, Peru. A large number of them wish to retire and to end their days in Miami, the capital of Cuban exile, since the "Magic City" represents for them what's most familiar with what they lost in Cuba.

It is hypocritical and profoundly wrong to call affirmative action for minorities "racism in reverse," while treating affirmative action for bankers, farmers and powerful white men as entitlements.

— Paul Rockwell

7

Angry White Guys for Affirmative Action

by Paul Rockwell, John Russo & Larry Hendel

For more than 25 years, opponents of affirmative action for women and people of color have overlooked a key American reality, the role of affirmative action in the lives of white men.

Opposition to affirmative action is based on selective inattention to the social props on which white men themselves depend.

Now is the time, before the 1996 elections, to redefine the terms, to expand the frame of reference in which affirmative action is discussed.

Most of us recall the first heated arguments over preferential programs that took place over 25 years ago in the teach-ins about the war in Vietnam.

In the 1960s, the first big affirmative action debate was not about minority programs. It was about college students who were getting draft deferments during the hate wars in Indochina.

It is easy to forget that minorities were overrepresented on the involuntary battlefields of Asia. Black and brown kids from working-class neighborhoods were being sent to die abroad, while primarily white college youth were building their own careers through one form of affirmative action, college draft deferment.

Some professors, judges and journalists who oppose affirmative action today took advantage of affirmative action (draft deferments) in college years ago.

Minority programs are only a small part of the spectrum of preferential policies in the United States. It is time to consider the extent to which white males are intertwined with policies of preference: tax breaks for corporations, subsidies for middle-class homebuyers, mass transit subsidies for white suburbs, bank bailouts for desperate bank executives, selective allotments for refugees and price supports for corporate farms.

These are all shot through and through with consideration of need and preference. Special consideration may be valid or invalid, but preference for those perceived to be in need is a basic concept for American society.

In the last 50 years of social engineering the vast majority of direct beneficiaries of affirmative action policies were not minorities—they were white males.

Preferential social policies for those in need were not invented by civil rights leaders. Under Franklin Roosevelt, whom most white American still revere, the New Deal embarked upon a massive affirmative action approach to social crises.

With the critical exception of segregation, Americans approached their social problems—unemployment, the poverty of senior citizens, the re-entry needs of veterans and GIs, farmers needing price supports—through planned social engineering.

The post-World War II Marshall Plan, a plan that provided billions of dollars for training and jobs, was a massive affirmative reaction plan for Europe. Former enemies got free training programs in Europe that were denied to Black GIs at home in America.

The New Deal concepts became unpopular only after they were applied to the crisis of segregation. It was not affirmative action itself but the extension of affirmative action to minorities and women, that caused the backlash.

We hear a lot about "angry white males" today. Well, we too are angry white males. But contrary to the caricature, we support affirmative action. As white men whose own families got free medical care or unquestioned access to higher education through the GI bill, who shared in the social uplift of the New Deal, we support affirmative action for those who are still left out.

We are not tear-jerk liberals or millionaires who can afford to appear magnanimous. It is out of our own self-interest, as direct beneficiaries of social engineering, that we support programs of inclusion.

The late Mitch Snyder, advocate for the homeless, once gave an address to an affluent, white audience. He asked members in the auditorium: "Who lives in federal-subsidized housing?" No one raised a hand. But then he asked homeowners to identify themselves. All hands went up, after which he pointed out that homeowners are subsidized.

Tax breaks for homebuyers may not be wrong. What is wrong is the smug psychology of California Gov. Pete Wilson and the Pat Buchanans, who take advantage of all kinds of breaks for themselves, while denying affirmative action for the most oppressed areas of society.

We hear a lot about the so-called stigma for affirmative action for minorities and women. We are told that affirmative action harms the psyche of African Americans, Latinos and women. It is a strange argument.

Veterans are not stigmatized by the GI Bill. European are not stigmatized by the Marshall Plan. Corporate farmers are not stigmatized by huge water giveaways and million-dollar price supports. The citizens of Orange County, a Republican strong-hold, seeking a bailout to cover their bankers' gambling losses, are not holding their heads in shame. The $500 billion federal bailout of the savings and loan industry, a fiasco of deregulation, is the biggest financial set-aside program in U.S. history. Its beneficiaries feel no stigma.

Affirmative action is already part of the fabric of American life. We are all bound together in a vast network of affirmative action, the mutual support systems we take for granted.

It is hypocritical and profoundly wrong to call affirmative action for minorities "racism in reverse," while treating affirmative action for bankers, farmers and powerful white men as entitlements.

Black families are forced to inhabit deteriorating crime-ridden apartment complexes, while white (often single) elderly people are sheltered in safe, well-maintained buildings with amenities such as...air conditioning, laundry rooms, and splendid security systems

—Craig Flournoy

8

Federally Subsidized Housing in America: Still Separate and Unequal

by Craig Flournoy

Willie Lewis and Blanche Rosenberg both live in federally assisted housing in Los Angeles. The eligibility and rental guidelines governing both are basically the same. Mr. Lewis, age 56, and Mrs. Rosenberg, age 85, also have the same landlord, the Housing Authority of the City of Los Angeles.

Mrs. Rosenberg, who is white, says she is more than satisfied with Las Palmas Gardens, the elderly-only development in West Los Angeles where she has lived since it opened in 1979. She and the other elderly residents—nearly all of whom are white—say maintenance is excellent. And the residents say they seldom worry about street crime at the complex because of the protection provided by guards, computerized emergency systems, and enclosed parking lots with electronically activated gates.

"I love it here," says Mrs. Rosenberg, a native of New York. "If anything breaks they fix it immediately. And I feel very secure here."

Mr. Lewis and his wife Birdell, who are black, say they feel like prisoners in Nickerson Gardens, a sprawling public housing project in the Watts area of Los Angeles. Mr. Lewis and his wife say they often are afraid to go outside because of the gangs and the drug-related violence. Security for the Lewises and for the other 1,000 black families and elderly persons in Nickerson Gardens often depends on a 12-foot-high, grease-coated fence that encircles much of the project.

"You know why they put that fence up?" says Mr. Lewis, gesturing toward the black wrought-iron fence with long spikes that point inward toward the project. "They think we're animals, so they're fencing us in."

The disparity between Las Palmas Gardens and Nickerson Gardens is not unique. The two are part of a national system of 60,000 federally subsidized rental developments that The Dallas Morning News found to be largely separate and unequal.

Separate means that most of the nearly ten million residents of federally assisted housing lived in racially segregated apartment complexes in 1984. Numerous federal lawsuits and studies by the government and the private sector have documented pervasive racial segregation in public and private housing.

Unequal means that virtually every predominantly white occupied development was significantly superior in condition location, services, and amenities when compared to projects that house mainly blacks and Hispanics. At least that's what my partner George Rodrigue and I found in visits to 47 cities and 74 towns across the nation.

In fact, we did not find a single locality in which federal rent subsidy housing was fully integrated nor one where services and amenities were equal for whites and minority tenants living in separate projects.

The U.S. Department of Housing and Urban Development (HUD) is responsible for funding and overseeing more than 90 percent of the nation's federally subsidized rental housing. Many current and former top officials with HUD agreed with our "separate and unequal" findings. HUD General Counsel John Knapp, the agency's chief legal officer, said in response to our central finding: "I don't doubt that there is a good bit of that."

Our inquiry found that hundreds of suburban communities-from Birmingham, Michigan and DuPage County, Illinois to Fulton County, Georgia—have refused to accept subsidized housing for families, housing for which minorities have the greatest demand. This refusal has played a pivotal role in perpetuating the overwhelmingly white makeup of these communities while leaving millions of minorities locked in inner-city ghettos.

There were almost 3.7 million households in 1984 whose rent was subsidized by the federal government. We found that almost nine of every ten of these apartments were provided in the last tow decades, after Congress approved the landmark Civil Rights Act of 1964 that included the Title VI provision prohibiting racial discrimination in all federally funded programs. However, we found that HUD often has ignored the illegal operation of federally assisted developments by many local housing authorities and private developers. Except in isolated instances that have had little national impact, five presidential administrations have steadfastly refused to invoke the strongest penalties and most effective tools provided under federal fair housing laws.

Our 14-month investigation revealed a "new segregation" in the current system of almost 3.7 million federal rent subsidy apartments.

Laurence D. Pearl, a top official in the HUD office responsible for enforcing anti-discrimination laws in federally subsidized housing, said simply that "perhaps we've accepted too little." Mr. Pearl, director of program compliance in HUD's Office of Fair Housing and Equal Opportunity, also said that racial segregation in the country's 11,500 public housing projects is "definitely a nationwide problem." And Mr. Pearl said solving the problem "rivals in magnitude what I think went on with [desegregation of] the [nation's] schools."

The racial segregation and unequal conditions that pervade federally subsidized rental housing have more than legal implications. Gary Orfield, a University of Chicago housing expert and a HUD consultant, said racially segregated housing "cuts off access to jobs. It cuts off access to education. It leads to disinvestment as the ghettos and barrios expand. It leads to eventual definition of most cities in racial terms and to their inability to finance basic services as poverty grows with the ghettoization cycle. It can devastate entire cities."

126

Racial segregation in federally assisted rental housing is not a new development. Since the inception of such housing in 1933, housing authorities from Dallas to Detroit intentionally separated tenants into white projects and black projects with federal consent. By 1964, the government had helped fund the construction of about 540,000 public housing apartments. Families lived in almost three of every four of these modest apartments in separate, but often roughly equal, projects.

Our 14-month investigation revealed a "new segregation" in current system of almost 3.7 million federal rent subsidy apartments. The new segregation differs from the old in two key ways. First, the whites who benefit the most now are the elderly rather than families. Second, today's system of federally subsidized rental housing is significantly more unequal in the housing and services provided to whites and minorities than in previous decades. The pattern in most cities and towns is a throwback to the days of the antebellum South: the deteriorating, barely habitable housing goes to the blacks; the newer, well-maintained and sometimes lavish housing goes to the whites.

More than 1.5 million blacks live in public housing projects that house both families and elderly persons. Many live in older urban areas in projects vacated by whites in the 1950s and 1960s as surrounding inner-city neighborhoods became increasingly occupied by minorities. Others live in decaying high-rises originally intended to house urban renewal refugees.

The names of many of these older, minority-occupied public housing projects have become synonymous with the worst in slum housing: Chicago's Cabrini-Green, where more than 3,500 black families live in high-rise buildings and row houses often controlled by street gangs; Kansas City's Wayne Miner Court, a half-vacant, virtually all-black complex of high-rises and low rises so deteriorated that local officials want to demolish it; and, in Dallas, the overwhelmingly minority-occupied West Dallas projects, where more than a third of the almost 3,400 units are vacant and boarded up because of years of official neglect.

"It becomes a serious danger when public housing becomes totally black," said William Wynn, deputy assistant secretary in HUD's Office of Fair Housing and Equal Opportunity. "At the ones that I have seen that became totally black, there is disparity of services. It becomes an area where there are not too many supportive services. It also becomes an area where crime seems to run rampant. And it also becomes an area where the laws of the [housing] authority are not readily enforced."

The "winners" in today's new segregation have been elderly whites. Based on both eligibility and need, they won a disproportionate share of the almost 3.3 million federal rent subsidy apartments provided during the last 20 years. HUD figures show that the white elderly did particularly well in the competition for the most costly of these apartments—the more than 2.2 million units in which the federal government helped finance construction costs and agreed to subsidize rents. An examination of who lived in these 2.2 million apartments in 1984 shows:

- The elderly lived in more than 1.1 million or 50 percent of these apartments. This is twice the level of their eligibility. Elderly households accounted for less than 23 percent of the nation's renters eligible for the vast majority of federal rent subsidy housing in 1981, the most recent year for which HUD has information.

- Whites lived in 75 percent of the almost 1.5 million newly built apartments for which racial data is available. White house holds comprised 64 percent of the nation's renters eligible for subsidized housing in 1981.
- In the Section 8 New Construction program, which produced more newly built apartments during the past decade than any other rent subsidy program, elderly whites did exceedingly well. In 1984, there were 583,000 Section 8 New Construction units, most of them in privately-owned developments; elderly whites occupied 63 percent of these apartments. Yet HUD's most recent data show that elderly white households accounted for 17 percent of the country's renters eligible for subsidized housing.[1]

Many local housing authorities have also stopped or severely curtailed the construction of family projects during the last 20 years. Despite waiting lists dominated by families, many cities and towns have concentrated on building government subsidized apartments for the elderly, often under the public housing program, sometimes under new programs such as Section 8, and sometimes under special local programs. This trend is typified by the Seattle Housing Authority, the largest landlord in the Pacific Northwest.

Since 1967, the Seattle Housing Authority has built 36 developments restricted to elderly and handicapped tenants. Whites occupy almost nine of every ten of the nearly 3,300 apartments in these complexes, most of them in white neighborhoods in the Northern part of the city. Meanwhile, from 1942 to 1984, the housing authority built fewer than 600 family apartments, or fewer than 15 per year. Blacks and other minorities occupy about 70 percent of these apartments.

However, the housing authority's waiting list reveals that families have the greatest demand for housing. Families make up almost two-thirds of the more than 2,200 applicants on the public housing waiting list. And the number of families applying for apartments in Seattle's Section 8 Existing program is so large that no applications have been taken since May of 1982.

Meanwhile, Housing Management Director Ron Oldham said Seattle has been so successful in its efforts to serve the elderly that "there is an excess supply of one-bedroom units both in public housing and in Section 8 [Existing]."

What explains the dramatic shift in federal rent subsidy housing over the last two decades toward construction of elderly-only developments? The programs providing the vast majority of apartments, such as public housing and Section 8, have the same basic eligibility requirements and rent guidelines. We found, however, that HUD offered developers a financial incentive to build or rehabilitate elderly-only Section 8 developments. HUD regulations, issued during the Ford administration, allow the private owners of newly constructed and renovated Section 8 elderly-only developments to charge five percent higher rents than the agency allows for Section 8 family projects. The Carter administration refused to eliminate the regulations in 1979 despite findings by the U.S. General Accounting Office that the practice "acts as a penalty for developers contemplating family projects."[2]

Despite waiting lists dominated by families, many cities and towns have concentrated on building government subsidized apartments for the elderly.

The News found that an equally dramatic shift toward elderly only projects also occurred in the public housing program although HUD offers no financial incentive to local housing authorities to build elderly-only developments. Federal figures show that in 1984 the elderly lived in more than half of occupied public housing apartments built since 1964. By comparison, the elderly occupied about one-quarter of all public housing units in 1964. HUD's latest racial occupancy figures show that whites lived in almost two of every three public housing apartments occupied by the elderly.

Robert Weaver, appointed by President Johnson in 1966 as HUD's first secretary, said the primary reason for the shift is racial. Many communities made a conscious decision to build public housing for the elderly rather than for families, Mr. Weaver said, because they knew from waiting lists that "the demand among families for public housing was much greater among blacks than among whites. This is tied, of course, to the whole question of schools, [and] it's tied to the whole question of amenities."

Tenants often put the current situation in eloquent perspective. Georgia Hysaw, a 54-year-old native of Bakersfield, California who has lived for 28 years in an overwhelmingly black occupied public housing project there, described the situation this way: "We are still segregated and unequal, and it certainly isn't by choice."

In our visits to 47 cities across the country, we found that many elderly-only projects are equipped with sophisticated emergency and security systems, central air conditioning and heating, community centers, and laundry facilities. Through a combination of public and private resources, these developments routinely provide their mostly white tenants with free shuttle bus service for shopping, meals for one dollar, in house medical care, and arts and crafts facilities staffed by instructors.

In Rhode Island, the Providence Housing Authority so neglected the Roger Williams Housing Project—once the well-maintained home of more than 700 white families—that today it is a rat-infested slum housing just 40 families, all but three of them black.

At the Kinder Park Apartments in suburban Philadelphia, an elderly resident can walk from building to building through enclosed, air-conditioned walkways protected by a computerized security system to reach a circular sunroom with sky light and fountain.

At the Crown Tower high-rise in Omaha, Nebraska, an elderly tenant can play a piano inside the first floor community center, shoot a game of pool inside the billiards room, or take ceramics classes from an instructor.

The Rosa Parks Senior Apartments in San Francisco once were rat-infested firetraps that mainly housed minority families. Renovated at a cost of ten million dollars, the building today provides its elderly residents with social workers for counseling and a hot tub for relaxation.

The 150 million dollar Angelus Plaza complex in Los Angeles is the nation's largest federally subsidized rental development for the elderly. Security measures are as elaborate as the landscaping. They include 24-hour protection by guards, closed-circuit cameras, and a multi-story parking garage. Each apartment includes wall-to-wall carpeting, central air conditioning, and a balcony. Each apartment is also linked to a sophisticated computerized emergency system that allows each tenant to alert the building manager, who receives a printout with the tenant's apartment number, physician, and medical history.

But it is the social services and recreational activities that, according to tenant Joe Rybacki, make his apartment at Angelus Plaza "just like heaven." These services are showcased in the terraced, six-story Agape Social Services and Activities Center. There, Angelus Plaza tenants are provided with meals costing as little as one dollar, an 11,000-volume library, a ceramics studio with two kilns, and a medical clinic staffed by two physicians. Tenants also can get free psychological counseling, free legal assistance, interest-free loans, and vans to take them shopping.

Conditions are far different at most family public housing projects, which are heavily occupied by black and Hispanic families and elderly persons. In our visits to 47 cities, we found few amenities and even fewer social services.

In Rhode Island, the Providence Housing Authority so neglected the Roger Williams housing project—once the well maintained home of more than 700 white families—that today it is a rat-infested slum housing just 40 families, all but three of black.

In Kansas, the Topeka Housing Authority provides each of its three predominantly white-occupied high-rises for the elderly with a community center and tornado shelter. Only one of the three predominantly minority-occupied family projects has a tornado shelter. Topeka's three family projects had recreation centers but lost them when the Topeka City Commission voted to stop funding the facilities. Tenant Imogene Burns recalled, "We practically got down on our knees and begged [the commissioners] to let us keep the center, but they didn't pay attention to us."

In California, the Kern County Housing Authority shut down the only community center it provided to the 230 households living in the Oro Vista and Adelante Vista projects in Bakersfield, both of which are 90 percent black. The housing authority spent almost 600,000 dollars to install central air conditioning and heating, new carpets, and a new fire alarm system in Plaza Towers, a 14-year-old elderly-only development that is 90 per cent white. The housing authority has never replaced the air coolers at the 43-year-old Adelante Vista family project or at the 31-year-old Oro Vista family project.

When asked about this, Paul Castro, the deputy director of the Kern County Housing Authority, said, "As hot as it is in Kern County, a good cooler is absolutely necessary. Some [black family project] tenants just have to buy their own."

In Oklahoma, the Lawton Housing Authority recently spent 1.4 million dollars to install central air conditioning and heating and to construct a maintenance building at the 11-story Benjamin O. Davis high-rise for the elderly. The complex, which is equipped with a nurse call button in each apartment, laundry facilities, arts and crafts room, community center and sprinkler system, is 96 percent white. Elderly minorities are harder to attract, according to Lawton Housing Authority Director Retta Seabolt, because they "just prefer to be out where they can touch the ground."

At the Lawton View family project, blacks live in 130 of the 135 apartments. Lawton View has none of the comforts and conveniences of the high-rise. Annie Anderson, the manager of the family apartments, said that "a lot of tenants [in Lawton View] call in with legitimate complaints. It should be equal."

A series of congressional acts, HUD regulations, and U.S. Supreme Court decisions spanning two decades have banned racial segregation and other forms of discrimination in housing.

After passage of the Civil Rights Act of 1964, HUD issued regulations prohibiting any action that would "subject a person to segregation or separate treatment in any matter relating to his receipt of housing." In 1968, Congress approved Title VIII, better known as The Fair Housing Act, which prohibited racial discrimination in the bulk of the nation's public and private housing. The lawmakers also directed all executive agencies, HUD in particular, to act "affirmatively" to remedy the effects of past racial segregation and discrimination in housing.

However, except in isolated cases, the administrators of Presidents Johnson, Nixon, Ford, Carter, and Reagan have failed to enforce Title VI and Title VIII aggressively. Top HUD officials from the Johnson administration to the Reagan administration have approved funding for the construction of subsidized projects knowing that tenants would be racially segregated.

Mr. Weaver, the first secretary of HUD, acknowledged that he and other HUD officials knew that some cities and local housing authorities would segregate tenants by race. Mr. Weaver said he tolerated the illegal segregation because he did not want to arouse further opposition to the 1968 Fair Housing Act. Mr. Weaver said that since then "the reason that the 1968 Act wasn't enforced to the degree that it could be enforced was because there wasn't the will to enforce it."

HUD's failure aggressively to enforce fair housing laws under five presidential administrations, Mr. Weaver said, is "purely a case of the federal government not carrying out its responsibilities."

Congress has provided HUD with powerful penalties to ensure that city officials, local housing authorities, and private developers comply with fair housing laws.

The 1964 Civil Rights Act authorizes HUD to cut off federal assistance to an agency or individual who engages in racial discrimination. Under the Housing and Community Development Act of 1974, HUD can suspend, reduce, or stop the flow of Community Development Block Grant funds to a city that violates fair housing laws or does not act "in a manner to affirmatively further fair housing." And HUD is empowered to refer violations of fair housing laws and of the 1974 Act to the Justice Department for prosecution.

With few exceptions, the eight HUD secretaries during the past 19 years have not invoked the laws' strongest measures. For example:

- No HUD Secretary has ever used the authority provided under Title VI to cut off federal funds to a local housing authority, private developer, or landlord who operated a federal rent subsidy development. HUD Secretaries have threatened to cut off funds in 11 instances, but never followed through. Yet an internal 1981 HUD report concluded that "public housing remains racially segregated...in violation of Title VI of the Civil Rights Act of 1964 and Title VIII of the Civil Rights Act of 1968."[3]
- Top HUD officials from the Johnson administration to the Reagan administration have approved funding for the construction of subsidized projects knowing that tenants would be racially segregated.
- HUD officials in the last 10 years have never asked the U.S. Department of Justice to sue a locality for violating the Housing and Community Development Act, despite what the U.S. Commission on Civil Rights has said are HUD's own "well documented findings of discrimination."[4]

- Top HUD officials seldom have revoked Community Development funds from communities despite widespread evidence that many either were violating fair housing laws or failing to make a good faith effort to provide low-income housing, one of the Act's primary goals.
- HUD continues to rely on an 18-year-old plan for selecting and assigning tenants in public housing, despite findings by the Justice Department as early as 1970 that "most public housing...[projects] were segregated and the tenant selection and assignment policy [of HUD] could be a contributing factor."[5]

The U.S. Commission on Civil Rights may have best summed up the situation when, in 1979, it completed its most comprehensive examination of fair housing enforcement. "For more than a decade," the Commission said, "the Departments of Housing and Urban Development and Justice...have largely failed in their responsibilities to prevent and eliminate discrimination and segregation in housing."[6]

During the course of our project, we interviewed one HUD Secretary from each of the last five presidential administrations. Some, like Carla Hills, who served as HUD Secretary under President Ford, said the administration strongly supported her enforcement efforts and that they resulted in a sharp reduction in racial segregation and discrimination in housing.

Others, such as Mr. Weaver and the late Patricia Roberts Harris, who served as head of HUD during the first two years of the Carter administration, said no administration has effectively enforced fair housing laws. Mrs. Harris said fair housing enforcement "wasn't a high priority. I must say I consider that one of the areas where we left much to be desired."

Samuel R. Pierce Jr., the current head of HUD, said racial discrimination in federally subsidized housing is inseparable from one of the nation's fundamental problems: racial prejudice. "My God, it's a bad country we live in, prejudice-wise," said Secretary Pierce. "It's terrible here, that's what it is."

Secretary Pierce also said that as much as government may try to enforce the nation's fair housing laws, that "in the last analysis it will be [up to] the people" to end discrimination in public and private housing.

However, Antonio Monroig, Pierce's assistant secretary in charge of HUD's Office of Fair Housing and Equal Opportunity, said that vigorous enforcement by the government would change discriminatory behavior. He cites the deep-seated changes in the Jim Crow South sparked by the Supreme Court's 1954 ruling that racially segregated public schools were unconstitutional. "We pursued it [enforcement of civil rights laws] down South, where they had separate bathrooms, they had separate seating in the movie houses, everywhere," said Mr. Monroig.

"But it [the Brown decision] was a law; [other] laws were passed. They were enforced, and it has changed. And I don't think that anyone in the South at this point thinks that blacks should be on the second floor or at a different water fountain. The only thing is that with housing, it [enforcing anti discrimination laws] is a little more difficult," Mr. Monroig said. "It will take time."

End Notes

1. Occupancy data provided by several HUD studies. Eligibility data derived from HUD's Division of Housing and Demographic Analysis "Trends in Subsidized Housing, 1974–1981," Washington, D.C., March 1984, pp. 26–27, 44–45.
2. U.S. Comptroller General, "Evaluation of Alternatives for Financing Low and Moderate Income Rental Housing," Washington, D.C., September 30, 1980, p. 62.
3. Robert H. Covell, Office of HUD Program Compliance, "A Management Control Assessment of the HUD Tenant Selection and Assignment Policy," Washington, D.C., December 14, 1981, p.12.
4. U.S. Commission on Civil Rights, *The Federal Fair Housing Enforcement Effort* (Washington, D.C.: U.S. Government Printing Office, 1979), p.55.
5. As quoted in Covell, op. cit., p. 7
6. U.S. Commission on Civil Rights, op. cit., p. 231.

Privilege is invisible to those who have it.

—Margo Adair and Sharon Howell

9

To Equalize Power Among Us

We Need to Keep Ourselves in Check in Whatever Ways We Have Privilege

by Margo Adair & Sharon Howell

Despite our best intentions we find, more often than not, that we duplicate the patterns of power we find so abhorrent in dominant culture. Following are some guidelines to help us equalize relations. *Privilege is invisible to those who have it.* To create a context which embraces diversity, in which no one is marginalized, a conscious and ongoing effort is required. By noticing and changing what we take for granted, we make room for everyone's contribution. This list is offered as a way to help privileged group members reflect on their own behavior:

Don't interrupt.

Do take responsibility to learn about the history, culture and struggles of other groups as told by them.

Don't unilaterally set the agenda.

Do make sure the context welcomes everyone's voice and listen.

Don't patronize.

Do appreciate efforts to point out mistakes. (You must be doing something right, or no one would bother to tell you what's wrong.)

Don't assume you're more capable.	Do expect discomfort when relating to people different from yourself.
Don't trivialize the experience of others.	Do address the many dimensions of accessibility, including such things as money, space, transportation, child-care and language.
Don't challenge tone, attitude or manner.	Do notice what you expect from and assume about others, and note what experiences formed your ideas.
Don't assume anyone is more "suited" for anything.	Do name unacknowledged realities, so that the parameters of the situation expand to include everyone's experience.
Don't take responsibility for, think for, or speak for others.	Do remember that others speak about more than the conditions of their own group.
Don't assume someone is exceptional compared to the "average" person of their group.	Do regard people as whole human beings with families, interests and ideas beyond those of the particular task.
Don't assume an individual speaks for or has the same opinions as others from their group.	Do take responsibility for equalizing power.
Don't be the only one controlling the organization's resources.	Do name dominating behavior when you see it.
Don't reduce difficulties to personality conflicts.	Do encourage pride in your own and other's ancestry and history.
Don't assume the root of a problem is misunderstanding or lack of information.	Do understand individuals in the context of their social history.
Don't ask others to explain, prove, or justify themselves.	Do look for political differences rather than personality conflicts.
Don't mimic other cultural traditions or religious practices.	Do ask questions.
Don't expect to be treated as an individual outside of your group's history.	Do struggle over matters of principle and politics.
Don't flaunt how you may be different than others of your group.	Do respect disagreements.
Don't take up all the space or always speak first.	Do make accessible all information and so others can decide if they are interested.

136

Don't ignore or minimize differences by emphasizing similarities.

Don't overlook history and equate all oppressions as equal.

Don't expect "others" to educate you about their group's history, conditions or sensibilities.

Don't expect others to be grateful.

Don't defend mistakes by focussing on good intentions.

Don't take everything personally.

Don't assume everyone has the same options you do.

Don't try to guess what's needed.

Don't assume that the visible reality is the only one operating.

Don't expect to be trusted.

Do appreciate the risk a person takes in sharing their experience with you.

Do take risks.

Do trust others.

IN THE WAYS WE'VE BEEN OPPRESSED

In addition to keeping ourselves in check regarding whatever ways we possess privilege, it is vital that we stop constraining ourselves—stop keeping ourselves in check, in the particular ways that relate to how we have experienced being an "outsider." *We have to take the risk of putting our experience into the center.* We can no longer afford to collude with our own oppression by accommodating and/or not acknowledging our own power. It is our experience that is needed to inform and shape decisions.

It is also important to remember that offensive behavior is not necessarily calculated to protect power. It is often simply a result of ignorance. Those with privilege have never needed to understand the experience of others. They are frequently oblivious of how their behavior reinforces the status quo.

Don't hesitate
to ask them for a
presentation that
will honor the
Polish American
taxpayers during
Polish American
Heritage Month. Invite
the entire Polonia to
attend as well as
the news media.

10

Things to Do During National Polish American Heritage Month

1. Request the elected leaders in your area to present proclamations and greeting at a public event to leaders in the Polish American Community. Don't hesitate to ask them for a presentation that will honor the Polish American taxpayers during Polish American Heritage Month. (Sample proclamations are available upon request.) Invite the entire Polonia to attend as well as the news media.

2. Unite all Polish American organizations for a Mass for the intention of Polish Americans. Encourage each parish to have a Mass for the intention of their parishioners. Have a reception with Polish pastries and refreshments in the parish hall following the Mass. Ask all Polish American clergy to participate in your activities.

3. Sponsor an event to honor General Pulaski (October 11th is the anniversary of the death of Pulaski). Organize a wreath laying ceremony before a portrait of Pulaski and possibly award the coloring contest prizes during that event. Invite everyone from your area to attend along with the Polish American organizations and Polonia.

4. Display Polish and American flags in homes, organizations' headquarters, banks, businesses, etc. Ask your local organizations to fly the Polish flag alongside the American flag during the entire month of October. (Information on purchasing a Polish flag is available from the national committee.)

5. Organize an essay contest in your local schools. Award prizes during a school assembly or public event to encourage participation (you can obtain prizes from local businesses or organizations). Ask your area teachers to help organize and judge the essay contest.

6. Coloring contest on General Pulaski. This type of contest is very popular with the children. Ask some of the local art students to organize and judge the entries. Ask a local printer to reprint the artwork for you committee with the name of his business at the bottom as advertising.

7. Organize a library display of Polish books, arts and crafts, wycinanki and paintings by Polish American artists. Contact local artists and request them to display their works at the local library, parish hall, organization hall, public building or office building lobby.

8. Children's recital in local organization headquarters, school hall or recreation center. There are many children groups that would participate and appreciate this type of exposure for their students. Invite the public as well as the Polonia to attend the children's recital.

9. Display National Polish American Heritage Month posters. Posters are available by contacting the Polish American Heritage Month Committee at the address listed on this suggestion sheet. Ask all of your local stores, banks, supermarkets, churches and organizations to display Polish American Heritage Month posters throughout the month of October.

10. Contact your local radio, television and newspapers to tell them about Polish American Heritage Month and its activities in your area. If they are advertising the various activities, compliment them; if they have not complied with your request to advertise activities, call and complain about their lack of interest.

11. Ask all local radio programs to mention your local events in October as part of their community bulletin board or public service announcements. Press releases pertaining to the national celebration can be obtained by writing to the national committee.

12. Ask local organizations, banks, businesses and elected leaders to place "POLISH AMERICAN HERITAGE MONTH SALUTES" in local newspapers and on radio programs. Place a salute each week during the month of October in local newspapers, this will remind everyone about POLISH AMERICAN HERITAGE MONTH. (The national committee has an artwork for the newspaper salutes which is FREE upon request.)

13. Call upon your area high school students and college students of Polish descent to help with press releases and other activities. Polish American Heritage Month will be very successful if we get everyone involved. Members of your organizations have children and grandchildren that could volunteer some time for this very worthy cause.

14. Senior citizen groups could sponsor a Polish American Day Lunch or Dinner with a guest speaker or entertainment.

15. Local Polish American organizations could sponsor a lunch or dinner reunion day to get the people together for a Polish American Heritage Month celebration.

16. Hold a fundraiser to help the Polish American causes in your area or to help the needy children in Poland.

17. Sponsor a Polish American evening social with music, food and entertainment.

18. Contact the other Polish American organizations to see what they will be planning during the National Polish American Heritage Month and possibly unite your efforts.

19. Solicit several area businesses to donate towards a highway billboard that reads "WE SALUTE POLISH AMERICANS DURING OCTOBER." List their names on

the billboard, it's great advertising. (Sample billboard artwork available upon request)

20. Wear red and white or "Polish and Proud" buttons to your local events and encourage others to do the same.
21. Tell friends and family about National Polish American Heritage Month events and invite them to attend your local celebrations.
22. Encourage everyone you know to join a Polish American organization.
23. Encourage everyone to read a book about Polish American contributions or a book written by a Pole or a Polish American.
24. If there is a Polish American radio program in your area ask them to do something special during regular programming throughout the month of October.

Discussion Questions
Part III: Solutions for a Changing American Society: Economics and (Under)Development

1. Discuss one specific economic situation facing women in the United States today.

_____

_____

_____

_____

_____

_____

_____

2. List 5 proposed solutions for decreasing racism and sexism in American society.

_____

_____

_____

_____

_____

_____

_____

Asian-Americans do face
widespread prejudice,
discrimination, and barriers
to equal opportunity.
Asian-Americans are
frequently victims of racially
motivated bigotry and
violence; they face significant
barriers to equal opportunity in
education and employment;
and they do not have equal
access to a number of public
services, including police
protection, health care, and
the court system.

—U.S. Commission on Civil Rights, 1992.

Part IV

Integrating Race, Class, and Gender: Socio-Political Movements

It is often said that "where there is oppression, there is resistance." People respond to the conditions of their social and economic environment in a variety of ways. This is certainly true when people seek solutions to racial, gender and class discrimination.

The selections in Part IV illustrate some of the perspectives that minorities and women have taken in response to the different oppression they face. It is only possible to present a very small cross-section of these responses, but the student can get a sense of some problems that minorities and women encounter, as well as some of the ways in which they have struggled against these problems.

While African-Americans have often struggled against the sources of their oppression, their resistance has taken many forms. "Black Past, Black Present," demonstrates that there is still a need for affirmative action for minorities and women. One of the most controversial social and political topics of the present decade involves the role of immigrants to America. Some critics of immigration blame immigrants for a multitude of social and economic problems. This position is refuted in "Irish and Blacks Share Oppressed Histories."

"Solutions to Black Male Prison Crisis," are presented, as well as "Gender Policing" and "Evidence of Environmental Racism."

Oftentimes, males are blamed for these socio-political problems, as in "Masculinity, Violence and War," and if not males, then those of who are physically different, as in "Size Discrimination is a Civil Rights Issue."

**[Affirmative action]
is not about slavery.
It is not about the past. It
is about oppression that
continues daily, whether
in the form of disparity
of school financing, the
disproportionate number
of black youths.**

—Vernon McClean

1

Black Past, Black Present: Real-Life Lessons About Why Affirmative Action Matters

by Vernon McClean

February is Black History (Herstory) Month, celebrating the achievements of African-Americans. It is also a time when African-Americans in New Jersey are under attack, specifically in a bill on affirmative action introduced by two Republican members of the state Assembly, Kevin O'Toole and Michael Carroll.

I would like to tell these Assemblymen a story. Let's pretend, just to make the story more interesting, that the man involved, who is black, is press secretary in the Whitman Administration. The story goes like this: When the man was 11 or 12 years of age, he used a restaurant restroom and, as he was leaving, encountered a white man entering the restroom. The white man stopped, saw an unflushed urinal (our man had flushed his) and proceeded to muse loudly about the nasty habits of "niggers."

"After that," our man said, "even if I was alone, every time I left a restroom. I flushed all the toilets. I was determined that no one would ever come behind me and find an unflushed toilet."

This is a true story, according to the African-American columnist William Raspberry, who recounted it as an episode in the life of a man who is now a prosperous Washington lawyer. I retell it in the context of the Whitman Administration to make the point that it could happen anywhere. It could happen here.

When I first began teaching at William Paterson College in Wayne, a predominantly white college, I always overprepared and usually traveled to class with a shopping bag of books. I felts that if students challenged me, I could point to the books (written by *white* scholars) to validate my point. I am being embarrassingly honest; I still do this, but the load of books has gotten smaller.

The point I am making is that racism (some of it internalized as in the examples above) is alive and well in New Jersey, and therefore we continue to need affirmative action.

Each semester, students tell me how their friends couldn't get into William Paterson College because some "unqualified" black person with a low S.A.T. score was admitted instead. (For the record, there are few black students at this state college, which is supported with tax dollars, many of them from black, Latino and poor white taxpayers.)

I point out to students that it's not fair to use the S.A.T. exam as the sole basis of admission. Doing that, I argue, would be the same as my using one exam to judge them, excluding their class participation, written projects and bountiful assortment of other required assignments.

Another argument I hear from students is that affirmative action has led to excesses in preferential treatment. Perhaps it is because blacks are like flies in buttermilk. We are obvious. That is, students seldom complain about geographic quotas or set-aside programs for children of alumni at Ivy League institutions. Rather, as poor whites and blacks (and honestly, it is the economically poor whites and blacks who are forced to attend state colleges in New Jersey and elsewhere) we foolishly fight each other about the myth of the excesses of affirmative action.

Then there's the bootstrap myth, the argument that other ethnic groups managed to pull themselves up by their own efforts. Yet history indicates that all kinds of people have received government help in New Jersey, whether it was bilingual programs for Germans, housing aid for Italians, subsidies for white suburbs or bailouts for desperate bank executives.

Finally, it is common to hear my students (especially white women who are not aware that they also benefit from affirmative action) say that they do not know what blacks are complaining about, since they have all the power today; that blacks can't expect white people to keep paying today because blacks were slaves in the past.

For us, as black citizens in New Jersey, the issue is not about slavery. It is not about the past. It is about oppression that continues daily, whether in the form of disparity of school financing, the disproportionate number of black youths in county jails or the number of blacks, especially children, who are dying because of lack of good medical care.

Because we are dying, we need affirmative action. It is about the black present.

Let us not accept the myth that New Jersey blacks have overcome all obstacles and thus there is not more need for affirmative action. Let us use Black History Month to eliminate barriers to everyone in New Jersey—regardless of race, class, gender or other conditions.

The purpose of
this essay is to foster
a more accurate
understanding among
Irish-Americans and
African-Americans
of each other's history
and culture, and to
suggest ways in which
we can learn from
each other.

—Vernon McClean

2

The Ties That Bind: Irish-Americans and African-Americans

by Vernon McClean

The traditional view of Saint Patrick's Day among many in the African-American community is that of drunken white men carousing down the streets of Chicago. This superficial image is an inaccurate portrayal of the past and present realities of the Irish-American experience. The purpose of this essay is to foster a more accurate understanding among Irish-Americans and African-Americans of each others' history and culture, and to suggest ways in which we can learn from each other.

There are many similarities as well as differences. Both groups were immigrants to these shores, but the conditions of the two groups' migration were drastically different. The Irish migration to the United States, while often resulting from harsh conditions, was voluntary, whereas the African-American experience was one of forced enslavement. And after settling in America, the Irish were able to attain positions of power and leadership in such institutions as the Roman Catholic Church and big-city political organizations, but African Americans for many years remained a servant class.

EARLY LIFE

Just as there were laws limiting the number of African-Americans (including Caribbean) immigrants to the United States, the same was true of the Irish. They, too, were limited by racist laws. Just as many Africans labored as servants (domestics), the same was true of many Irish.

Just as the Irish crossed the Atlantic in dangerous ships, the same was true of our African foreparents. Just as recent African-Americans (especially Caribbeans) have headed straight for American urban areas, the same was true of the Irish. And just as African-Americans lived together in crowded apartment houses owned by others, the same was often true of the Irish. (They lived in crowded apartment houses called *rookers*.)

Just as African-American women encountered sexism as immigrants, the same was true of the Irish women. Most of the Irish women who came to the U.S. in its early history were unmarried and were force to work as domestics (as Caribbean and African-American women continue to do today.)

And just as African-Americans continue to be stereotyped as lazy and unintelligent, the same has been true of the Irish. As a matter of fact, for a time the Irish were regarded as "the missing link" between the gorilla and African-Americans.

The sociologist Andrew M. Greeley, in his *That Most Distressful Nation* (Chicago, Quadrangle, 1972), reported that "Practically every accusation that has been made against the American blacks was also made against the Irish: Their family life was inferior, they had no ambition, they did not keep up their homes, they drank too much, they were not responsible, they had no morals, it was not safe to walk through their neighborhoods at night, they voted the way crooked politicians told them to vote, they were not willing to pull themselves up by their bootstraps, they were not capable of education, they could not think for themselves, and they would always remain social problems for the rest of the country." (p. 91 in Feagin—See references at the end of essay."

In the 1860s, *Harpers Magazine* observed that the Irish "have so behaved themselves that nearly 75% of our criminals are Irish, that fully 75% of the crimes of violence committed among us are the work of Irish men..." (p. 116 in Steinberg). And, among the prostitutes, we are told that "in the middle of the nineteen century, it was the Irish who...figured most prominently, among the streetwalkers..." Substitute the word "black" for "Irish" and this sounds remarkably similar to the stereotype propagated in some quarters more than a century later.

Just as African-Americans in their early history were forced to cross picket lines to support their families, the same was true of the Irish, who did not hesitate to use retaliatory violence (rather than the non-violence practiced by most blacks in the U.S.). The Irish, for their part, also created secret organizations like the Ancient Order of Hibernians, which will parade on St. Patrick's Day.

Although African-Americans and Irish-Americans sometimes see themselves as rivals competing for influence or jobs in such organizations as police departments and in industries such as construction, in many areas both African-Americans and Irish-Americans have found themselves shoulder-to-shoulder: both groups have been key components of the Democratic party, labor unions, etc.

In their social and cultural lives, Irish-Americans and African-Americans shared more similarities than are often recognized. In their early years in the United States, like African-Americans, many Irish remained single. "One out of six of each sex never married, according to Steinberg (p. 164). As a matter of fact, jobs were more readily available for Irish women than men (because the women worked mainly as domestics).

This not to say that our dual history was one of continuous cooperation. Many Irish refused to help African-Americans attain their emancipation from slavery, often because they feared black competition for jobs. According to Steinberg, "The Irish immigrants...became...racist as any segment of northern society simply because they competed with blacks for jobs at or near the bottom of the occupational ladder."

An unfortunate example of this occurred during the U.S. Civil War. In July, 1863 New York "exploded into the bloody Draft Riots, when Irish mobs ravaged New York City for four days, randomly lynching blacks, [because the blacks were considered the cause of the war and a threat to Irish jobs], razing a black orphanage and driving blacks out of the city." (Steinberg, p. 177). A further indication of the tension between blacks and Irish could be seen in this August, 1862 commentary in the *Boston Pilot*, and Irish-Catholic newspaper: "we have already upon us bloody contention between white and black labor...The North is becoming black with refugee Negroes from the South. These [black] *wretches* crowd our cities, and by overstocking the market of labor, do incalculable injury to white hands."

CONCLUSION: OUR COMMON HISTORY

While acknowledging some important differences, African-Americans and Irish-Americans need to realize that we have a common history of being oppressed. Black Americans—for the sake of our self-esteem alone—need to realize that the same racist statements regarding violence and crime which are made against us, were made against other white ethnic groups and especially against the Irish. Thus, instead of fighting each other, we can learn from each other's struggles.

As both groups continue to strive for equal rights, on St. Patrick's Day we need to remember the words of Martin Luther King, Jr. from a Birmingham jail, "Injustice anywhere is a threat to justice everywhere. We are caught in an inescapable network of mutuality tied in a single garment of destiny. Whatever affects one directly affects all indirectly."

The proliferation of drugs in the black community and the growth in inner-city gangs in the last ten years is the result of a deliberate federal policy to do nothing. When you have policies like that, is it any wonder that a community would collapse on itself?

—Ed Wiley III & Jacqueline Conciatore

3

Solutions to Black Male Prison Crisis Elusive and Difficult

by Ed Wiley III and Jacqueline Conciatore

In the past six months, the U.S. prison population jumped by 46,000, an increase that exceeds both semi-annual and annual records.

If trends remained constant, Black men were a significant portion of the new prison population and will represent over 40 percent of all inmates by year's end. That latter figure has alarmed many educators, who warn of "the disappearance of the Black male" from our college campuses.

Efforts to emphasize rehabilitation over incarceration do not appear to have strong public support, a fact to which legislators and policymakers are sensitive, observers say.

The resistance is fueled by a lack of conclusive evidence that prison education programs and other rehabilitative efforts reduce crime. Without public faith in rehabilitation, some prison officials say they are operating against a backdrop that veers from education and looks toward prison as the final solution.

Outside the debate over prison education, however, there is consensus: In order to save the man, start with the boy.

The nation saw a 7.3 percent surge in the prison population from January through June 1989, according to the Bureau of Justice Statistics (BJS). The increase of 46,004 inmates is the largest increase recorded for the 64 years the government has been keeping track of prison populations. In fact, the six-month increase, which brings the total prison population to 673,565, was larger than any recorded annual increase, Said Tom Hester of the bureau.

Although the proportion of Black men in prison seems to have held steady over the last 15 years—Black people were 48 percent of the prison population in 1974 and 46 percent in 1985, according to a recent National Research Council report—the number of all prisoners has increased at an alarming rate.

"The numbers are the big difference," said one official with the Virginia Department of Corrections. "Fifteen years ago, there were 5,000 prisoners here, now there are 14,000..." The state's prison population during that time has been consistently 30 percent white and 70 percent Black, he said.

Experts cite many reasons for the disproportionate number of Black male prisoners: lack of economic opportunity, lack of accessible adult male role models, inequity in our justice system. Education also plays a big role. As former chairman of the Virginia parole board Bobby Vassar, put it: "I don't think it's a coincidence that a small percentage of people who have college degrees end up in prison."

Indeed, about 94 percent of all state prisoners in 1986 had never gone to college, according to BJS. About 28 percent were high school graduates, while 41 percent had not gone past the 11th grade. Such a correlation between educational attainment and incarceration, as well as the continuing swell of inmates into prisons that are already severely overcrowded, have caused some prison officials to look to prison education programs as a way to reduce recidivism.

But policymakers and legislators don't perceive rehabilitative efforts as being popular with the public. (How the public in fact perceives rehabilitation is anyone's guess: in a recent NAACP Legal Defense Fund survey, only 11 percent of Blacks and 9 percent of whites said they thought the best way to cut crime was to "send criminals to prison and keep them there a long time.")

LACK OF EVIDENCE

"Nothing works." This was the sentiment many people gleaned from studies, many undertaken in the 70s, which said rehabilitation programs don't prevent a return to crime. One well-known study was conducted by the late prison scholar Robert Martinson.

The Martinson study came at a time when the public was fed up with crime and when the prison officials were demoralized by the return of prisoners, said Dr. Rick Linden, a Canadian sociologist who conducted his own study of research on prison education programs. Legislators seized the opportunity to take a politically popular stand and divert resources, he said. "What better thing to cut than something that doesn't work...especially if you're looking for places to cut corners?" he said.

It's easier to state a tough position against criminals," Vassar said "Everyone wants to be tough on crime."

In his study, Linden found that there were in fact few evaluations of prison education programs, and those that exist were poorly conducted. Evaluations do show that inmates benefit from education programs in terms of learning, but that does not necessarily translate into lower recidivism, he said.

Vassar says he was troubled by the pessimism that followed the 1970 studies. "Nothing works—*everything* works. What is 'works?' Most people have the notion that parole doesn't work, only because what gets the attention are those cases that don't," he said. "I felt a deep sense of something going way awry" when policy-makers accepted the "nothing works" idea, he said.

Rehabilitative efforts are not helped by the instances when prisoners on work release or ex-convicts commit crimes, both Virginia officials said. "Belief in rehabilitation has been weakening over the last 10 years and last year as a result of the Willie Horton case, it has been extinguished," said the VA Department of Corrections official.

"The Horton incident just eroded public confidence in work-release. There is no support for alternatives...'Build more prisons'—that's the only answer—absolutely," he said.

Such a view is "very short-sighted," he said, "but the political fall-out is too great" and politicians don't take any other position, he said.

Offenses committed by ex-prisoners or those on work-release or furlough means "less emphasis on programs and more emphasis on security and punishment," said Vassar, who now is deputy commissioner of the State Department of Social Services.

Such incidents feed into a "psychological affinity in the country for incarceration," he said. "You commit a crime, get caught, get tried, fairly of course, and get sentenced and that's it. No one seems to go to the next step —*Then what?* If you do that, what are you trying to accomplish?"

START AT THE BEGINNING

If people can't seem to agree on the value of prison education programs and other rehabilitative measures, almost everyone agrees that more emphasis should be placed on the frontside, devising strategies to save youths—particularly Black youths—before they become ensnared by the penal system. Such measures must be accompanied by changes within the societal structure, including the job market and criminal justice system.

As Norvall Morris, prison expert and University of Chicago law professor puts it: "You don't wait 'til someone's in prison to try to help him."

"There is a big chunk of these in prison who are there because they saw no other option," said Dr. Asa Hilliard, Fuller E. Callaway Professor of Education at Georgia State University. Hilliard speaks regularly to inmates about Black history and Black pride. "Many of them hear TV talk about what you're supposed to aspire to, but they had no means to get there," he said.

Hilliard and other experts say that if Black males are to be steered away from a criminal lifestyle, society must employ an education and socialization process that deals with motivation and self-esteem as early as the preschool years.

Says Dr. Mary Rhodes Hoover, an ethnic studies professor at San Francisco State University and a leading authority on reading and linguistics: "If the education system would stop miseducating Black male children, we would not have the large employment problem; thus, we wouldn't have the serious problems of crime and incarceration among Black males."

Citing research by Dr. Amos Wilson (*Developmental Psychology of the Black Child*), Hoover says that although Black children show superior development over all groups in the infant stage—i.e., they walk first and speak first, using more detailed vocabulary and phrasing—they never get credit for their potential once they hit kindergarten.

Further, Hoover says, teachers—most of whom are unfamiliar with the "buoyancy of Black culture"—will likely place the child in a slow or retarded class. "And if they start out in a slow group, research shows that is where they are likely to remain throughout their life experience, "she said, adding that Black males comprise roughly 70 percent of those in classes for the mentally retarded. Hoover supports mandatory workshops for teachers to help them understand that "they have to stop looking at Black males as having behavior problems and realize that they are vibrant, buoyant children from a dynamic culture."

Dr. Wad Nobles, director of California's Institute for the Advanced Study of the Black Family, Life and Culture, Inc., agrees that society must attack the negative images that paint Black males as the "enemy."

He contends that racism and oppression are intensified by the fact that the nation's economic base has shifted from physical production of materials to mental production of ideas. "Now the Black man is viewed as being of no value," Noble says. "Therefore, many Black males see drugs and drug trafficking as the only method of economic survival, he says. "Black men are not valued by society. The are not being sought after in the legitimate employment market. The solution offered doesn't say, Let's do something to invest in the potential of Black men; let's invest in their education.' The answer is, "These Black men are dangerous, so let's invest in more prisons..."

Hoover says that Ralph Ellison's depiction of the Black male as "The Invisible Man" sums up the Black experience in America. He views the nation's dismal employment picture for Black males as proof that society has abdicated its responsibility to take care of all its citizens. She said that 50 percent of all Black males are either unemployed, not participating in the labor force or not accounted for. The comparable figure for white males is 20 percent, she says.

But if national leaders were serious about improving conditions for Blacks—the only way to address the growing Black prison population—they would enact the kinds of programs that snatched the nation from the jaws of the Depression in the 1930s, Hoover said.

Unfortunately, says Hoover and others, society has ignored trends which suggest that the nation's security and economic development depend upon its ability to educate and prepare all groups for future job demands.

Dr. Manning Marable, professor of political science and a research associate for the Center for the Studies of Ethnicity and Race in America at the University of Colorado, Boulder, also blames societal neglect and a "blame-the-victim" mentality for much of the problem. Marable has been a frequent critic of both presidents Reagan and Bush for their attempt to solve the crime crisis by building more prisons and hiring more judges. "Bush's approach has been to address the problem by repressive means," Marable says. "The root of the crime problem is the failure of federal policy toward urban development and treatment of minorities."

In pushing for a "systematic" approach, Marable says that current federal policies have had much to do with the growing Black underclass. "The proliferation of drugs in the Black community and the growth in inner-city gangs in the last ten years is the result of a deliberate federal policy to do nothing," he says. "When you have policies like that, is it any wonder that a community would collapse on itself? If there are no real jobs at decent wages, it's only natural that people—any people—resort to drugs, prostitution and petty theft to survive."

Marable says that the only way to address the rising Black prison population is by shifting the nation's priorities. He urges national leaders to support a stronger policy of full and fair employment, comprehensive public health care, massive support for education at all levels, improvements and expansion of public housing and transportation ("New jobs don't mean anything if you can't get to them") and initiatives for combatting crime that focus on community-based intervention, rather than efforts to expand the penal system.

Since 1978, the American penal population has increased by 50 percent. "For Blacks, we have the highest per-capita prison population in the free industrial world, including South Africa.

"It's a nightmare," Marable said. "It's almost impossible for any young man who grows up in Washington, DC to reach age 40 without having been stopped and arrested by police," he said, adding that drug-related crimes and murder are at an all-time high. "More Black men will die in Washington, DC this year than the number of Palestinians in the occupied West Bank."

That reality is fueled by the fact that the most prevailing consciousness among Black people today is one of survival, according to Haki R. Madhubuti, an award-winning poet, editor, publisher and educator.

In an article, titled "Were Corners Made for Black Men to Stand On," Madhubuti writes, "Black life is affected by overcrowded prisons, too few homes, overstressed minds, fat bodies and a communicative network that legitimize the easy, the quick and 30-second answers. America's context and content is built upon a subtle and effective ideology of white world supremacy that few people understand. For those that do, many are unwilling to voice the call to resist."

Marable says that alternative sentencing for nonviolent offenders should be used more frequently, stressing more concentration on work-release programs, group counseling and preparatory education programs. "There are too many people in prison who don't belong there," he said. Moreover, Marable continues, "When you look at sentencing patterns, Blacks, Latinos and Hispanics get longer sentences than whites for identical crimes."

He cites a 1968 California Department of Corrections study of state inmates which found that on average, of the first-time offenders who committed auto theft, whites were sentenced to 19 months in prison, while Blacks received 24 months; for marijuana use, Blacks received 36 months, compared to 26 months for whites. Rape resulted in 40 months for Blacks, nine more than for their white counterparts. Another example of the imbalance in the justice system can be seen by the fact that in the history of the U.S., there has never been a white executed by the state for the rape or murder of a Black person, Marable adds.

Nobles said that society often ignores questions about race because of the guilt and animosity such feelings produce. "When people teach about racism, if you don't handle the guilt associated with one group of people victimizing another for centuries, then it becomes a negative experience," he said. "How do you teach people of color about racism without their developing a righteous hatred. "How do you handle the issue without creating a legacy of hatred, because when you look at the history of what Europeans have done in the world, there is real cause for hatred?"

But disseminating the kind of information that will tear down racial barriers is not the responsibility of any one group in society, many educators agree. Dr. Shirley Lewis, executive director of The Black College Fund administered by the United Methodist Church, calls for churches, university officials and the whole of Black community—males and females—

to take up the fight. "I think that all of society—and that certainly includes the wives, mothers, sisters and sweethearts—needs to have a political orientation in addition to an intellectual and educational one," Lewis said.

"That's important, because we need to help Blacks begin their academic lives by making them understand that academic excellence is a part of our tradition that began in Africa.

"We need to help them value literacy at an early age and make sure Black students receive intellectual skills while maintaining their appreciation of Black heritage."

In the final analysis all parties agree that the Black male crisis in the prison system will continue unabated unless the educational, corrections, political, civil rights, religious and private sector together and earnestly begin to seek meaningful solutions. The key questions are when will this effort begin and how effective it will be.

Maintaining a social order that is both sexist and heterosexist requires a constant stream of homophobic messages to keep people fearful of being perceived as either gender inappropriate or as other than heterosexual.

—Arlene Holpp Scala

4

Gender Policing

by Arlene Holpp Scala

Suzanne Pharr, in *Homophobia: A Weapon of Sexism* (1997), argues that there are three weapons of sexism: homophobia, violence, and economics. In the hetero-patriarchy, hetero-sexuality is compulsory (Rich 1980). Maintaining a social order that is both sexist and het-erosexist requires a constant stream of homophobic messages to keep people fearful of being perceived as either gender inappropriate or as other than heterosexual. Heterosexism flour-ishes as long as "norm" concepts are maintained. Heterosexist sex, gender, and sexuality norms depend on a "blurring" of the three identities (Scala 1997). For example, a "normal" female is assumed to be feminine and heterosexual , and a "normal" male is assumed to be masculine and heterosexual. A female who is masculine, i.e., gender inappropriate (abnor-mal), is assumed to be lesbian, and a male who is feminine is assumed to be gay. "Blurring" makes female or male "gender inappropriate" behavior a signal that a person is queer.

Lesbian baiting and gay baiting is a form of homophobic behavior that is routinely used to encourage all people to conform to sex, gender, and sexuality norms. Lesbian baiting and gay baiting refers to the tactic of calling or implying that a person is lesbian or gay when her or his behavior is perceived to be gender inappropriate. The intent of "baiting" is to make a person feel badly about her/himself and to cause her/him to retreat to the "appropriate" sex/gender box.

In recent years, transphobia (the fear and hatred of transgendered people) has expanded my understanding of societal gender and sexuality policing. "Transgender" is the term used for people whose gender presentation does not conform to society's expectations for their birth sex or for their perceived biological sex. Some transgendered people are transsexuals (people who have had surgery and/or hormone treatment to alter their birth sex) and others are gender outlaws.

I made the connection between lesbian baiting, gay baiting, and transphobia in the context of my personal experience living with a trans-identifying butch lesbian. In my relationship with my partner, I have become keenly aware of the constant harassment that she lives with the moment she steps outside our doorway. What she experiences is gender harassment. To most people she looks more male than female, but there is enough ambiguity in her appear-ance to confuse most passers-by. This confusion often results in what I term "low-level harassment." I say "low level" because the harassment is usually done with facial and body language—looks of disgust, sneers, numerous other negative facial messages and body mes-sages that include stopping dead in one's tracks. Laughter, whispers, or audible comments such as "What is it?" are also commonplace. My experience of walking by the side of a transgendered female has made even clearer society's investment in the dualistic sex/gender system, a system that also requires compulsory heterosexuality. I have found that lesbian baiting, gay baiting, and gender harassment are powerful weapons used in the hetero-patriarchy against people who transgress society's gender expectations.

To better understand "baiting" and gender harassment it is helpful to understand the connection between sexism and heterosexism. Sexism encourages the socialization of females and males as opposites by designating distinct characteristics and roles for males and "opposite" characteristics and roles for females. In the gender-role system, if one does not act like a male, masculine, one is identified as behaving like a female, feminine. A binary sex and gender system only allows one possibility for behavior perceived to be "mutated" (Hopkins 1992). In other words, if one's behavior is not masculine, then it must be feminine. If one is not a female then one must be a male. Heterosexism compels females to be feminine; to be feminine means to be attractive and and attracted to males. Heterosexism compels males to be masculine; to be masculine means to desire to have sex with females.

When a female does not conform to standards of femininity, she is assumed to be a non-female, and heterosexist beliefs name that female a lesbian without knowing anything about her sexual orientation. By the same token, when a male does not conform to standards of masculinity, he is assumed to be a non-male, a homosexual. It is not uncommon for non-masculine males to be called a "girl" or a "woman" by other men. When one's behavior does not conform to gender expectations, one is perceived to be like the other sex, i.e., homosexual. Both sexism and heterosexism rely on gender roles.

I became interested in lesbian baiting and gay baiting when I gathered data in a Women's Studies class for a study of heterosexism. I analyzed students' sex-role socialization autobiographies as well as their responses to questions about their awareness of heterosexism. In my initial study, I never asked students if they were lesbian baited or gay baited. Yet, when they wrote their sex-role socialization stories, numerous accounts of what I recognized as lesbian baiting and gay baiting emerged. A story told by Tracy makes clear the function of lesbian baiting:

> In fourth grade my goal was to be on the Yankees. I can remember a classmate, Danny, saying, 'Girls can't be on a professional baseball team.' So I said, Then I'll be the first!' Then he said that I was going to be a lesbian when I grew up. 'A lesbian? What was that?' I thought. I asked my teacher about it and she sent Danny to the principal's office to be scolded. I then realized it was something bad. I still had no idea what it meant. My teacher even told me it was something bad and he should never call anyone that. It was then when I decided it was a curse word, so when I felt like calling someone a bad name it was 'lesbian'. It didn't matter if you were a boy or girl, you were a lesbian.

Tracy's dream to play for the Yankees was identified as deviating from the female gender-role expectation by Danny based on the stereotype that only males (presumably heterosexual) would desire to play professional baseball. Danny then "baited" Tracy by telling her that she would grow up to be a lesbian. Although most of the participants in my study tried to conform to gender-role expectations, Tracy did not explicitly state that she gave up her dream to play for the Yankees. However, Tracy learned a powerful homophobic message. She concluded that the term "lesbian" stood for something bad: "I then realized it was something bad." Although Tracy "still had no idea what it meant," her teacher told her "it was something bad and he [Danny] should never call anyone that." Tracy came to her own conclusion about the term "lesbian."

Tara, an athletic young woman, was another student who reported being called a lesbian. Athletic young women are always vulnerable to lesbian baiting because athletic ability is perceived to be a masculine trait. In her sex-role socialization autobiography she wrote that in middle school she was a "jockette." Her story follows:

> Two girls in my class decided to make up a rumor about me; they spread the rumor that I was a lesbian. At first I couldn't believe that these girls could spread something like that. Then I got angry because I thought what if people believe this. But everyone laughed.

Tara's story about lesbian baiting revels that the girls who baited her "decided to make up a rumor about me; they spread the rumor that I was a lesbian." According to Tara, the two young women who lesbian baited her actually conspired to hurt her. This example seems to fit with Pharr's (1997) contention that lesbian baiting is used as a weapon. They "decided to make up a rumor" and "they spread the rumor that I was a lesbian." In Tara's case, the lesbian baiting actually did not work. Tara was a very well liked student whose femininity and heterosexual dating had convinced everyone that she was a gender appropriate "normal" teenager, even though she was an athlete.

Paul wrote about "baiting" in his sex-role socialization autobiography. His account is interesting in that he wrote his five-page essay in the first person pronoun to the second-person pronoun, thereby distancing himself from the "baiting":

> In junior and high school years peers always pressured you into 'gender appropriate' behavior. My buddies would go to another guy that you like guys and not girls. You would reassure them by saying that you have a crush on the girl standing in the hallway by her locker. You always wanted to make a point to everyone that you were not a homosexual.

Paul's story seems to reveal a practice common among adolescent males, the practice of proving one's masculinity by indicating heterosexual behavior by conforming to the stereotype. This story shows how young men taunt one another and make them "prove" their heterosexuality. Ann Pellegrini, a feminist theorist, says that males prove their heterosexuality by recognizing the homosexual possibility and then denying it (1992). I noticed that Paul's account reveals a "ritualistic" gay baiting: "My buddies would go to another guy that you like guys and not girls." Then, "You" would "reassure them by saying that you have a crush on the girl standing in the hallway by her locker." Paul's story indicated that gay baiting was routine among the young men in his junior and high school social circle. By announcing a crush on a young woman a young man was able to simultaneously announce that he was "not a homosexual."

Paul's story shows that males need to disprove homosexuality by showing a romantic interest in females or by giving peers evidence of sexual conquests (scoring), and failure to do this results in gay baiting.

American society is dependent on gender roles as a way of maintaining the social fabric, particularly the capitalist economic system. Mean stereotypes about lesbians, gays, bisexuals, and transgendered people are instrumental in encouraging "appropriate" gender role behavior. As HIV/AIDS educator Jonathan G. Silin (1995) states, "Homophobic stereotypes are critical maintainers of the social fabric, assuring the economic and biologic reproduction of the family through adherence to appropriate gender roles" (p. 196)

Homophobic name-calling or implications seems to be the most effective tactic for policing gender. The fear of being labeled lesbian or gay leads heterosexuals and homosexuals alike to monitor their own behavior carefully to avoid any appearance of gender nonconformity. Most young people engage in an intricate web of societal gymnastics in order to appear both gender appropriate and heterosexual. Gender policing makes females and males conform to dualistic gender and sexuality standards.

Environmentalism has often been criticized as a predominantly white, upper middle-class movement that is more sensitive to wildlife and the wilderness than to human needs.

—Charles Lee

5

Evidence of Environmental Racism Out of Sight, Out of Mind

by Charles Lee

Most of us have never heard of Gauley Bridge in West Virginia. This is the site of the worst recorded occupational disaster in U.S. history. During the 1930s, hundreds of African American workers from the Deep South were brought in by the New Kanawha Power Company, a subsidiary of the Union Carbide Corporation, to dig the Hawks Nest tunnel. *Over a two-year period, approximately 500 workers died and 1,500 were disabled from silicosis, a lung disease similar to Black Lung.*

Men literally dropped dead on their feet breathing air so thick with microscopic silica that they could not see more than a yard in front of them. Those who came out for air were beaten back into the tunnel with ax handles. At subsequent congressional hearings, New Kanawha's contractor revealed, "I knew I was going to kill these niggers, but I didn't know it was going to be this soon." An undertaker was hired to bury dead workers in unmarked graves; he agreed to perform this service for an extremely low rate because the company assured him that there would be a large number of deaths.

Some 40 years later, during the 1970s, a new vision began to emerge within the peace movement. This broad and influential movement in modern society began to grapple with a fundamental question about itself, its calling, and the premises upon which its actions were based. The question was this: Is it moral to advocate for peace without justice? Indeed, is it even possible to achieve peace without justice?

Out of the questions, a concept called peacemaking emerged. Not to be confused with peacekeeping, which implies the preservation of the status quo, this concept highlights the connection between peace and the protection of human rights. The religious community very naturally gravitated toward the debate.

These developments bring to mind the need to raise a similar set of questions within another influential and expanding social movement-that of environmentalism. Particularly in the United States, a linkage between justice and the environment has yet to be made by environmental groups. The question needs to be posed. Can there truly be a healthy environment without justice?

The working paper for the recently launched World Council of Churches' World Convocation on Justice, Peace and the Integrity of Creation attempts to provide an answer. It states that "while it has special application to the natural world, the term integrity reminds us of human society as well, which is part of nature in the broadest sense. It reminds us, too, of social evils such as racism, sexism, unfair land distribution, political and economic oppression by dominant groups, and other manifestations of the human sin of greed and the thirst for power." Set in the context of disasters such as that at Gauley Bridge, the connection can hardly be overstated.

Another answer, based on fundamentally different assumptions, is provided by Dr. Norman W. Jackson executive director of the United Church of Christ Council of American Indian Ministry:

> The western Christian perspective, which spawns a whole set of assumptions, emerges from thousands of years of interpreting Genesis 1:27-28. This is based on humanity being created in God's image, to have dominion over the earth, and to subdue it. Indian creation stories have very different affirmations. Generally, humanity is understood to be an integral part of creation like everything else, with no authority or powers for domination and subduing creation. The integrity of creation means living in integral harmony with creation, which means justice and peace. Hence, indigenous peoples believe that justice, peace and the integrity of creation "is not only a wrong sequence, but betrays a fatally flawed understanding of the nature of creation, humanity's place and role in creation, and how justice and peace are achieved.
>
> The western Christian understanding of justice and peace seem to assume that human relationships are qualitatively different from the relations of the remainder of creation. Indians, however, believe justice and peace to be expressions of harmony, not conviction one adds in an attempt to ascribe integrity of creation. As long as humanity believes it can manage creation, it will manage it for self-perceived, short-term, self-interest, oblivious to the consequences of disharmony and the limitations of creation.

The question of the role of justice also reveals the highly analogous social and class bases of the peace and environmental movements. Environmentalism has often been criticized as a predominantly white, upper middle-class movement that is more sensitive to wildlife and the wilderness than to human needs. Its leaders readily concede that African-Americans, Hispanics, Asian/Pacific Islanders, Native Americans, and other racial minorities in the United States are largely absent from its ranks.

There is ample reason, historically, for the distrust and disaffection that racial minorities have for the environmental movement. In 1970, for example, during Earth Day activities at San Jose City College, organizers bought a brand new Cadillac and buried it. The Black Student Union demonstrated in protest, contending that such money could have been better spent on the problems of the inner cities.

Lois Gibbs, a mother who led the struggle at Love Canal in New York and who is now director of the Citizens Clearinghouse for Hazardous Wastes, once characterized the nation's attitude toward hazardous wastes as "out of sight, out of mind." These words appropriately describe the manner in which modern industrial societies have treated environmental pollutants over the past century. Such an approach has proven to be highly flawed as the vast accumulation of toxic, radioactive, and other hazardous contaminants in our air, water, and soil now threaten the very survival of our planet's ecology.

Besides being an apt description of the way pollution has been handled, however, Gibb's remark is a commentary on social relations. As the following examples will show, "out of sight and out of mind" is where the poor and powerless live and work.

- The nation's largest hazardous waste landfill, receiving toxic materials from 45 states and several foreign countries, is located in predominantly African-American and poor Sumter County, in the heart of Alabama "black belt."
- The predominantly African-American and Hispanic South Side of Chicago, Illinois, has the greatest concentration of hazardous waste sites in the nation.
- In Houston, Texas, six of the eight municipal incinerators and all five of the municipal landfills are located in predominantly African-American neighborhoods.
- African-American residents of a West Dallas neighborhood whose children suffered irreversible brain damage from exposure to lead from a nearby smelter won a $20 million out-of-court settlement.
- Pesticide exposure among farm workers, predominantly Hispanic, causes more than 300,000 pesticide-related illnesses each year. A large percentage of farm workers are children and women of child-bearing age. This exposure may be directly related to the emergence of childhood cancer clusters in McFarland and Delano, California.
- Navajo Indians were used as the primary work force for the mining of uranium ore, leading to alarming lung cancer mortality rates. In addition, the Navajo community in Shiprock, New Mexico, where more than 100 tons of uranium mill tailings flooded the Rio Puerco River, is one of the numerous Native American communities near uranium mills and nuclear facilities.
- Three executives in Illinois were convicted of murder in the death of a Polish immigrant worker from cyanide poisoning. The plant employing the worker hired mostly Hispanic and Polish immigrants who spoke and read little English. The skull and crossbones warning labels had been erased from the plant's cyanide drums.
- Puerto Rico is one of the most heavily polluted places in the world. For example, Puerto Rico's underground aquifers have been contaminated by massive discharges from pharmaceutical companies, oil refineries, and petrochemical plants. La Ciudad Cristiana, a small community near Humacao, is the only community in North America that was relocated due to mercury poisoning.
- The Marshall Islands, Bikini, and other islands in the Pacific have been devastated by nuclear bombing and other weapons testing. The effect of radiation exposure is now a major health problem in these areas.

To understand the causes of these injustices, it is important to view them in a historical context. Two threads of history help to explain the disproportionate impact of toxic pollution on racial and ethnic communities. The first is the long history of oppression and exploitation of African-Americans, Hispanic Americans, Asian Americans and Pacific Islander and

171

Native Americans. This has taken the form of genocide, chattel slavery, indentured servitude and racial discrimination in employment, housing, and practically all aspects of life in the United States. We suffer today from the remnants of this sordid history, as well as from new and institutionalized forms of racism.

The other thread of history is the massive expansion of the petro chemical industry since World War II. Between 1950 and 1980, the production of synthetic organic compounds increased from less than 10 billion pounds to more than 350 billion pounds a year. Each year, approximately 1,000 new compounds are added to the 70,000 in use in 1980. In addition, nuclear weapons facilities and nuclear reactors have the capacity to make entire regions uninhabitable for decades, if not centuries. Recent revelations about leaks from nuclear weapons facilities suggest that these weapons may be potent killers even without ever being used.

Nor are these problems limited to the United States. The problems of pesticide misuse, toxic waste dumping, and other domestic environmental threats all have international dimensions, particularly in the Third World. Of special concern is the continuing production and export to the Third World-by U.S. corporations-of pesticides that have been banned or restricted for use in the United States. In addition, the world was shocked by the catastrophe in Bhopal, India, where leaking methyl isocyanate killed thousands and crippled tens of thousands. Recently, leaders of African nations at a summit meeting of the Organization of African Unity denounced the dumping of toxic wastes in Africa, calling the practice "toxic terrorism" and "a crime against Africa and the African people."

It was against this background that the residents of the predominantly African-American Warren County, North Carolina, approached the United Church of Christ Commission for Racial Justice in 1982, asking for assistance in their protest against the proposed siting of a polychlorinated biphenyl (PCB) landfill near the community of Afton. This culminated in a campaign of civil disobedience that resulted in more than 500 arrests, including Dr. Benjamin F. Chavis Jr., director of the United Church of Christ Commission for Racial Justice; Dr. Joseph Lowery of the Southern Christian Leadership Conference; and Congressional Delegate Walter Fauntroy (D-D.C.).

Fauntroy subsequently requested a study on the demographic patterns of communities surrounding hazardous waste landfills. In 1983, the U.S. General Accounting Office (GAO) found that three out of the four landfills it looked at in the Southeast were located in predominantly poor and African-American communities. The GAO study, though limited in scope, was the first to document that poor and racial minority communities are indeed disproportionately impacted by hazardous waste sites.

In 1986, the United Church of Christ Commission for Racial Justice decided to undertake the first comprehensive national study on the demographic patterns associated with the location of hazardous waste sites. This study, titled Toxic Wastes and Race in the United States: A National Report on the Social and Socio-Economic Characteristics of Communities Surrounding Hazardous Waste Sites, was released in April 1987. Its findings led Bejamin Chavis to conclude the existence of "environmental racism."

The study found that the racial composition of a community is the single variable best able to explain the existence or non-existence of commercial hazardous waste facilities in that area. Racial minorities, primarily African Americans and Hispanics, are strikingly overrepresented in communities with such facilities; in fact, communities with a single hazardous waste facility were found to have twice the percentage of racial minorities as do communities without such a facility (24 percent vs. 12 percent). Communities with the highest level of hazardous waste activity-that is, having two or more facilities or one of the nation's five largest landfills-have three times the minority representation of communities without facilities (38 percent vs. 12 percent).

Furthermore, three of the five largest landfills in the nation are located in predominantly African-American or Hispanic communities. These three sites account for more than 40 percent of the nation's total capacity for commercial hazardous waste disposal. The largest of these, in Sumter County, Alabama, accounts for almost one quarter of the nation's capacity.

The location of "uncontrolled" toxic waste sites, numbering approximately 20,000 at the time of the study, shows an equally striking racial imbalance. African-Americans are particularly heavily represented in the populations of metropolitan areas with the largest number of uncontrolled sites. Although African-Americans comprise 11.7 percent of the total population, they make up 43.3 percent of Memphis, which has 173 sites; 27.5 percent of St. Louis with 160 sites; 23.6 percent of Houston with 152 sites; 23.7 percent ofCleveland with 106 sites; 37.2 percent of Chicago with 103 sites, and 46.1 percent of Atlanta with 94 sites. Overall, three out of five African-Americans or Hispanics in the United States live in a community with one or more uncontrolled hazardous waste sites. This represents more than 15 million African-Americans and eight million Hispanic Americans.

The report made a series of recommendations, directed at the federal, state, and municipal governments; at the civil rights, environmental, and religious communities; and at local communities themselves. It was aimed at making the public cognizant of an issue that is not presently at the forefront of the nation's attention. Of paramount importance is the need to initiate education, organizing and mobilizing efforts to confront these pollution problems in racial minority communities. The report concludes that hazardous wastes and environmental pollution should be made a priority issue at all levels of government.

In response to this report, Rep. John Conyers (D-Mich.) Wrote, Toxic Wastes and Race is a powerful indictment of those who argue that poor health and other problems in Black, Hispanic, and minority communities are self-inflicted. The findings of this impressive study are as chilling as they are compelling." In addition, Dr. Barry Commoner, noted environmentalist and activist, pointed out that the report "shows that there is a functional relationship between poverty, racism, and powerlessness and the chemical industry's assault on the environment.

Commoner's remarks begin to address the question posed at the beginning of this article: whether or not there can he a healthy environment without justice. They make the link between environmental pollution and issues of racial and social equity. The unwritten law governing corporate decision making around toxic pollutants seems to have been "Do what you can get away with," otherwise known as "malignant neglect." Communities that are poorer, less informed, less organized, and less politically influential become likely targets for the dumping of toxic wastes and other abuse from polluters.

The growing activism among racial minority communities about environmental issues is encouraging. For example, the Southwest Organizing Committee, a community group in

Albuquerque, New Mexico, used voter registration and block organizing in predominantly Hispanic neighborhoods to get political leaders to address underground water contamination, nitrate poisoning, and other severe environmental problems in that area. The predominantly African-American and Lumbee Indian area of southeast North Carolina was able to prevent the local siting of the first commercial low-level radioactive waste incinerator. This effort was spearheaded by the Center for Community Change, a group now in the midst of a fight to stop the placement of a regional chemical waste treatment plant along the Lumbee River.

In a smaller situation, the residents of Hancock County, a 78 percent African-American county in Georgia, recently stopped the proposed placement of a garbage incinerator in that county. In Louisiana in November 1988, a coalition of civil rights community activists, environmentalists, and labor unions organized the "Great Louisiana Toxics March" along the "cancer corridor" between Baton Rouge and New Orleans. Finally, pesticide poisoning caused the largely Hispanic United Farm Workers Union to initiate another national boycott of California table grapes, called the "Wrath of Grapes."

Since the inception of the environmental movement, it has become evident that modern industrial society, no matter what benefits are forthcoming, will not find alternatives to harmful production practices without pressure from a highly mobilized people. In the case of hazardous wastes, for example, the stated goal of national legislation is reduced production of such wastes. Research has shown that not only will this be technologically feasible but economically beneficial. Nonetheless, the United States has made very limited progress in this area.

Perhaps the real explanation for this lack of progress was expressed by the Rev. Leon White, of the Commission for Racial Justice and a primary organizer of the Warren County protests. White said, "As long as there are poor and minority areas to dump on, corporate America won't be serious about finding alternatives to the way toxic materials are produced and managed."

Racial minorities in the United States and their brothers and sisters around the world clearly bear a disproportionate burden of pollution. This fact is directly related to the economic, political, and social oppression that they also bear. If we are serious about cleaning up the environment, we must begin to link these issues. The environmental movement needs to undergo a transformation, similar to that which took place in the peace movement, toward becoming a just environmental movement.

Since the Warren County protest, a growing number of African-American, Hispanic, Native American, and Asian/Pacific Islander communities have become conscious of environmental racism and have actively taken up the fight against toxic pollution. Their efforts must not only be embraced and supported but also used to articulate a new understanding of the basic premises and goals of the struggle to clean up our environment.

It is at least conceivable
that we can re-work
masculinity in a way that
sustains a struggle
without reproducing the
enemy. In much this sense
feminism has been
re-working feminity. In
doing this it will be useful
to remember the hidden
riches of masculinity,
as well as its horrors.

—Bob Connell

6

Masculinity, Violence and War

by Bob Connell

ONE

In 1976 there were 22 million people under arms in the world's 130-odd standing armies. The figure today may be a little higher. Probably 20 million of them are men. I have not seen any global totals by sex, but there are figures for particular countries which serve as pointers. In the major NATO forces in 1979-80, for instance, 92% of the US military forces were men; 95% of the French and British; 99.3% of the German. From what is commonly known about other countries, these are not likely to be exceptional figures. The vast majority of the world's soldiers are men. So are most of the police, most of the prison warders, and almost all the generals, admirals, bureaucrats and politicians who control the apparatus of coercion and collective violence. Most murderers are men. Almost all bandits, armed robbers, and muggers are men; all rapists, most domestic bashers; and most people involved in street brawls, riots and the like.

The same story, then, appears for both organised and unorganised violence. It seems there is some connection between being violent and being male. What is it? And what light can an analysis of masculinity, apparently a question of individual psychology, throw on the question of violence on a world scale?

There is a surprisingly widespread belief that this is all "natural." Human males are genetically programmed to be hunters and killers, the argument runs. The reason is that ape-man aggression was a survival need in the prehistoric dawn, while the ape-women clustered passively round their campfires suckling and breeding.

Right-wing inflections of this argument thus explained and justify aggression, competition, hierarchy, territoriality, patriarchy, and by inference private property, national rivalry, armies and war. Crude versions of this doctrine are part of the stock rhetoric of modern fascism. More sophisticated versions are developed by "sociobiologist" in the universities.

Remarkably, there is now a feminist version of this argument too. The line of thought is that human males are naturally predatory and violent; patriarchal power is thus an expression of men's inner nature. Rape and war become synonymous. A poster slogan reads: RAPE IS WAR, WAR IS RAPE. Even serious and thoughtful attempts to reckon with the connection between sexual dominance and war, like Penny Strange's pamphlet *It'll Make a Man of You,* talk freely of "male cosmology," "male violence," "male values" and so on.

Two things have gone wrong here. One is that biological speculation has substituted for hared analysis. A critical examination shows practically no grounding in evidence. The sociobiologists' pre-history is speculative, their anthropology highly selective, and their mechanisms of selection and inheritance simply imaginary. By equally convincing evolutionary speculation one can "prove" that men are naturally co-operative and peaceful. In fact it has been done, by Kropotkin in *Mutual Aid.*

More important, perhaps, is the confusion of concepts in phrases like "male power," "male violence," "male culture," "malestream thought," "male authority." In each of these phrases a social fact or process is coupled with, and implicitly attributed to, a biological fact. The result is not only to collapse together a rather heterogeneous group (do gays suffer from "male cosmology," for instance; or boys?). It also, curiously, takes the heat off the open opponents of feminism. The hard-line male chauvinist is now less liable to be thought personally responsible for what he says or does in particular circumstances, since what he says or does is attributed to the general fatality of being male.

That this is a point where argument and emotion have got tangled is not accidental. There is a basic theoretical problem here. The social categories of gender are quite unlike other categories of social analysis, such as class, in being firmly and visibly connected to biological difference. It is therefore both tempting and easy to fall back on biological explanation of any gender pattern. This naturalisation of social processes is without question the commonest mechanism of sexual ideologies. That biological difference underpins and explains the social supremacy of men over women is the prized belief of enormous numbers of men, and a useful excuse for resisting equality. Academic or pseudo-academic versions of this argument, male-supremacist "sociobiology" from Tiger's *Men in Groups* through Goldberg's *THE Inevitability of Patriarchy* to present, find a never-failing audience.

If we cannot do better than this in getting to grips with the connection between masculinity and violence, then the left might as well pack its bags and go home, turn on the VCR and play *Threads* until the missiles arrive. For if it all stems from the biological fact of maleness, there is nothing that can be done.

We can do better, and the basis for doing so is well known. It is to recognise that war, murder, rape and masculinity are social and cultural facts, not settled by biology. The patterns we have to deal with as issues of current politics have been produced within human society by the processes of history. It is the shape of social relations, not the shape of genes, that is the effective cause. "Male" and "masculine" are very different things. Masculinity is implanted in the male body, it does not grow out of it.

This argument implies a very different approach to the nature of gender from the natural categories appealed to by both sociobiology and cultural (or eco-) feminism. Such an understanding has been emerging from the work of other groups of feminists (in Australia, research such as Game and Pringle's *Gender at Work* and Burton's *Subordination),* and others. Broadly, gender is seen as a structure of social practice, related in complex ways to biological sex but with a powerful historical dynamic of its own.

That general framework suggests two lines of approach to the question of masculinity and war. One is to investigate the social construction of masculinity. The other is to undertake a social analysis of war. In what follows I'll suggest some points about both.

Two

Given a framework of social analysis, we can look at the familiar images and archetypes of manliness in a clearer light. They are parts of the cultural process of producing particular types of masculinity. What messages they convey are important because they help to shape new generations.

One of the central images of masculinity in the Western cultural tradition is the murderous hero, the supreme specialist in violence. A string of warrior heroes—Achilles, Siegfried, Lancelot and so on—populate European literature from its origins. The twentieth century has steadfastly produced new fictional heroes of this type: Tarzan, Conan, James Bond, the Jackal, the Bruce Lee characters. If you walk into a shop selling comics you will find a stunning array of violent heroes: cops, cowboys, supermen, infantry sergeants, fighter pilots, boxers and so on. The best of the Good Guys, it seems, are those who pay evil-doers back in their own coin.

This connection between admired masculinity and violent response to threat is a resource that governments can use to mobilise support for war. The most systematic case in modern history was the Nazis' cult of Nordic manhood, reaching its peak in the propaganda image of the SS-man during World War II. In a different context, a cult of masculinity and toughness flourished in the Kennedy and Johnson administrations in the USA, and helped commit that country to war in Vietnam. Fasteau documents this in one of the early books to come out of the American "men's movement," *The Male Machine*. I can remember the process operating on young men of my generation in Australia, whose conservative government sent troops to support the Americans in Vietnam. Involvement in the war was presented as standing up to threat, and opponents were smeared as lily-livered effeminates. In the fullness of time support for napalm raids and carpet bombing by B-52s became the test of manliness. In the aftermath of the TWA jet hijacking, Reagan has been playing this tune again, trying to rouse American feeling against the threat of terrorism to provide a cover for his own military operations in central America.

Yet there is a good deal of scepticism in response to Reagan. And in the previous case, Western opposition to the Vietnam war did grow: Together with the Vietnamese resistance it eventually forced the American military to withdraw. The cult of masculine toughness is not all-powerful. This should alert us to some complexities in masculinity and its cultural images.

It is striking that the *Iliad* centres not on Achilles' supremacy in violence, but on his refusal to use it. And what changes his mind is not his reaction to threat, but his tenderness—his love for his friend Patroclus. Siegfried and Lancelot, not exactly gentle characters, are likewise full of hesitations, affection, and divided loyalties.

The image of heroism in modern figures like Tarzan and James Bond is a degraded one. The capacity for tenderness, emotional complexity, aesthetic feeling and so on has been deleted. More exactly, they are split off and assigned only to women, or to other, inferior

179

types of men—such as the wimps, poofters and effeminates who evaded the Vietnamese war. (Part of the legend of Achilles was that he put on a dress and lived among women in order to evade the Trojan war.)

We know very little of the history of masculinity as distinct from the history of men; the detailed research has not bee done. We know enough to understand that such changes in images of heroism are part of the historical process by which different kinds of masculinity are separated from each other, some exalted and some spurned. A crucial fact about men is that masculinity is not all of a piece. There have always been different kinds, some more closely associated with violence than others. This is why one should not talk of "male violence" or of "males" doing this and that—phrasing which smuggles back in the idea of a biological uniformity in social behaviour.

As any given moment some forms of masculinity will be hegemonic—that is, most honoured and most influential—and other forms will be marginalized or subordinated. The evidence about these forms is very scattered, as the question is only just coming into focus as a research issue. Some points are clear. Modern hegemonic masculinity is defined as heterosexual (not true of all societies or all periods of history), and sharply contrasted with homosexual masculinity (in our society the type case of subordinated masculinity). Some other forms of subordinated masculinity are temporary—like that of apprentices in a strongly-masculinized trade. There are kinds of masculinity that are not directly subordinated but rather marginalized by a process of social change that undermines their cultural presuppositions— the patriarchal masculinity of many immigrant men from Mediterranean countries is an important case in Australia at present. And there are struggles about what form of masculinity should be hegemonic—for instance the contest going on in the ruling classes of capitalist world between professional/managerial and entrepreneurial/authoritarian masculinities. (The victory of Reaganism in the US is an important shift in the style of American patriarchy as well as in the precise locus of class power.)

THREE

In some civilisations the hegemonic forms of masculinity stress restraint and responsibility rather than violence. I believe that was true, for instance, of Confucian China. In contemporary Western society, hegemonic masculinity is strongly associated with aggressiveness and the capacity for violence. Modern feminism has shown us one of the bases for this: the assertion of men's power over women. This relationship itself has a strong component of violence. Wife-bashing, intimidation of women in the street, rape jealousy-murder, and other patterns of violence against women are not accidental or incidental. They are widespread and systematic, arising from the tensions of a power struggle. This struggle has many turns and twists. Even in a society that defines a husband as the "head of the household," there are many families where wives actually run the show. Bashings may then result from an attempt to re-assert a damaged masculine ego. In other cases domestic violence is a direct expression of the husband's power, his belief that he can get away with anything, and his contempt for women in general or his wife in particular.

180

So there are many complexities and contradictions. The main axis, however, remains the social subordination of women, and men's general interest in maintaining it. The masculinity built on that bedrock is not necessarily violent—most men in fact do not bash women—but it is constructed, so to speak, with a door open towards violence.

Gay liberation has shown us another dimension: hegemonic masculinity is aggressively heterosexual. It defines itself in part by a vehement rejection of homosexuality. This rejection very often takes violent forms: arrests, frequent bashings, and occasional murders. Homosexual men seem to arouse particular fear and loathing among tough "macho" men. This fact has led many to think the violence is an attempt to purge the world of what one suspects in oneself. In psychoanalytic terms, there is a current of repressed homosexual feeling buried somewhere in hegemonic masculinity. This, again, suggests the importance of the tensions and contradictions within masculinity. It is by no means a neat package.

In much of the writing about men produced by the "men's liberation movement" of the 1970s it was assumed that violence was simply an expression of conventional masculinity. Change the macho image, stop giving little boys toy guns, and violence would be reduced. We can now see that the connection of masculinity and violence is both deeper and more complex than that. Violence is not just an expression; it is a part of the process that divides different masculinities from each other. There is violence within masculinity; it is constitutive. Once again, this is not to imply that it is universal. Real men don't necessarily bash three poofters before breakfast every day. For one thing, TV does it for them. Part of the pattern of contemporary masculinity is the commercial production of symbolic violence of an unprecedented scale, from Tarzan movies to Star Wars, Space Invaders, World Series Cricket, and now Rambo.

FOUR

It is very important that much of the actual violence is not isolated and individual action, but is institutional. Much of the poofter-bashing is done by the police; much of the world's rape is done by soldiers. These actions grow readily out of the "legitimate" violence for which police forces and armies are set up. The state is an instrument of coercion; this remains true whatever else about it varies. It uses one of the great discoveries of modern history, rational bureaucratic organization, to have policy-making centralized and execution down the line fairly uniform. Given this, the state can become the vehicle of calculated violence based on and using hegemonic masculinity. Armies are a kind of Hybrid between bureaucracy and masculinity.

But to make this connection with an undifferentiated "masculine violence"—as, say, Fernbach does in *The Sprial Path*—is to misunderstand the way armies work. Generals, notoriously, die in bed. They are not themselves "violent men," and would be bad generals if they were. Of course they need violent men under their command as front-line troops, or at least as organisers of front-line troops—men like the grim Sergeant Croft of *The Naked and the Dead* (a novel that strikingly makes the point about different masculinities).

It is the *relationship* between forms of masculinity—physically violent but subordinate to orders on the one hand, dominating and organisationally competent on the other—that is the

181

basis of military organisation. The two need not overlap at all. Heinrich Himmler, the commander of one of the most brutal military organisations in recent history, never killed anyone personally. When present at any execution where some brains splattered on his neat SS uniform, he threw a screaming fit.

Even this is to understate the matter. In modern armies the majority of soldiers are not combatants at all. Most are in support services, as transport workers, administrators, technicians, maintenance worker, cooks, etc., and have no competence as fighters at all. The proportion of this kind of worker in armies has grown markedly over the last century and a half with the increasing technologisation of warfare, as several major developments have reduced the need for cannon-fodder and increased the need for supply workers. The US made two great contributions to the art of war in the 1940s—nuclear weapons and logistics. Logistics was certainly more militarily effective at the time. And you don't want Rambo types driving your jeeps and supply trucks.

Automatic weapons (machine-guns and quick-firing artillery), self-propelled military vehicles (tanks and aircraft), and ultimately long-distance weapons that eliminate the front' (strategic bombers, nuclear missiles) have successively intensified the trend. They have made more and more important in military organisations of third kind of masculinity, the professionalised, calculative rationality of the technical specialist.

The first stage of this was the rise of the "General Staff" to a central position in European military organisation by the early twentieth century. The idea of a General Staff was a group of planners, separate from the command of combat units, who worked out overall strategies as well as technical issues of supply. The "Schlieffen Plan" for the German attack on France in 1914 marked the ascendancy of staff over line commanders. In no sense did this mean a shift away from violence—the violence of war was growing on an unprecedented scale. The man who was the 20th century's most successful general, the Soviet Chief of Staff Georgi Zhukov, was notorious for his disregard for human life. He accepted huge casualties in order to gain advantage in battles of attrition at Moscow, Stanlingrad and Kursk (the battles responsible for the ultimate defeat of Hitler).

The second stage was the mobilization of physical scientists on a large scale into weapons research, culminating in the Manhattan Project. The friction within the Manhattan Project, and the crisis of conscience suffered by the unclear physicists immediately after the explosion of the Hiroshima and Nagasaki bombs, are measures of the difficulty of integrating this kind of worker into the military. But the huge growth of nuclear weapons research establishments in the USA and USSR since then shows that the initial difficulties have been overcome. The end of the world has been made technically possible by this achievement in human relations.

FIVE

In the past, as well as being the main actors of war, men have also been the main victims. Napoleon's wars killed mainly soldiers. The harnessing of high technology to the bureaucratic state has steadily changed this. Hitler's mass extermination campaigns, and the Anglo-

American firebombing of Hamburg, Dresden and Tokyo, were an organised turning of conventional weapons to the killing of whole populations. The nuclear arsenal has been directed against whole populations from the start.

It has thus become a matter of urgency for humans as a group to undo the tangle of relationships that sustains the nuclear arms race. Masculinity is part of this tangle. It will not be easy to alter. The pattern of an arms race, i.e., mutual threat, itself helps sustain an aggressive masculinity.

Nor can the hegemonic pattern of masculinity be rejected totally. To achieve disarmament in reality means conducting a long and difficult struggle against an entrenched power structure. This calls for some of the qualities hegemonic masculinity exalts—toughness, endurance, determination and the like. It is no accident that hegemonic masculinity has been important in radical movements in the past: in unionism, in national liberation movements, and in socialist parties.

Yet we know masculinity is not fixed. It is at least conceivable that we can re-work masculinity in a way that sustains a struggle without reproducing the enemy. In much this sense feminism has been re-working femininity. In doing this it will be useful to remember the hidden riches of masculinity, as well as its horrors. There are cultural resources in subordination masculinities, and in patterns lost or bypassed in recent history.

"Size Discrimination is
a Civil Rights Issue."
Studies have shown
that fat people are less
likely to be admitted to
elite colleges, are less
likely to be hired for a
job, make less money
when they are hired,
and are less likely to
be promoted.

—NAAFA

7

Size Discrimination Is a Civil Rights Issue

The myths and stereotypes about fat people held by American society are often used to justify treating fat people as second-class citizens. This treatment has a devastating effect on the quality of life for fat people:

EMPLOYMENT

Fat people are denied employment, denied promotions and raises, and sometimes fired, not due to factors of competence, but due to an arbitrary standard of "acceptable" weight.

EDUCATION

Fat people are often not accepted into graduate programs, and are sometimes harassed and expelled, not because of their grades or conduct, but because they do not fit the school's "image".

HOUSING

Fat people are sometimes denied the opportunity to rent apartments and houses by biased landlords.

ACCESS TO QUALITY MEDICAL CARE

Fat people are often refused treatment, misdiagnosed, or told that every condition is weight-related by biased health care providers.

PUBLIC ACCOMMODATIONS

Fat people are often denied access to public transportation, airline travel, theatres and restaurants because seating is not available to them.

SOCIAL

Fat people are fair game for ridicule and public humiliation, because they do not look "acceptable."

Each of these is a type of discrimination based on size. NAAFA, the National Association to Advance Fat Acceptance, is committed to ending size discrimination in all forms.

Discussion Questions
Part IV: Rethinking Race, Class, and Gender:
Socio-Political Movements

1. Compare and contrast a socio-political movement in your community or state with one discussed in Part IV.

_____

_____

_____

_____

_____

_____

_____

2. In the space provided below, write a brief essay examining the history of your own ethnic group. Use the blank pages at the end of this book if more space is needed.

_____

_____

_____

_____

_____

_____

**What is FED-UP about?
I am fed up with
Rightwing Christians
preaching against
lesbians and gay men
and upholding
heterosexuals as those
chosen by christ and
anthropomorphic god
called "Father."**

—Suzanne Pharr

Part V

Prognosis for the Future:
Religion and Health

Religion and Health Care are intertwined with issues of race, class, and gender. For example, recent studies have indicated that AIDS which affects black and Latina women more than men are affected by religion. The intersection of religion and health are discussed in "Combatting Racism and Sexism in Health Education," and "AIDS: What the Black Much Must Do." There are other issues which impact on religion and health. Examples (and solutions) are presented in "Circumcision: An American Health Fallacy," and "Daddy, Why is Your Penis Different from Mine."

These selections make it clear that racism, sexism, and classisms have a harsh impact on both the wellness of millions of Americans and on their ability to receive quality medical care.

The Judeo-Christian ethic also plays a vital role in undergirding the "moral fiber" and world view of American society. Critics of this ethic have often characterized it as a tool for sexist, heterosexist, and racial oppression. In their religious institutions, as in the larger society, ethnic minorities, women and gays must either accommodate and adapt to the prevailing dogma, or else reinterpret these dogmas and reorient them towards an alternative form of theology. The selections in PART V, among other questions, explore the various dimensions of these processes.

With regard to race, class, and gender, traditional Christian churches have often been criticized as "being part of the problem, not part of the solution." Several selections in this chapter examine the role of the church in grappling with some of the important religious and social questions of today. The traditional Christian church has finally come to grips with some of the problems that growing numbers of men have had in relating to religious institutions. This issue is analyzed in "The Men's Movement: Challenge to the Church's Ministry." "Coping With Biblical Fundamentalism: Solutions" offers some ideas for countering the growing influence of this Religious Right.

Finally, "On Family Values" proposes a "feminist ethic" as the answer to the problems of the corruption and dishonesty that is so rife in American society today.

As with racism, dealing with sexism in the classroom requires us to first confront our own sexist behaviors and attitudes.

—Maryanne Galvin

Combating Racism and Sexism in Health Education: Some Issues, Responsibilities, and Solutions

by Maryanne Galvin and Donald A. Read

Of the numerous parallels between racism and sexism, three are most significant to us. Others exist, of course, but these three are continually used against minorities and women with injurious effect.

Race and sex stereotypes are the first and single most handicapping factors still facing us today in American society. Stereotypical images in movies, in books, in the news and entertainment media, and finally, in our own minds, tend to deny minorities and women pride in themselves and a desire or will to change. The use of these stereotypes—from the ancient image of the shuffling, absentminded servant in the film "Gone With the Wind," to the contemporary Brooke Shields in the sleek designer jean ads—have detracted from a positive self image for minority groups and women.

These stereotypes exist historically in education as well as in the media, and they have been reinforced by a discriminatory legal system. The nation's public schools regularly purchase and use textbooks and other learning materials which still exclude blacks to a significant degree from their pages and place girls and women in denigrating and stereotypical roles.

A black or Chicano student might wonder whether he or she ever existed after delving into the textbook world. A girl surely might ask if she could be anything other than an elementary school teacher, a secretary, a housewife, or a nurse. And although strides are being made with regard to minorities, this is not true with regard to women. All too many negative images of women still appear on television, particularly in advertising. Madison Avenue has used girls and women to sell every conceivable product through smoothly professional hustling of sexual messages. After all, women equal sex and sex sells.

A second parallel between sexism and racism is in the extent to which the law and our system of justice have perpetuated the oppression of minorities and women. Our government and laws began by describing blacks and women as non-persons. The Constitutional Convention declared a slave equal to only three-fifths of a man. Only white males were included for purposes of voting and taxes.

Thus from the beginning our nation's lawmakers gave minorities and women second-class status. Except for the 19th amendment, Congress did not act until 1964 to safeguard the rights of minorities and women.

More contemporary evidence can be found in the continued struggle to seek passage of the Equal Rights Amendment, and the suggestion of tax exemptions to segregated schools by the Reagan Administration. Some would, in fact, view the Reagan Administration as establishing a new record for cynicism and social reaction.

A third example of the parallels between sexism and racism exist in the form of physical violence, and fear of physical violence, that is often used to keep blacks and women in line. Racist attacks throughout the country have escalated recently in number and intensity. If, for example, the slaughter of five demonstrators by the Ku Klux Klan in Greensboro, NC., recently was not appalling enough, the newspaper coverage of the atrocity was. Virtually every account that moved across the national wire services carried the outrageous suggestion, either implied or outright, that the victims of the massacre somehow deserved what they got when carload of admitted Klansman drove up to a demonstration at a mostly black housing project and opened fire with shotguns and automatic riffles. In yet another example of outright racism, in the midst of the child killings in Atlanta, a Ku Klux Klansman appeared on national TV news and proudly stated, "I am a racist." These attacks can only be viewed as reminding blacks that whites are still in charge. In a comparable way the raping of women is a societal oppression. It reaffirms "superiority" in the male attacker and is executed with wanton disregard for the person attacked. (And it must be noted, rape is on the increase across the United States.)

WHAT IS HEALTH EDUCATION DOING?

We are not aware of any concerted, organized effort within health education as a collective body to help our generation of young people become more aware of the tenacious, persuasive, and particularly, the subtle components of the social disease of racism and sexism. And it is an educational problem health education in the specific sense and education in the broad sense.

If it is, as we see it, a function of health education to help free human beings from the constrictions of unhealthy lifestyles, of irrational fears, and hatreds, and it is a prime function of education to attempt to liberate the human mind and the human spirit, then it is most certainly a function of education in general, and health education more specifically to deal with racism and sexism within its curriculum at all levels.

Any socially concerned person would have to acknowledge the possibility that it is, perhaps, incumbent upon the educational system to incorporate into its curriculum the teaching of the social, political, and interpersonal implications of racism and sexism. Is it not more crucial for social studies to teach ways of becoming a more social and authentic person with all people regardless of race or sex, than to stress such dates as when the Roman Empire collapsed? Is it not equally as compelling to teach preventative character decay as to instruct in methods of preventive medicine and dentistry in health education? There are so many possibilities of creative approaches to this idea, only waiting to be instituted by teachers who dedicated to the development of more positive, loving people and a more caring society. Somewhere in the overloaded circuits of nutrition, sexuality, accident prevention drug abuse, etc., there must be a vacant outlet to plug in the teaching of positive human relationships, to identify racism and sexism and the need for change in our society today if we hope for a better life and world tomorrow.

As humanists, our cynicism is tempered by an optimism about the potential for just such a curriculum. With that in mind, we would like to offer the reader some possibilities for establishing a curriculum of affect in combating racism and sexism in your school and your program in health education.

SOME CONSIDERATIONS IN ESTABLISHING A CURRICULUM OF AFFECT

The task confronting us as educators and facilitators of change is developing ways to identify the issues of racism and sexism within each of us as individuals and in the school and community at large. How can we help young people come out from behind the myths they have accepted and perhaps unknowingly perpetuated, which ultimately confine all of us?

We see as some of the goals of a program/curriculum in combating racism and sexism a helping young people to:

- Recognize and clearly define the concepts of bias, sexism, prejudice, bigotry, hatred, and racism.
- Describe and examine racism and sexism in its institutional, cultural, and individual forms.
- Explore, identify, and clearly articulate one's own personal feelings, including fears, surrounding the issues of racism and sexism.
- Identify and articulate ways in which one's own racist and sexist attitudes and behaviors negatively affect self and others.
- Develop new, more positive, ways of acting and behaving which can hopefully lead to an elimination of racist-sexist attitudes and behaviors in self in others.
- Act on these new attitudes and behaviors in all interpersonal interactions.

There are some key factors to facilitating a truly effective program in combating racism and sexism. First, and probably most important to us, is that the teacher must have a very sensitive understanding of racism and sexism. This includes both an awareness of one's own personal sexist/racist attitudes and behaviors, plus an ability and willingness to discuss all ramifications of racism and sexism as they apply to self and others.

Central to the above, and to any class or workshop that would deal with racism and sexism as described in this discussion would be the willingness and ability of the participants to practice self-disclosure. Self-disclosure as defined by the late Sidney M. Jouranrd means an

193

ability on the part of one person to disclose his or her true feelings to another.

Self-disclosure would be an important dimension of the classroom or workshop. The willingness to communicate one's beliefs, or "saying one's self," becomes vital when establishing a classroom climate where trust can develop and where studying one's self is a priority. Even though the formal research is inconclusive, previous experience of the authors in a variety of educational settings indicates that the need "to say one's self" is deep-seated.

We want to be known by others as much as we want to know ourselves; the meaning is derived out of the dynamic of the relationship, not before it. So, the class becomes the place where mutual, shared self-disclosure can be attempted in a relatively safe environment. As we "say ourselves" while in relationships, the others become mirrors for our thoughts, and we have the opportunity to use that information to alter the way we see ourselves.

Recognize also that the classroom is by a microcosm of the larger work of the student, and any truly effective program dealing with racism and sexism must, if at all possible, also involve the entire school. Other teachers, administrators, and students should be part of any awareness program. Such strategies as inservice training for administrators, all faculty, and supportive staff; the adoption of a multicultural, non-racist and non-sexist curriculum; and the setting aside of an entire week devoted to racist/sexist issues are prime examples of a commitment to an educational and social environment that provides an atmosphere of respect and support for all its members.

Finally, to close this part of our discussion, some comment needs to be made about grading. The traditional use of grades in a program as envisioned here simply is not appropriate. To suggest that letter grades be used to judge some arbitrary level of accomplishment about how much self-awareness one has gained, or that he/she is less racist than another, is in direct opposition to the ideas presented here. At the very most a "pass, no report" might be tolerable if some form of course evaluation were found necessary by the school.

A CURRICULUM OF AFFECT IN COMBATING RACISM

If you would like some encouraging information as to why a curriculum in combating racism might just prove successful, consider this: sociologist Thomas Pettigrew has found that approximately one-fifth of the whites in the United States are unprejudiced against minorities and about one fifth are highly prejudiced to the extent of being set in their ways. This leaves three-fifths (a majority) who are prejudiced against minorities in conformity with custom and current practice. Pettigrew believes the conformers could make the adjustment easily and without any great personality change if they were educated to conform to a different set of customs and circumstances.

In this latter group, the conformers, that we as teachers can have the most positive effect on, but only if a truly concerted effort is made to confront and deal with the issue head on. Racism is hard to understand in a vacuum. People hold racist attitudes without being consciously aware of them. Institutions, the media, and people in general perpetuate racist values, sometimes without intention. Thus, any realistic unit dealing with racism must include students' examining:

- What are our own and other's hidden prejudices against blacks and other minorities?
- What factors contribute to these discriminatory attitudes?
- What forces perpetuate them?
- How are these attitudes reinforced by individuals, the media, one's own school and society at large?
- What are the negative effects of hidden prejudices and discrimination on minority groups?
- What can we as individuals do to lessen or eliminate racism in our school, neighborhood, town?
- What can we do as a class to change attitudes in our school?
- Where and how do we start?
- How do we evaluate the results?

Any unit dealing with racism will most often deal with black people in American society. Blacks represent the largest minority group in the country and are the most visible. As you begin to develop and work with the unit on racism, however keep in mind that other minority groups are victims of racism; and you and your students will wish to enlarge your knowledge and understanding of these other groups and their plight.

The explosiveness of the issue of racism, the potential for hurt feeling, and the fear that lurks in the minds of people who may see their comfortable ways of life threatened require that the teacher handle this subject carefully. Keep in mind that you are guiding students toward a new awareness of facts about racism within themselves, their school, their hometown, job, etc. Most of all, you should always stay aware of the fact that you are not "selling" your position on this or any other controversial issue. A climate of openness in which opinions may be shared freely, questions asked, and the answers given or discovered by students should be your goal. A final caution: one should never convey (either overtly or covertly) that inherent racism exists within any student or students. The atmosphere should be one of openness, trust, and caring.

As you introduce the unit on racism, raise the possibility that during class discussions, students may make what would undoubtedly, in some other setting, be interpreted as racist remarks. Unless students are free to make these statements in class, how will they bring them to awareness, to be challenged, to change their attitudes and behaviors? What are some ground rules which the class would like to develop relative to this possibility? How can students help each other in the honest search for answers or a more enlightened view? How confidential can discussions held in the class be? What is the meaning of trust and how is it developed?

Neither teacher nor students should view the opinions of minority group students as representative of the total group. The black student should not be expected to speak for all black people nor to be an authority on the history, economics, social class structure, religion, etc., of all black people. The same is true for Puerto Rican, Oriental, Chicano, or other minority group youngsters in your class.

In developing your design, try to plan for time between sessions for all students to reflect on and integrate the materials and concepts into their own life frame. For example, provide reading materials before beginning the program. In this way students can begin thinking and raising questions in their own minds.

Finally, plan for some follow-up sessions. The more reinforcement participants have, the more they may be able to change. It is difficult to become anti-racist in a racist society. Your students will need support to make changes in and around themselves. Structure that reinforcement into the design and impress upon your students the need for support. In this vein, your students may wish to share their learning experiences with others. Invite another class in for an especially interesting activity, present a panel discussion in the assembly, or ask a group to prepare articles for the school newspaper.

Rather than providing the reader with some effective strategies that can be used in bringing about an awareness of racism in self and others in the classroom, we would like to provide two resources that offer very creative strategies and suggestions:

An instructional kit for teachers, *Violence, the Ku Klux Klan and the Struggle for Equality*, has been published jointly by the Connecticut Education Association, the NEA, and the Councial on Interracial Books for Children. Copies of the 72 page guidebook are available for $4.95 from the Council on Interracial Books for Children, 1841 Broadway, New York, NY 10023.

A book on curriculum and strategies is Judy H. Katz's *White Awareness: Handbook for Anti-Racism Thinking*. Norman, Oklahoma: University of Oklahoma Press, 1950.

A CURRICULUM OF AFFECT IN COMBATING SEXISM

As with racism, dealing with sexism in the classroom requires us to first confront our own sexist behaviors and attitudes. For example, see if you can relate to the following questions in terms of your own teaching:

- Do you use the same standards and the same punishment for students regardless of sex?
- Do you value and encourage independent and assertive behavior in both male and female students?
- Do you encourage male and female students to share jobs equally?
- Do you display test, films, and pictures of girls and women as well as boys and men assuming a variety of androgenous behaviors?
- Do you distribute your time equally between male and female students in class?

This checklist provides only a cursory introduction to many routes educators might embark upon in evaluating themselves and their classroom environments for instance of sexism.

A number of observational studies conducted in American preschools, elementary, and high schools have documented that educators' (and counselors', nurses', administrators') sex-differentiated behaviors institute a different type of sex discrimination directed toward boys and girls.

Some findings show that educators praise as well as criticize boys more frequently than girls. One study concluded that boys were asked more direct questions by the teacher than girls. Boys were also praised more frequently when they gave correct answers and criticized more often for incorrect answers or failures to respond.[1]

These findings are significant because they indicate that the educator's sex-differentiated behavior tends to place a greater pressure on boys than on girls to achieve a pattern that reinforces the one produced by similar sex-differentiated parental behaviors.

Researchers have found that school personnel approve of girls more than boys because they fit better the desirable institutional-type behavior of dependent, docile, passive, and obedient children who do not disrupt the classroom routine.[2] It seems that school personnel's ideal of a school child coincides with the "feminine" stereotype, a fact that may appear to be beneficial to girls in the short range but which is clearly detrimental to them in the long range.

Current findings have shown that an important component for effective teaching is the ability to establish a "fair" classroom environment, one in which girls and boys are regarded as equals. As school personnel enter the classroom, so, too, enter their socially influenced beliefs about "appropriate" behaviors, values, and careers for boys and girls. Students oftentimes receive an avalanche of negative subtle and no so subtle messages from teachers and school personnel which limit their options and restrict their aspirations. The athletic girl who is super in math and science, assertive with peers, and capable of becoming a corporate president if she so chooses, may receive a variety of negative messages from teachers and parents. So too, the poetic boy, training to be a preschool teacher is often subtly disapproved of by school staff, parents, and peers. A starting point for those interested in expanding awareness would be to contact any of the sources listed in our references to begin assessing your environment (books, design of classroom, pattern of interaction, etc.) for implicit sex bias.

However, research also tells us that most school personnel are complete unaware that they treat their male and female students differently. So, the stereotype messages continue, and the potential of children is most certainly limited in some ways.

A curriculum of affect that we are suggesting should aspire to provide choices—perhaps provide a means to an end of this limiting cycle of sexism in the classroom. Focus on school personnel expectations and interactions will help teachers, counselors, nurses, administrators to examine how they view boys and girls—and how they expect each of them to behave.

A closer look at how expectations can be translated into behaviors is also illuminating. However, more than provide information, our goal is to help you develop practical skills to counteract problems of sex bias and stereotyping in your own environment—both between teacher and students, and between student and student. Try this exercise as a thought stretcher:

Jym was walking down the corridor one day when he bumped into an old friend. This conversation followed:

---

[1]Brophy, J., and Good, T. Teachers Communication of Differential Expectations for Children's Classroom Performance: Some Behavioral Data, *Journal of Educational Psychology*, 61: 365–370, 1970.

[2]Good, T. *Reaction of Male and Female Teacher Training to Descriptions of Elementary School Pupils. Technical Report No. 62*, Center for Research in Social Behavior, University of Missouri, Columbia, 1972.

Jym: Hi!

Friend: Hi! How are you?

Jym: Fine. What have you been doing since you graduated from high school? I haven't seen you since then.

Friend: Well, I tried college for a few years, but didn't like it, so I went to work. I really enjoy being involved in a job.

Jym: What do you do?

Friend: I got a job five years ago with an architectural firm in their drafting department. You remember that was the one thing I really liked in school?

Jym: Yes.

Friend: I also got married three years ago, and this is my daughter.

Jym: What's her name?

Friend: It's the same as her mother's.

Jym: (to daughter) Hi, Sally!

How did Jym know the daughter's name was Sally? Sally, of course, is the friend. This brief exercise and several like it could be used to demonstrate how perceptions of appropriate sex roles "box" people in and limit their ability to take the fresh approach needed for problem solving and creative living in our classrooms today.

One important jumping off point for interrupting this cycle of oppression is the redefinition of one's self in one's own terms. Paulo Freire, a multi-cultural educator with the whole world as his classroom, states that becoming aware involves developing the ability to "name" one's self. To name oneself is to move from being object to being subject. Abraham Maslow points out in *Toward a Psychology of Being* that "...the unfamiliar, the vaguely perceived, the mysterious, the hidden, the unexpected are all apt to be threatening. One way of rendering them familiar, predictable, manageable, controllable, unfrightening and harmless, is to know them and understand them."

One means of making things controllable and less threatening is by comprehension—especially through activities in the classroom, such as the exercise you just read. The curriculum in the classroom can provide a place for expressing the mysterious, the unfathomable, the emotional, and for giving them structure—for naming them. Language can be a means of clear and precise expression. For instance, poetry can offer one succinct means of recording experience, which combines the immediacy of specificity with emotionality. The conventional school teacher, nurse, administrator seeks to generate alternative flexible ways of being in the world. The goal of the many exercises listed in our references is to provide experiences and to introduce appreciation for androgenous living for all. Suggestions for self-actualization, practical hints for integrating "masculine" and "feminine" learning styles, and healthy approaches to androgenous modes of learning and perceptions are for the most part just being developed.

The crucial element in the pedagogy of any academic subject matter is the teacher, who must establish an atmosphere of trust and mutual respect that allows students to respond openly and spontaneously as they connect their lives with the content at hand. An instructor can create an environment in which the exchange of ideas and opinions is the norm, allowing students to acknowledge their feelings and thoughts in such an environment. Her or she can use such rich subject areas as sexuality, family life, emotional wellness, etc. in helping students learn to know themselves better and to go beyond the self to the greater social context of respect and care for all humankind.

We suggest that change must be accompanied by awareness—awareness of one's own attitude toward sexism and sex stereotyping behavior. Consciousness is an awareness of one's self in relation to one's environment. The following services offer strategies, curricula, and suggestions to examine your own social process and to disseminate in your particular environment.

TABS: Aids for Ending Sexism in School. A Quarterly Journal, 744 Carroll Street, Brooklyn, NY 11215

Sex Equity Handbook for Schools. Sadker and Sadker, Logman NY & London: 19 West 44 Street, New York, NY 1982. Provides practical field tested strategies for curriculum material, including specific lesson plans, unit activities teachers can draw upon for models; up-to-date Resource Directory of organizations providing material for training assistance, as well as detailed information on how to organize and conduct adult sex equity training. The book and information can be found at: Women's Educational Equity Act Publishing Center, Educational Development Center, 55 Chaple Street, Newtown, MA 02160 (toll-free. 800-225-3088)

Peer-Resources for Ending Sex Bias in the Schools. Selected introductory listing of books and other resources aims to help educators, parents and community groups recognize sex bias in an educational setting, understand how it does harm, and effect action against it. Focus is on Kindergarten through high school. PEER-Project on Equal Education Rights, 1413 K Street, N.W., Suite 900, Washington, DC 20005 (phone 202-332-7337).

A FINAL NOTE

In dealing with racism and sexism, keep in mind its complexity, its pervasiveness, and its entrenchment in our society. Change often comes slowly. Students may leave the classroom with little or no apparent change in their perspectives but, in time, begin to see both racism and sexism and themselves in a new light. The process of developing awareness, accepting and owning one's own racist/sexist attitudes and behaviors, and developing ways to change is a difficult task. The teacher's job is to help and guide toward change.

"After separating [the] outer and inner lips (labia majora and labia minora) with her fingers, the old woman attaches them with large thorns onto the flesh of each thigh."

—Edward Wallerstein

2

Circumcision: An American Health Fallacy

by Edward Wallerstein

Speculation as to the origin of and reasons for primitive genital surgery is rather fruitless. Clitoral surgery has been employed for hundreds, if not thousands, of years. It has been estimated that at the present time there are 20 to 25 million women who have undergone clitoridectomy in Africa alone, and in dozens of other places throughout the world. According to Fran P. Hosken, more girls undergo clitoral surgery today than throughout history. Ms. Hosken is waging a one-woman crusade against female genital mutilation. She publishes The Women's International Network (WIN) News to disseminate worldwide information on women's health problems, with special emphasis on clitoridectomy.

Proponents of clitoridectomy present the surgery in a positive light. Jomo Kenyatta, the western-trained leader of Kenya, not only encouraged the surgery but wrote of it in such glowing terms that John Gunther said that Kenyatta make "it sound like a picnic at Vassar." Kenyatta, in his thesis at the London School of Economics under Bronislav Malinowski, described the operation (1962):

> [The person performing the surgery]...takes out...the operating...razor, and in quick movements, with the dexterity of a Harley Street surgeon, proceeds...with a stroke...cuts off the tip of the clitoris.

Other writers on Africa, such as Colin Turnbull, take an idealized view of African culture and see it as superior to that of the West's. In his recent book, Man In Africa, Turnbull described both male and female circumcision and characterized them as displays of courage with no word of criticism. However, in 1972 a French physician provided a very different picture of Pharaonic circumcision as currently practiced in Somalia. (It takes a strong stomach even to read the description.)

> After separating [the] outer and inner lips (labia majora and labia minora) with her fingers, the old woman attaches them with large thorns onto the flesh of each thigh. With her kitchen knife the woman then pierces and slices open the hood of the clitoris and begins to cut it out. While

another woman wipes off the blood with a rage, the woman (or operator) digs with her fingernail a hole the length of the clitoris to detach and full out that organ. The little girl screams in extreme pain, but no one pays the slightest attention.

The woman finishes the job by entirely pulling out the clitoris and then cuts it to the bone with the kitchen knife. Her helpers again wipe off the spurting blood with a rag. The woman then lifts up the skin that is left with her thumb and index finger to remove the remaining flesh. She then digs a deep hole amidst the gushing blood. The neighbor women who take part in the operation then plunge their fingers into the bloody hole to verify that every remnant of the clitoris is removed.

Thousands of women have died or sustained serious injuries or infections as a result of such surgery. Some Protestant missionaries tried to convince tribal leaders to abandon clitoridectomy, but to no avail. Presbyterian missionaries from Scotland were singularly unsuccessful in Kenya. The rejection of the Presbyterian appeal was as much political as medical. The Presbyterians were viewed by Kenyans as the representatives of British imperialism who were denying Kenya freedom and independence; many of the country's leaders, including Jomo Kenyatta, were jailed by the British. Support of the custom of clitoridectomy was therefore considered an anti-British stance and a matter of national pride.

The attitude of Catholics to clitoridectomy is worthy of special note. Jesuits in Ethiopia banned the ritual in the 16th century because they thought it was a Jewish rite. They later allowed the surgery, but only after the people swore they were not Jews. In the 17th century, the matter was brought before the Pope, who sanctioned the surgery as necessary because women who retained their clitorises could not find husbands and therefore could not have children. Ms. Hosken estimated in 1979 that in Kenya today two-thirds of the Catholic girls have undergone clitoridectomy. Some medical missionaries clitoridectomize tribal women in hospitals under aseptic conditions, using anesthesia.

Proponents of clitoridectomy established a "medical" rationale. A non-excised woman is considered unclean; the clitoris is said to interfere with menstruation, childbirth, and impregnation, and is considered the cause of impotence in males. In sum, the clitoris is dirty, dangerous, and disgusting. By far, the most important "medical" reason for clitoridectomy is the claim that the clitorises of Third World women, if not cut off, will grow to monumental proportions. One early traveler in Ethiopia described the clitoris in its natural state as being as "long as a goose's neck. Few carried the exaggeration to that extreme.

What man, in his right mind, would want to marry a dirty, ugly woman who was sterile and who would made him impotent? Jomo Kenyatta wrote that: "No Kikuyu would think of marrying an uncircumcised girl." But Kenyatta and others added another aspect: clitoridectomy was said to subdue sexual urges and make the woman more faithful. The reduction of female sexuality was, and is an important element in the acceptance of clitoridectomy in underdeveloped countries.

One African tribal leader provided a fascinating rationale:

A woman has two different and separate areas where she experiences desire and excitement: the clitoris and the vagina.

God has given woman a clitoris so she can enjoy it before marriage and still remain pure...One does not cut off the clitoris in small girls because they use it to masturbate. Only when they are ready to procreate is it removed—and once it is they feel deprived. Their desire then is concentrated in one place only and they promptly get married.

The similarity of this differentiation between the clitoris and vagina is strikingly akin to that of Freud's Freud maintained that the clitoris was the initial source of sexual pleasure, but as the woman matured emotionally and sexually, the vagina replaced the clitoris as the source of orgasm.

The acceptance of clitoridectomy is not limited to tribal leaders. One African man, responding to an attack on his surgery by African physicians wrote:

> …an uncircumcised woman is much more interested in sex, and this would undermine the family.…It would be too hard on a man to regularly satisfy all his wives…where circumcision is not practiced debauchery and prostitution are the rule.

Nor is this view held only by African males. Two American writers (1977) reported a more extreme position with regard to clitoral hypertrophy and hyper-sexuality among African women. They stated that social scientists postulate that primitive man actually killed off those women who had a high sex drive: "For the sexually insatiable woman would neither work the fields nor care for the family, but would prowl around in endless quest for men to gratify her. No source is given for this statement, nor is any proof offered.

Until recently, no one bothered to verify or challenge these "facts." However, Ms. Hosken reported that thousands of Ethiopian women, examined in family planning clinics, revealed no unusual clitoral hypertrophy. Nor have thousands of African women who refused clitoridectomy in recent years exhibited bizarre sexual behavior. The propagation of the hypertrophy and nymphomania myths is racist. The myth still persists that black men have enormous penises, insatiable desires, and unlimited capacity, and the same myth is also applied to black women. Both, of course, are untrue.

There is no doubt that the circumcision and clitoridectomy procedures described above continue to be practiced. The New York Times reported in 1974 that Islam also "tolerates female circumcision" and in 1977 that 90% of Somalian teenagers had undergone Pharaonic circumcision including infibulation.

Many Westerners have been shocked by this mutilation of women and have protested against the practice, among them the London Spectator (1949), John Gunther (1953) and Shirley Maclaine (1971). The New York Times and the Paris Match carried articles in 1977 describing the practice and the protest. Yet, according to Fran P. Hosken, no african leader has spoken out against clitoridectomy.

Recently, women in many parts of the world have protested this ritual. In reporting the proceedings of the First International Tribunal on Crimes Against Women, 1976, the New York Times, stated that the most impressive testimony was provided by Third World women who reported on the practice of clitoridectomy in many African and Arab countries. What is new about the clitoridectomy protest is that it is coming from many Third World women themselves, who are struggling against these practices in their own countries and in the international arena. The elimination of centuries-old practices, especially those that are degrading to women, is often a difficult and protracted effort. For example, in Moslem countries some women who took off their veils were murdered, often by their husbands. In many African countries, a women who is not excised (clitoridectomized) is considered illegitimate and cannot inherit money, cattle, or land.

Some customs have been banned. In the Upper Volta, scarification is prohibited. Ethiopia banned cutting off the uvula, the U-shaped tissue in the back of the throat. In some areas, the elaborate excision rituals have been abandoned, but the surgery has been retained.

Some similarities between African clitoridectomy and Jewish circumcision practices are startling. In Ethiopia, the operation on girls is performed on the eighth day. In some areas of Nigeria the clitoris is nicked, not ablated, to draw blood. In several countries the infant is named after the excision ceremony. Whether these similarities are simply coincidences or a reflection of a common origin is unknown.

The World Health Organization (W.H.O.) held a seminar on clitoridectomy and infibulation in Khartoum, Sudan, in February 1979, under the title "Traditional Practices Affecting the Health of Women." Most of the male delegates wanted the traditional practices maintained and argued that the surgery should be done in hospitals. The women delegates were adamant in calling for total discontinuance of the practices. Although the attendance was sparse (10 countries), resolutions were passed calling for the abolition of all female genital mutilation. This does not mean that such surgeries will cease forthwith, but it is at least the first step by the W.H.O. to eliminate the practices.

If the lack of more vigorous African protest against excision is difficult to comprehend, it should be borne in mind that when clitoridectomy was introduced in the United States and practiced on a large scale, there were no significant protests from women or men. It may seem unfair to compare American and Third World clitoridectomy, because there was little or no pain involved in the American surgery. Although pain is a serious factory in the primitive surgery, it was not of any consequence in the United States, since any surgery to the clitoris and/or adjacent tissues was and is performed under anesthesia. The critical factor is that clitoridectomy, whether performed as an initiation rite or as a medical procedure to stop masturbation, etc., is dehumanizing.

We used to believe that circumcision did not hurt male babies...Now it seems clear that this mutilation is very painful.

—Dick Gilkeson

3

Daddy, Why Is Your Penis Different From Mine?

by Dick Gilkeson

About a month ago my five-year-old son finally asked why his penis is different from mine.

Fewer and fewer men are simply opting to have their sons circumcised "because we are." It is no longer, if it ever truly was, a strictly medical procedure. We now know that the practice does not curtail masturbation, and that doctors have a large financial stake in keeping this unnecessary surgery going.

Historically, these kinds of rationalizations and peer pressure seemed to be what drove the practice in the U.S. "Hygiene" has most often been the reason for this procedure; however, that excuse presumes that we males are too ignorant to wash our genitals.

With so few documented medical reasons for this practice, it is hard to imagine how we reached the point as a nation where 85% of our boys were regularly circumcised at the peak of cutting in 1980. It remains the second most frequently performed operation in this country today, directly involving 58% of our boys. These statistics are very confounding when one considers that in Great Britain, by contrast, only one percent of the males currently undergo this ritual cutting. The reality is that we are the last major nation on Earth to engage in widespread non-religious circumcision.

Circumcision is one of the oldest operations on record. The Egyptians performed it more than 5000 years ago. The Hebraic practice is believed to have originated with Abraham, who circumcised himself at age 99 following a divine revelation. He then circumcised his son Ishmael and all the males of his household, including his slaves. When Isaac was born, he was circumcised on the eighth day—creating the sacred ritual still followed today.

Those who take the Bible literally are unlikely to be swayed by current thinking. I can understand their reluctance to abandon the practice in light of the passage in Genesis 17:10 that states:

"This is my covenant, which ye shall keep, between me and you and thy seed after thee: Every man child among you shall be circumcised."

It must be truly difficult for the very small minority of Jewish people who are currently breaking with their tradition by creating alterative bris support groups. Their circumcision ceremonies are being conducted as tradition has dictated, but without cutting.

Moslems have a culturally defined use for circumcision as well as a religious one. Moslem boys are routinely circumcised at age 12 as a rite of puberty. This ritual cutting is also delayed in several other cultures to test the males' ability to withstand pain, and thus demonstrate their readiness to become adults. Body mutilations of young males still abound around the world. Most lead to further desensitizing of young males as part of creating brave men.

I say it's time to rethink the purposes served by the binding of feet, knocking out of teeth, piercing of noses, lips, and ears, excising of clitorises, and mutilating of male foreskins. Can it possibly be that we need violence to teach us not to do violence? Surely that is not the case in the most criminally violent country in the world.

Our tradition has not always existed. Actually, among the non-Jewish population in this country, prior to 1920, the circumcised male was the exception. This changed dramatically in the 20s and 30s. After World War II the practice became almost universal for newborn males.

We are told on page 37 in *Love's Body,* by Norman O. Brown, that the piece of flesh that is cut is "the size of a quarter containing more than three million cells, twelve feet of nerves, one hundred sweat glands, fifty nerve endings, three feet of blood vessels...and [the] penis's own personal lubrication...An essentially internal organ has been made permanently external with the drying out and desensitization that accompanies any moist sensitive skin adapting itself to frequent contact with an often abrasive world."

Dr. Thomas Ritter, a writer on this subject, tells us that the exposed glans becomes dry, less purple-red, less smooth, less expansive, develops a layer of keratin, and is less sensitive.

This makes it easy for me to accept reports where men circumcised as adults describe their sexual pleasure as having been dramatically decreased. They felt that their penises began to toughen, not unlike callouses on our hands, and they felt like they were "wearing a glove." They describe their sexual experience as shifting from color to black and white. They felt their foreskins bad protected their glans and provided a great deal more sexual stimulation to that exposed area during sex play and intercourse prior to their surgery.

Do we really want this for our sons? Let's look at the arguments:

The foreskin serves a definite purpose. It is nature's way of protecting the sensitive glans from irritating urine or feces. It also protects our urinary opening from becoming susceptible to ulcers, inflammation, or narrowing.

The American Academy of Pediatricians has stated that there is no medical reason to circumcise a baby. Arguments relating to hygiene are unfounded in my experience, and in the vast majority of the population I can barely remember the couple of times in my son Kyle's five years that I had to put cream on his penis because he had a minor infection. Infections which may or may not have been related to having a foreskin.

Actually, the problem of painful erections is far more common among males who have had too much tissue removed in their circumcisions, rather than among uncircumcised males.

This operation, like all such operations, could cause death, infection or hemorrhage; too much skin could be removed, or not enough mucous membrane, or so forth—depending on the skill of the person with the knife. That it may cause psychic damage is apparent in the emergence of foreskin restoration clinics where men are able to regain their natural covering by stretching or grafting to overcome their foreskin obsession and again become "completely male."

We used to believe that circumcision did not hurt male babies because they were so easily calmed when hugged or suckled immediately following the cutting. Now it seems clear that this mutilation is very painful. Just ask anyone who has heard their baby scream at the moment of cutting. A baby, can't be given general anesthesia, and local anesthesia distorts the area too much for successful surgery.

The argument against circumcision is that, "He'll look different than his father and many of his peers. With 42% of newborns currently keeping their foreskins, it's not clear who will look different than whom. As far as my son knowing he looks different from me—he has blue eyes. I have green. He'll likely have little body hair. I have plenty. And so forth. It was certainly no big deal for my son when we talked about our differences. I believe this one is way overplayed.

Regarding cleanliness—circumcision is credited with removing the need to regularly cleanse smegma, a normal accumulation of penile secretions and naturally shedded skin cells, from the foreskin. Unchecked buildup of smegma may cause irritation and even a painful infection of the foreskin called balanitis.

This one too is overplayed. Very little extra effort is needed to remove smegma in the case of uncircumcised males. During baths the smegma should be simply wiped from the tip. This advice also applies when white "pearls" or lumps of smegma appear under the foreskin indicating that normal separation of foreskin and glans is occurring....

One other reason given for cutting has been that it corrects phimosis, (from the Greek word meaning "muzzling"), a condition where the foreskin cannot be retracted over the glans. This condition, however, rarely causes problems except in very unusual circumstances such as when urination is blocked or erections are painful. Usually even when these dysfunctions occur they may be relieved with remedies less painful than circumcision.

One other potential problem related to uncircumcised males is called paraphimosis. Here a tight foreskin, if forcibly retracted, may get stuck behind the glans trapping blood and causing swelling. Normally even this condition may be relieved well short of circumcision.

On balance, I believe there is little to recommend circumcision for the population in general. Given that belief and my own and my wife's decision to leave Kyle uncut, here is some advice for other fathers (and mothers) who have, or will have, uncut sons:

The foreskin of an intact boy should never be pulled back because it is attached to the glans and the opening is typically only big enough for urination. It will work its way back naturally. In most boys this occurs by age three or four, but it may gradually occur all the way until a male is about eighteen years old. Even at eighteen if the foreskin is not fully retractable but no discomfort accompanies erections, nothing needs to be done. If this condition is somewhat painful, gradual stretching or a small dorsal slit are often all that are needed. A general regular washing of the penis does not require retracting the foreskin since the natural penis is well "packaged" like one's tongue and keeps itself clean.

Forcing the foreskin back may not only cause pain and bleeding, but also scarring. This may result in a foreskin that does not stretch normally, a condition called adhesion, which may need to be treated medically.

Most problems now arise from over-fastidiousness. The natural secretions are intended as aids in intercourse and other functions; so, the best advice is to wash as needed and let nature take its course.

Most of what we are given at birth serves a useful function. Who among us really believes we can improve significantly on the functionality nature has endowed us with?

Do we really believe we can fool mother nature?

As you can tell, I have become quite biased regarding this issue after having reviewed a sampling of the available literature. Apparently the major insurance companies agree with my position as very few are now covering the costs of this "unnecessary surgery." Their reluctance, and not articles such as mine, is currently the primary reason that the incidence of this practice is declining.

IDS (or Income Deficiency Syndrome) is a disease for which there are many simple solutions.

—Sharon McQuaide and
John Ehrenreich

4

IDS: The Shameful Disease

by Sharon McQuaide and John Ehrenreich

Brief Description of the Disease: Often called the epidemic of the eighties, this stigmatizing disease causes great emotional, mental, and physical pain. Effects of the illness range in seriousness from embarrassment to death in the gutter. Physical examination reveals lesions of clothes, malnutrition, psychic scarring, crushed hopes, battered spirits, and bruised hearts.

BIOLOGICAL FACTORS THOUGHT TO BE OF CASUAL SIGNIFICANCE:

1. Genetic predisposition: If one or both of your parents had the disease, you are more likely to have it.
2. Infectious disorder: IDS victims cluster together and can therefore be inferred to infect and reinfect each other.
3. Racial predisposition: Individuals with darkly pigmented skin are predisposed to contracting IDS.
4. Allergic disorder: Some IDS victims are thought to have an allergic reaction to the "American Dream."
5. Hormonal factors: Testosterone helps to combat the disease: nearly one female-headed family in three is poor, where only one in eighteen families with an adult male present is poor.

Epidemiology: IDS hits more women than men; children; people of color (who are almost four-fold overrepresented); the elderly (although this group have responded favorably to Social Security treatment); and those living in the South and rural areas, although certain urban ghettos are hotbeds for the disease. The prevalence of IDS is rising in the eighties, and the gap between the health of those stricken with IDS and those who are not is widening. It is also known that the true prevalence of IDS is greater than those who are receiving treatment.

Associated conditions: High rates of institutionalization; high risk of low-birthweight babies; a disproportionate number of homicide and crime victims; shorter life expectancy; in the past, association with high rates of septic abortions, which faded in the sixties and seventies but may be returning; and exposure to occupational and environmental hazards.

Psychological Effects: Hopelessness; anger; despair; frustration; random or directed rage; depression and a sense of powerlessness, some times expressed through drug addiction, alcoholism, and sociopathy; low self-esteem; misplaced self-blame; and withdrawal.

Disease Exacerbators: Unequal opportunity; inferior education; loss of social services and unemployment benefits; fewer tax breaks; regressive taxes; and cuts in welfare, food stamps, housing subsidies, Medicaid, and Medicare.

Treatment of the Disease: Money; jobs; education; social services; political leadership which sanctions humanitarian rather than militaristic values; moral leadership concerned with the quality and dignity of all human life.

Prevention of the Disease: Radical redistribution of wealth; restructuring of the political power system; noncompetitive value system; elimination of racism, classism, sexism, ageism.

There are many theories which attempt to explain the existence of this disease, and how it selects its victims.

One popular theory is that those afflicted by IDS deserve the disease because they did not fight the illness as strongly as the nonafflicted did. A spokesperson for this position might say something like this: "IDS victims have made certain choices I wouldn't have made; they have used the options life has offered them differently from the way I would have. If people are going to insist on being born black and female, and then choose to live in a high-crime district, what else can they expect beside what they get? They make these choices and then expect sympathy and handouts (which only make them worse). People who choose to be poor shouldn't be rewarded by having money thrown at them. The sense of entitlement of IDS victims is gross." IDS carriers are seen by some as merely victims of their own poor choices and unfortunate character flaws.

Political scientist Edward Banfield writes with confidence about his observations of those stricken with IDS:

> The lower-class person lives from moment-to-moment, he is either unable or unwilling to take account of the future or to control is impulses. Improvidence and irresponsibility are direct consequences of this failure to take the future into account...and these consequences have further consequences; being improvident and irresponsible, he is likely also to be unskilled, to move frequently from one dead-end job to another, to be a poor husband and father...lower-class culture is pathological...the lower-class individual lives in the slum, which to a greater or lesser extent, is an expression of his tastes and style of life...the subcultural norms and values of the slum are reflected in poor sanitation and health practices, deviant behavior, and often a real lack of interest in formal education. With some exceptions, there is little general desire to engage in personal or community efforts for self-improvement....(The lower-class person) is not troubled by dirt or dilapidation and he does not mind the inadequacy of public facilities...in the slum one can beat one's children, lie drunk in the gutter, or go to jail without attracting any special notice; these are things that most of the neighbors themselves have done and that they consider quite normal.[1]

---

[1] Edward C. Banfield, *The Unheavenly City Revisited* (Boston: Little, Brown, and Co., 1974), pp. 54, 63, 71–72.

According to Banfield, IDS begins when you find an individual who is not future-oriented and who has poor impulse control. The disease then progresses to the state of improvidence and irresponsibility which leads to wallowing in subcultural norms and slum values.

From an economist's perspective, IDS is like a vaccination. If one little part of you—that you don't care about anyhow—is given one little patch of chickenpox, then the rest of you will be safe from the disease. If one little part of the country (approximately 10 to 15 percent) has IDS—which is a necessary evil—then the majority of the country will be safely inoculated. Robert LeKachman is an economist who is critical of this use of "inoculation." He comments:

> [Unemployment at moderate rates] confers a good many benefits upon the prosperous and the truly affluent. If everyone could be employed, extraordinary high wages would have to be paid to toilers in restaurants, kitchens, laundries, filling stations, and other humble positions. Whenever decent jobs at living wages are plentiful, it is exceedingly difficult to coax young men and women into our volunteer army. Without a volunteer army, how can the children of the middle and upper classes be spared the rigors of the draft? [Unemployment also] calms the unions and moderates their wage demands…when people are scared about losing their jobs, they gripe less.[2]

The author of this statement is critical of techniques which cripple one group of people for the sake of the apparent "health" of another group; the well-being of one class of people is maintained at enormous cost to the health of another class.

Regarding the treatment of IDS, George Gilder in Wealth and Poverty, the bible of supply-side economics, prescribes work, faith, and love as the treatment of choice. he writes:

> [Any] effort to take income from the rich…and to give it to the poor…is sure to cut American production, limit job opportunities, and perpetuate poverty…The only dependable route from poverty is always work, family, and faith…But the current poor, white even more than black, are refusing to work hard…the maintenance of families is the key factor in reducing poverty…It is love that changes the short horizons of youth and poverty in the long horizons of marriage and career…The most important of the principles of upward mobility under capitalism [is] faith…faith in main, faith in the future, faith in the rising returns of giving, faith in the mutual benefits of trade, faith in the providence of God…[3]

Eschewing any effort to redistribute wealth from the rich to the poor, Gilbert advises the poor to have faith and "Think Rich" as an antidote.

In contrast to those who recognize the pernicious seriousness of the disease and the is articulated by Martin Anderson, President Reagan's domestic policy advisor in 1981–1982.

> The "war on poverty" that began in 1964 has been won. The growth of jobs and income in the private economy, combined with an explosive growth in government spending for welfare and income transfer programs, has virtually eliminated poverty in the United States. Any American who truly cannot care for themselves are now eligible for generous government aid in the form of cash, medical benefits, food stamps, housing, and other services.[4]

---

[2] Robert Lekachman, "The Specter of Full Employment," Harpers (February 1977): 40.
[3] George Gilder, *Wealth and Poverty* (New York: Basic Books, 1981), pp. 67, 68, 73.
[4] Martin Anderson, *Welfare* (Palo Alto: Hoover Institution, 1978), p. 15.

Sharing Anderson's perceptions are economists Sar Levitan, "[poverty has] almost been eliminated"[5] and Edgar Browning, "In a meaningful sense poverty had become virtually nonexistent in America by 1973."[6]

One final theory sees IDS victims as less diseased than the nonafflicted and contends that the poor (another name for IDS victims) are merely symptom bearers for an ailing nation.

---

[5]Quoted in Mark R. Arnold, "We're Winning the War on Poverty," National Observer (February 19, 1977): 1, cited by Anderson, Welfare, p. 20.

[6]Edgar K. Browning, *Redistribution and the Welfare System* (Washington: American Enterprise Institute for Public Policy, 1975), p. 2, cited in Anderson, *Welfare,* p. 20.

We are told overtly and in many subtle ways that our lives are not valuable because we are women...because we are black... because our primary emotional and/or sexual bonds are with women.

—Tonia Poteat

5

Taking The Home Out Of Homophobia: Black Lesbian Health

by Tonia Poteat

When I sat down to write about Black lesbian health, I was prepared to share information on breast cancer, HIV/AIDS, and substance abuse in our communities. But, as I thought more about it, I realized that the number one barrier to our health and well-being as African American lesbians is the debilitating effects of homophobia, racism, and sexism on our self-image and our access to quality health care. We are told overtly and in many subtle ways that our lives are not valuable because we are women, our lives are not valuable because we are Black, and our lives are not valuable because our primary emotional and/or sexual bonds are with women. Most of us internalize these messages at an early age, and learn to devalue ourselves and our sisters in the same way we are discounted by others.

In terms of institutional medical care, Black lesbians are in an extremely compromising position. Very few Black women have access to quality medical care. Because lesbian families are not legally recognized, a lesbian who may have health insurance cannot insure her female partner or their children. If we are fortunate enough to access health care; our health care provider usually base their practice on heterosexual assumptions and have little known edge, if any, about lesbian health. If we let them assume that we are not lesbian, we get care that may not be appropriate for us. If we come out, we risk being denied health care and being harassed verbally or physically.

Many times we are brutalized by our own communities (as well as by whites) if we are open about who we are. We are told that we are sick, that homosexuality is a white man's disease, and/or that we just need to find the right man to set us straight. When we choose to live honestly, we are subject to being beaten, raped, emotionally abused, and killed by those who question our basic right to live. If we choose not to "come out" we must also deal with the mental anguish of living in isolation and fear of being "quoted."

Homophobia creates barriers between Black lesbians and our heterosexual sisters. We are often silenced by those who fear being labeled lesbian themselves. We put up walls between ourselves and our sisters based on the well-founded fear that someone will find out and reject us or that someone will mistake our attempts at friendship and sisterhood for sexual advances.

Self-help is about breaking the silence that separates us as Black women and keeps us from being emotionally, spiritually, and physically well. It is based on our commitment to speaking the truth and to being heard with love and acceptance by our sisters. I challenge lesbians and non-lesbians alike to do the work it takes to make us all well.

I and many others
have searched through
the New Testament for
a single word about
homosexuality that is
attributed to Christ
himself and there is
not one on this subject
by the man who kept
the company of men
and held them dearest
to his heart.

—Suzanne Pharr

6

Why Rightwing Christians Should Fear Lesbians and Gay Men

by Suzanne Pharr

You may have noticed that it's very popular to create organizational names that are acronyms, such as ACT-UP (AIDS Coalition to Unleash Power) or FIRED-UP (Freedom Involves Responsibility Exposing Decadence & Upholding Principle), Kansas City's own. Some of these organizations, such as ACT-UP, have thousands of members, others have only one or two but give the impression they have hundreds. My newly formed organization probably falls in the latter category because it has only one member, and its name which looks like another acronym actually is only a group of letters standing simply for the words they make together. Mine is called FED-UP.

And what is it I'm FED-UP about?

I am fed up with Rightwing Christians preaching against lesbians and gay men and upholding heterosexuals as those chosen by Christ and an anthropomorphic god called "Father." I and many others have searched through the New Testament for a single word about homosexuality that is attributed to Christ himself and there is not one on this subject by the man who kept the company of men and held them dearest to his heart. So I want to know where Rightwing Christians get off drawing this hard line between heterosexuals whom they see as normal and good, and gay men and lesbians whom they see as perverted and evil.

I am fed up with this strange, relentless, hysterical, strident attack on lesbians and gay men. I've been thinking about what the Rightwing Christians are supporting with heterosexuality and what they (probably appropriately) fear about lesbians and gay men. And that's the subject of my talk today: how odd it is that Rightwing Christians should be so all-out supportive of heterosexuals, and given that peculiarity, how right it is that that they should fear lesbians and gay men.

Just what is it that Rightwing Christians see as so admirable about heterosexuals as a class? Now, I must admit that some of my best friends are heterosexuals, and so are all of my favorite family members, but to embrace them generally as a class? I'm sorry, but I think there needs to be major improvement across the board before I can do that. I'm going to tell you why.

For instance, in 1990 there were 68 women killed by men in Arkansas. Those murders were extremely brutal: women stabbed over 100 times, women dismembered with specialized instruments, women abducted & raped & killed, women shot in the face with a shotgun, women mutilated, etc. Almost all of those women were in some kind of relationship with their murderer: he was a husband, ex-husband, boyfriend, ex-boyfriend, etc. As far as we know, every one of those men was a heterosexual. Can I embrace that? No, I'm fed up with heterosexual men killing thousands of women each year.

The Department of Justice reported in March that there were over 100,000 reported rapes in the U.S. in 1990. They figure that only 1 in 10 rapes is reported, so you figure out for yourself how many rapes there really were.

These were acquaintance rapes, date rapes, family rapes, stranger rapes and of course, what is so seldom mentioned, marital rapes. And guess what? Probably 99% of these rapes—including men raping men in prisons—were committed by heterosexuals. Do we want to support these people? What is perverted and evil here?

There is now a remarkable body of documentation showing that there is violence in over 50% of marriages; that domestic violence accounts for more injuries to women than mugging, rape, and auto accidents combined; that the number one cause of homelessness for women is domestic violence; that the 1100+ U.S. battered women's shelters cannot begin to accommodate all the victims of violence. Domestic: that means husbands, boyfriends, lovers, family members. We're talking heterosexuality here—men and women, women getting beaten by men, their children witnessing it as a way of relating, as a way of life. No, thank you. After 15 years in the battered women's movement, I'm fed up. The body count is too great, and it never ends.

And then there is child sexual abuse; rape, molestation, incest. Diana Russell's studies indicate that one in four girls will be sexually assaulted before she is 18, and one in six boys; 38% of all women will be sexually assaulted in their lifetimes. And these are conservative figures. I think it is so morally wrong for anyone to sexually abuse a child—anyone—and here again, I have to wonder what group of people is being offered up as an ideal, as the preferred norm, when the Department of Justice tells us that 95% of those who sexually abuse children are heterosexual men? As you know that includes those who abuse boys; with few exceptions, they too are heterosexual men who are in positions of trust: family members, teachers, ministers, coaches, scout leaders, etc. Doesn't this make you sick? Should we be thinking of some way to keep heterosexual men away from children? If Rightwing Christians want to hold up these heterosexuals as normal and good, they can have them. Me, I'm fed up with the whole lot of what I would call perverts and am happy to be dissociated.

When I think of battering and child sexual assault, I think it would be better to use the word "homophobia" to mean fear of the home instead of gay and lesbian oppression.

And then there's a billion dollar pornography industry, forced prostitution, and the physical abuse of children. There's the KKK, the Aryan Nations, the S & L scam and the HUD scandal, the Iran-Contra affair, war games, and the destruction of the environment by big business interests—all led by visible heterosexuals, I'm afraid. I may have to create yet another group called WORN-OUT because just listing these heterosexual achievements is wearing me down to a nub, emotionally and physically.

I need to pick myself back up and get on to my second point: why Rightwing Christians probably should fear lesbians and gay men.

Of course, there are some murders, some battering, some child abuse, some pornography, etc., in the lesbian and gay community—because we inherited the ills of heterosexual society, I'm afraid (you can't escape the dominating culture)—but our numbers can't even begin to compare. We can't get into the same ballpark of destructive behavior with heterosexuals. However, Rightwing Christians aren't preaching sermons about heterosexuals or launching major campaigns to wipe them out through conversion techniques (sexual deprogramming) or incarceration. But they spend an incredible amount of time attacking gay men and lesbians for simply loving people of the same sex.

So why are Rightwing Christians so obsessed with lesbians and gay men? Because they fear the possibilities of change we bring to society. This is probably a legitimate fear for those who want to preserve the old order of domination and control, of violence and abuse. This particular variety of alleged Christians are really into social control: what people read, watch on TV, who people love and how they love, what people do with their own bodies, etc. There are rules and regulations for everything, and vague biblical references to justify censorship and suppression of people's right to be in control of their own lives. These people prefer for the world to be controlled by men, and white men, at that. In order for all of the abuses I just listed to exist, that is, in order for women and children, people of color, and the earth itself to be dominated and controlled by men, a fairly rigid hierarchical order must be maintained to support male power. Heterosexuality is a major piece of that order. It is, in fact, a linchpin.

To be lesbian or gay is to threaten that hierarchical order of male power and control. Let me explain.

First, lesbians. Lesbians are not "real women" because we live outside ownership by men. "Real women" know their place, and that place is to be subservient and subordinate. We lesbians at our best drive a stake right into the heart of male power and control because we offer an alternative to living emotionally and sexually dependent upon men. Lesbians construct whole, complete and satisfying lives in the company of women. We then are free to pursue friendships with men when there is a willingness to work at peer relationships. (Can you imagine? Real friendships with men?) We offer an alternative, radical vision that posits this possibility: that if all women, heterosexual and lesbian alike, could work to bring an end to their dependency upon men, then perhaps gender equality and liberation could be realized. I'm not talking about sex here but dependency. This independence of women would be the wedge that breaks open the male ownership of women which leads to social and economic dominance.

Gay men are especially hated because they are not part of the male system of ownership of women. Those who are visible—out of the closet—are a serious threat to male power and control because they make a clear break from traditional power and privilege that comes from heterosexuality. Those who are closeted of course still seek and receive heterosexual male privilege and in this way collude with our oppressors. It infuriates our Rightwing friends to see an open gay male who offers an alternative to the ownership of women and even goes so far as to offer a vision of female qualities within males. Both gay men and lesbians show us that there can be a blend of female and male characteristics within either gender, and in a better world, we would encourage the qualities of both in each person. Such a world would not have gender roles, and if we didn't have gender roles, how would it be possible for one gender to dominate the other? It is this possibility that puts terror in the hearts of Rightwing Christians.

If there is one social territory that Rightwing Christians think they own, it is the family. Here again is where they no doubt have good reason to fear gay men and lesbians, for we offer a vision of family that has the power to change the world. The traditional family system that the Fundamentalists still promote is man, woman, child—in that order—with the man being the head, the ultimate authority over the family. Any other configuration signals societal breakdown to them. And what is our vision? We say the definition of family is two or more people who are connected to each other through love, trust, commitment, shared goals and responsibilities. Isn't this a radical idea? And any combination of people can fit into this definition: blood relations such as a mother living with her children, two men with or without children, several people of the same or different sexes, a father and his children and his friends, two or more women with or without children, the traditionally married, divorced men and women with their new spouses and their ex's and the various children of all concerned, adult bothers and sisters, Maggie Kuhn and her intergenerational household—the combinations are endless. What is important is the quality of what connects them into what can truly be called family. We need to stop using the word family to describe just those ownership connections where so often controlling behavior and abuse destroy the lives of those caught in a legally defined configuration of people.

And one final word on family. Rightwing Christians need to stop spouting the same old tired lie about how lesbians and gay men have to recruit children because we cannot have any of our own. First of all, do they think that we are born without uteruses, wombs, eggs, sperm? Second, don't they recognize that we have our own children—from former marriages, adoption, foster care, alternative insemination? Their ignorance is hard to deal with.

I guess there is one other area where Rightwing Christians also feel some strong ownership: that's the area of love. On their radio shows, in their writings, at their anti-Choice rallies, etc. I hear them talk about love of one's fellowman, love of Christ, love the unborn child, love of one's neighbor, and yet amidst this abundance, I also hear such restrictions. That is, we are to give our genuine, full love to the right kinds of people; to others it should be very conditional—I would say patronizing—based on the recipient's willingness to change. Rules and regulations are everywhere about who is worthy of love and how and whom one should love.

For instance, lesbians and gay men. We would be worthy of love if we would simply change our sexual identity—rip it out, annihilate it, become something we are not, a heterosexual. Here again, they have such ignorance and confusion about what sexual identity is. Instead of recognizing as simply something that is, they see it as a matter of choice or coercion. For instance, they tell the world that women become lesbians because we have had a bad experience with a man. Now, I ask you—consider that thought for a moment. If that were the case, heterosexual women would be a small minority, for who is it that has escaped a bad experience with a man? Certainly not those 100,000+ women who reported rapes last year, those girls who were sexually assaulted, those who battered women, etc., etc. What kind of foolish explanation is this for the development of sexual identity?

And then there is the issue of who and how we love. It simply is not permitted to have such deep passionate, erotic love for someone of the same sex, to make family with them, to create a life of fullness and completeness. No wonder they fear us on this score. Our vision is totally in opposition to theirs because we say it is OK, in fact it is really very good and wonderful, to love any adult in a passionate, erotic, or platonic way. What is important is not who you love—their gender, or race, or class, or religion—but how you love.

What is wrong is imbalances of power, where one person dominates and controls the other, where there is physical and emotional abuse. So much of the violent abuse I named earlier in my speech was done in the context of what some call love: child rape and molestation, child physical abuse, date rape, marital rape, the battering of women. Who needs it? Maybe the larger question is, is love enough? These people usually say they love the ones they abuse. Are heterosexual pairings enough? No. It is behavior that counts, the daily acting out of kindness, trust, honesty, peerness, commitment and responsibility. We lesbians and gay men are on to something: we know that figuring out the how of loving people of every variety is necessary to bring about the massive social change necessary to make this world liveable.

These are just a few of the ways that lesbians and gay men threaten the world order of Rightwing Christians who are trying their best to hold on to the old miserable violence-filled ways of traditional male hierarchy. They yearn for that world where women and people of color lead restricted lives serving a world view where they are allowed little power. Me, I'm fed up with that world. My craw is full. Or to change my animal metaphor here, I'm fed up but I'm beginning to chew my cud and think more and more seriously as I gaze out at the world beyond the restrictive pasture fence. I'm yearning for freedom. I love the vision that lesbians and gay men provide; I love the visions of races and religions and cultures that are outside the dominating class; and I want to find more and more effective ways to bring all of us together—in all of our grand differences—to act out our vision for a better world. For each of us, that will mean getting the courage, no matter what the opposition, to act out blatantly the truth of who we are. For me, that means being as clearly and unmistakenly lesbian as I can be.

Maybe I could dissolve my new FED-UP organization and create a new one that has potential for more than one member. What do you think? Shall we call it RILED-UP? Or shall we call it ACT-OUT and bring to it our best Outness? Our most honest and true to ourselves selves? I ask you to join me tonight in acting out your most free and total selves. There's a new day of freedom coming in this land. The Rightwing Christians ain't seen nothing yet.

**Above all, we
must keep ourselves
centered through
contemplative prayer
and must pray for
our fundamentalist
counterparts, asking
that life teach them
(and us, as well) some
humanizing lessons
that will put us in
touch with our
feelings.**

—Virginia Ramey Mollenkott

7

Coping With Biblical Fundamentalism: Solutions

by Virginia Ramey Mollenkott

I am graduate of Bob Jones University and taught there, briefly. I'm also the only sister of a Moody Bible Institute theology professor who has cut me off from his family because of my various departures from a fundamentalist belief system. I know the fundamentalist mindset very well, on an experimental basis. I was in my mid-thirties before I gathered the courage to apply to the Bible the hermeneutic or interpretive principles I had learned in my doctoral studies at New York University. I remember well the incident that launched me on my journey of liberation, which for a fundamentalist must at least begin as a biblical journey. I was reading a feminist book in which the author claimed that there are two different versions of creation in Genesis, chapters one and two. Well, I had read Genesis hundreds of times and I was sure that this author was wrong. So I made a dive for my Bible and discovered that indeed there were two plots. In one, Adam and Eve were created simultaneously and given a mandate together, while in the other, Adam was created first, then all the animals and other phenomena, and finally, Eve.

This discovery caused me, as you might imagine, considerable shock and dismay. I had a Ph.D. in literature, and I realized that I would never have read Milton or Shakespeare in such a sloppy way. Yet here I was, being truly careless with the Bible, which I believe to be the inerrant word of God. What had happened to me?

What had happened to me was what happens to everybody who is in fundamentalism or who experiences a total conversion into the fundamentalist worldview. I learned to read through the fundamentalist interpretive grid which screens out anything that might interfere with the belief that the Bible is free of all error and contradiction. Just as a horse wearing blinders can't see the peripheral motions that might make it skittish, a fundamentalist who is looking through what I call the "inerrancy grid" cannot see the evidence that the Bible contains a variety of perspectives and approaches.

It took courage for me to begin to apply the perspectives of scholarly and contextual reading to the Bible. I was afraid that if I read the Bible with the same care that I gave to so-called "secular" literature (a distinction I no longer make), the whole basis of my belief system would collapse. And I was right, because my fundamentalist interpretive grid did collapse. But I discovered faith in the process. And I have discovered a deepened, broadened, heightened faith through the two decades of Bible study that have ensued.

I make this point about courage because I want to counter a popular misunderstanding about fundamentalism: the notion that fundamentalism is based on a profound personal experience of God in Jesus Christ. One the contrary, fundamentalism is essentially a rationalistic and almost completely cognitive form of religion. It stresses making an act of the will regardless of one's feelings; and yet feelings must impact every relationship.

In many ways I think the fundamentalist emphasis on commitment is a positive thing. I meet a great many leaders in liberal circles who have come out of fundamentalism and we compare notes about the passion of our commitment. But there is a tremendous danger in the denial of human instincts (we have seen some of the results of that in the recent TV evangelist scandal) and in the denial of the complexities of human reality. The Bible is understood to have the answer to every question, so any doubt or ambiguity is a sign of submission to delusion, possibly Satanic delusion. This leads to an isolation from one's own emotions, since one knows what one ought to feel and tries hard to feel that and nothing else. When one is alienated from one's own feelings, it is very difficult to care about other peoples' sufferings. Hence the hard, uncaring glint you may see in fundamentalist eyes when you try to make a point about human suffering.

As a child I was taught answers before I even knew there were questions, so that my life was denuded of mystery and awe. Later, as an adult teaching in fundamentalist colleges, I was faced with students who were bored silly with theology because it was so neat and pre-packaged and nobody dared to deviate too far from accepted views. It's very different now that I am at a state college; I can hardly get on with Milton's Paradise Lost because everyone is so blown away with the interesting questions that theology deals with. But at those fundamentalist colleges, no one could even admit out loud their boredom, because that would indicate their lack of spirituality. So everybody tried desperately to convince themselves that they were saved and kept satisfied by Jesus, because that's the way it was supposed to be. Now I am not denying that for some people there may have been some life-transforming experiences. But I can tell you that that life is tough for the many people who don't fit that mold.

Why is it that so many liberals think that fundamentalism is based on what I hear them call "a merely emotional experience?" People often say fundamentalism is idealistic, relying on faith rather than reason. Why do so many people think that fundamentalism is based on "mere emotion?" The answer is, I think, that many liberals are seduced by the language of fundamentalism into believing that everybody has had a profound first-hand experience of God's grace in their lives. The hymns, the prayers, the testimonies all claim that the experience is direct and authentic.

But the born-again experience is actually a cognitive assent to a set of propositions about the Bible, about Jesus, about the sinfulness of the self, and about whatever interpretations of the Bible are yielded up by the inerrancy grid. Far from having a direct personal experience of God's gracious presence in her life, the fundamentalist is told to distrust her own experience on the basis of such biblical passages as Jeremiah 17:9 (which played a great role in my own life): "The heart is deceitful above all things and desperately wicked, who can know it?" For years I could not believe anything that came out of my own deep self because I had memorized that verse and others like it and was convinced that at the core of me was corruption. As a counselor at the Billy Graham Crusades and as a Bob Jones University soul-winner, I was taught to have penitent persons pray after me a prayer asking that the Lord Jesus Christ wash away their black sins and place in them His nature, a new nature which would render their hearts, white and pure. (I trust that the racism and the sexism of that prayer are not lost on you.) Once a person had repeated this prayer, phrase by phrase, I was taught to assure them that they had been born again, even if they did not feel any different than five minutes ago. That was an important part of our pitch. Even if the convert didn't feel any different than five minutes ago, he or she was different eternally. And, of course, converts must then join a church which teaches everything through the inerrancy grid so that they will learn to obey the Bible in all areas of life. In my own case obedience included advice to go ahead and get married and pretend I was heterosexual because the feelings would follow. They didn't. A lot of damage has been done to a lot of lives this way.

Although belief by faith uses the experiential term faith, there is a tremendous difference (and I know it by experience now) between authentic faith experience and mere cognitive assent which is called belief. Liberal people would understand fundamentalists better if they always distinguished between the quiet wholistic experience of faith and the intellectual noisy rationalism of mere belief. Fundamentalists are forced to believe what they are told the Bible says, even if their instincts and feelings flatly deny what their minds tell them the Bible is saying. That's why they are sometimes shrill and cruel, because the internal dissonance is painful. For instance, if your whole worldview is based on the belief that the Bible is directly inspired by God, without any human input, and if you've been told the Bible requires of you a cheerful, monogamous, and heterosexual triumph over all wayward impulses, you feel desperately threatened by any facts or feelings to the contrary.

I can't emphasize enough that fundamentalism is rationalism that cloaks itself in the language of experience. When a person has had an authentic faith experience, he is able to listen openmindedly to diverse points of view without getting threatened. But if a person's worldview is based only on rationalistic belief in an airtight, limited, pre-packaged belief-system, then the better the evidence that somebody else introduces about an alternative approach to reality, the greater the distress and the more necessity for a Bible-thumping insistence on absolutes.

I think that it is very important to recognize that all shrillness and dogmatism stem from fear and inner dissonance. And the proper response to fear is not contempt and mockery, but compassion and patience, and sometimes a good deal of fancy footwork. By fancy footwork I mean the way Jesus responded to the questions posed to him by some of the fundamentalists of his day-trap questions. For instance, some fundamentalist types tried to trap Jesus by forcing him to choose between supporting either the Genesis passage about the husband and wife being one flesh or the Mosaic requirement about there being a writ of divorce. He would be damned either way, whichever he chose to support. Jesus neatly evaded this either-or dilemma by supporting those rabbis who defined the Mosaic divorce statement as a necessary accommodation to flawed human existence. Jesus insisted that men have to adhere to the same stringent moral standards that are applied to women. His male disciples got the point, because they immediately said, "O, maybe it's better for men not to marry!"

I've often thought about Jesus' example when I am asked trap questions by fundamentalists. I have tried within my own severely limited capabilities to respond in a similar fashion. I have treated their questions with respect, but have tried to strike through the mask to the questioners' underlying and unspoken assumptions, all the while trying to use approaches and language that will be comprehensible to the fundamentalist mind. For instance, one must never shove the Bible aside as irrelevant or erroneous; those are trigger phrases that force fundamentalist people to withdraw all credibility from one's remarks. I have often heard liberals joking about Paul's being a male chauvinist pig. This is very bad strategy if we care about liberating fundamentalist women and men. We have to learn instead (and this is a lot more work) to interpret the Bible in respectful and liberating ways and to present our interpretations through loving and patiently positive, but insistent, methods.

An important aspect of understanding that fundamentalism is a rationalistic religion founded on cognitive, doctrinal belief, rather than holistic faith experience, is the need to comprehend that biblical literalism is not literal acceptance of every passage in the Bible. Rather, it is a highly selective process that takes literally the passages that seem to agree with the worldview as a whole, and usually ignores those passages that might undermine that worldview. I call it the supermarket approach to the Bible. The fundamentalist puts into her cognitive basket whatever passages seem to suit her preconceptions and simply leaves on the biblical shelf those passages that are less gratifying. For instance, I once asked a fundamentalist preacher in my church how he interpreted Galatians 3:28, "In Christ there is no male or female," since our church refused to allow women to speak or pray or even to ask questions in meetings. Certainly no woman could be part of any deliberative or decision-making process. This preacher had repeatedly claimed to be preaching the whole counsel of God. He shrugged off my question and said, "I have no idea what it means" in a tone that indicated he could care less. So much for Galatians 3:28 as part of the whole counsel of God!

Incidentally, as a teacher of literature I would like to say that the supermarket approach is no more honest or attractive when liberals use it than it is when fundamentalists do. The only honest way to interpret a book, any book, is to confront every passage in relationship to every other passage and in relationship to the author and culture from which it sprang, as well as in conscious relationship to the interpreter's own preconceptions and culture. All of us wear an interpretive grid when we read. The idea is to be conscious of our grid and honest about it, and honest about the hermeneutical principles we are following, and faithful in applying them to the passage we don't like as well as to the passage we like.

I want to demonstrate now some of the ways in which the fundamentalists' supermarket approach operates. I do this not in order to make fun, but in order to underscore the fear that blinds people to contrary evidence once the have consented to the doctrine of inerrancy. The doctrine of inerrancy encourages people to read the books of the Bible, which were written over a period of ten centuries, without taking seriously their diverse historical and cultural contexts. So it is possible to hear preaching that treats every passage as if it were contemporary with every other passage. Thus any chosen passage can be interpreted atomistically, ahistorically, and treated as a theological proposition that claims one-to-one correspondence with the thoughts of God. After all, God wrote this book and God's thoughts are eternal. Although reformers like Calvin fully understood that the Bible was written in the language of accommodation to human understandings, contemporary fundamentalists have lost that awareness. So if Jesus speaks of God as father, that proves in some way that God is literally masculine. (God is also spirit, but somehow it is a masculine spirit). And in order to be faithful, one must use androcentric imagery, language, and pronouns. However, when confronted with the evidence that the same Jesus also spoke of God as a mother giving birth, as in John 3, the fundamentalist is forced to deny that evidence by any available means. And when all else fails, people just get disinvited from speaking on that subject, as has happened to me. Scripture is, above all, understood as a compendium logical propositions that cannot contradict each other.

Such selectivity is a matter of life and death to a fundamentalist, because the whole belief-structure stands or falls as a unit. So we shouldn't be surprised by slippery slope doctrines; they are basic to the thinking. I have said that fundamentalists ignore historical context, but even that is done selectively. For instance, two chapters in Leviticus, chapters 18 and 20, both prohibit, among other things, male homosexual acts and heterosexual intercourse during the woman's menstrual period. But contemporary fundamentalists take literally and absolutely the prohibition against male homosexual acts (some of them even pushing for the Levitical death penalty), while at the same permitting heterosexual intercourse during a women's menstrual period because times have changed and we now understand hygiene in a different way. One of the sex manuals by fundamentalists Tim and Beverly LeHaye upholds Leviticus 18 and 20 as absolute and forever set in concrete against male homosexual acts, but several chapters later says Leviticus 18 and 20 can be disregarded concerning heterosexual intercourse.

Fundamentalists are also selective about recognizing figures of speech in biblical literature. "If your hand offends you, cut it off" is recognized as metaphoric. (We may be grateful for that). But the sonship and brotherhood of believers is taken as literal, and the androcentric language is required for faithfulness. "Take, eat, this is my body," is recognized as metaphor, but "nobody comes to God except by me" is taken literally and forces fundamentalists to proselytize. "Go, sell all you have, and follow me" is understood as metaphor, but the fires of hell are understood as literal. Tithing ten percent of the family income is also understood as literal, which helps to explain the well-heeled affluence of the right-wing juggernaut.

Fundamentalists are particularly selective about paying attention to the literary genre or type of any given biblical passage. The Song of Solomon, for example, is recognized as a poem, a poem that "frankly celebrates marital love." I looked hard for the evidence that the lovers were married and haven't found it—but at least there is a recognition that the Song of Solomon is poetry. But the creation stories of Genesis chapters 1 and 2 are treated not as creation stories but scientific textbooks. They're even used as proof that God's intention for the entire human race is heterosexual marriage, an interpretation that ignores the rather obvious fact that if the intention of the story is to tell how the whole human race got here, it is necessary that the couple be heterosexual and also that the couple be fertile. If fundamentalists are right about the Adam and Eve story as mandating heterosexual marriage for every body, then all childless couples are automatically second-class citizens, and all single people are automatically second-class citizens—and that would include Jesus and some of the other disciples.

In addition, fundamentalists are forced by their grid into ignoring the now of grammar in individual passages. They can't allow themselves to see that if they use Romans 1 to flog homosexual people, they fall under the judgement of Romans 2:1, which is based on Romans 1. It reads, "You, therefore..." Therefore. What does that mean? It means on the basis of everything I just said, "You, therefore, have no excuse, you who pass judgement on the other, for you are condemning yourself, because you who pass judgement do the same things." That's a lollapalooza, isn't it? Similarly, fundamentalists can't allow themselves to see that the Ephesians 5 passage about wives and husbands is grammatically and logically governed by the lead-in verse, 5:21, which says "submitting yourselves, one to another, in fear of God, the wives to the husbands... "When pressed, I have heard fundamentalist preachers claim that mutual submission, which Ephesians 5:21 sets as the context for the discussion of husbands and wives, works between unmarried males and females, but is specifically forbidden to married males and females because the wife must submit to her husband as to the lord. Now since mutuality fosters intimacy, such an interpretation actually encourages more intimacy among unmarried men and women than between men and women who are married to each other!

The Ephesians 5 quotation about wifely submission reminds me to point out that fundamentalists are also selective about when they respect the context of biblical analogies. All analogies break down somewhere, and therefore must be interpreted within their original context. For instance, the Bible depicts those who trust in God as eagles, because eagles can renew their strength. Now that passage may not properly be understood to be calling Judaeo-Christian people predators. Eagles are predators, but that is not the context in which the analogy was set up. Fundamentalists interpret that analogy well enough, but when it comes to the Ephesians 5 analogy between the husband and the Christ, they act as if the context were Christ coming in power and great glory to judge the quick and the dead. But the Ephesians passage makes the analogy between the husband and the Christ only in the context of Christ's giving up the special perquisites of divinity and dying the death of a slave in order to establish the church. By shifting the context of the husband-Christ analogy from one of voluntary self-giving in service to one of commanding and controling, Fundamentalists misconstrue the meaning of the passage. So do a lot of liberals. I get upset when liberals accept the worst possible interpretations of passages instead of studying them a little harder!

Furthermore, fundamentalists are forced by their belief in inerrancy to avoid placing apparently contradictory passages side-by-side. If you believe the Bible never contradicts itself, then "Thou shalt not kill," which is so important in the abortion controversy, does not bear close comparison with the many commands in the Hebrew Scriptures to kill Canaanites or to kill various social offenders. And in the Christian Scriptures, Paul's remarks about obeying the government do not bear close comparison with other passages that describe Paul's own acts of civil disobedience. Studying such passages together, I have discovered, yields creative ethical stimulus. But it rarely happens in a right-wing Context.

234

Finally, fundamentalists are forced to be selective about which details to emphasize in any given biblical narrative. For instance, in Genesis 3, the story of the fall, the judge said to Adam that he would have to earn a living by the sweat of his brow and would have to eat thorns and thistles. To Eve, the judge said that childbearing was going to be painful and that the husband was going to be domineering. Now during the history of humankind, there was never any hesitation about using labor saving devices to alleviate the sweat on the human brow, and no fundamentalist I know of sticks to a diet of thorns and thistles. But there was a whole lot of hesitation historically about lessening the pain of childbirth. And the remark about husbandly rule over the wife is still interpreted not as a sinful state to be overcome, but as a prescription for people in all places and all times. As an interpretation of a single passage, all of this is highly selective. There's no integrity about interpreting a passage that selectively, upholding some statements as absolute, and regarding others in the same passage as completely relative. Such reading is certainly not literal in any consistent sense. If you're going to talk about biblical literalism, you need to make a major distinction between the kind of literalism you see in Orthodox Judaism, which is consistent and pays a price, and this kind of selective literalism.

Let me close with a couple of quick suggestions about dealing with fundamentalists. First, do not put down inspiration. And do not speak of textual interpolations, at least until trust is firmly established. Instead, point out that the Bible is not a magic book. If the Bible were magic, it would automatically translate itself into the language and the age level of reading of everybody who picked it up. But since God chose to work through human authorship and human languages and human translators, all of us are obliged to try to understand biblical scholarship, changing definitions of words, discoveries in various fields of human scholarship that impact our understanding of Scripture, individual attitude of human agents through whom the Scripture were given to us, and so forth. Second, point out that to deny the human aspect of Scripture is as erroneous as denying the humane aspect of Jesus. To deny Jesus' human aspect is Gnosticism, it's a denial of incarnation and embodiment. To deny the Bible's human aspect is biblical Gnosticism. Third, raise respectfully, but insistent, questions about the passages that have been denied or ignored and about the other selectivity issues I have mentioned. If a fundamentalist seems sincere, instead of discounting Scripture, go into it in great depth, with great contextual awareness and human honesty.

Fourth, raise questions about how well the belief system is holding up in the light of real life situations. What is the fundamentalist's feeling about the pastor's recent serious car accident? About the birth of a deformed baby? About the destruction of their home by fire or flood? Or, if a child turns out to be gay, do the fundamentalist parents feel they must be guided by fundamentalist attitudes towards homosexuality? Or would the hundreds of biblical passages about love and the specific passages about parenting take precedence and lead them to open themselves up to studying the more sympathetic and liberating evidence? And what about ordinary parental human responsibility or love yearning toward the child? In case of severe illness, handicap, or death, is the belief system sustaining the sufferer and those who are caring for the sufferer? If it is, in all decency, we support that. But, if it isn't, there may well be an opening for a more liberating faith to enter. Fifth, remember that there are various stages of moral development, that most people never move beyond stage four, and that people cannot understand a more comprehensive moral development than their own. We can understand those stages which are prior, but we cannot understand those stages that are beyond where we ourselves have moved.

Above all, we must keep ourselves centered through contemplative prayer and must pray for our fundamentalist counterparts, asking that life teach them (and us, as well) some humanizing lessons that will put us in touch with our feelings. Only when someone is in touch with their own pain, can they possibly care about the pain in Central America, or South Africa, or the suffering of our own poor people here in the United States; The spark of faith can jump only in an atmosphere of love, but the spark is generated by friction. We need patience in confronting fundamentalism, but it must be a revolutionary patience.

As I said
some time ago…
men are hurting
and the church
is not responding
well.

—Roy M. Oswald

8

The Men's Movement: Challenge to the Church's Ministry

by Roy M. Oswald

The Men's Movement has been gathering energy in the last five years, and its momentum appears to be on the increase. Books on the Men's Movement and men's consciousness-raising events are but two indicators. And this is in the face of declining participation on the part of men in our mainline denomination congregations. According to a recent poll taken in Minnesota, where church attendance is relatively high, fifty-nine percent of the women said they attended church weekly, compared with forty-five percent of the men. But we don't need a poll to know this. All you need to do is to look around at who in your local congregation is filling the pews. As I said some time ago in ACTION INFORMATION (March/April 1990), men are hurting, and the church is not responding well.

In this article I will share my sense of the five elements of the Men's Movement that the church should consider adopting. I need to acknowledge, too, that we need to be wary of some things about the Men's Movement. As James E. Dittes writes in, "A Men's Movement for the Church?" (Christian Century, May 29–June 5, 1991), the movement's focus on issues of identity "are sinfully individualistic when the church is called to deal with pressing and overwhelming issues of human suffering and the deathly scarcity of justice and peace."

Some parts of the movement are clearly faddish and will fade with time, such as the endless drumming at many men's events. And there are parts of the movement that reflect New Age religion, with its emphasis upon shamanism and Native American spirituality.

Quite rightly, the movement mourns the loss of the tribal rites of passage common among primitive cultures. Men in the movement claim these rites have been trivialized in our culture or watered down into pseudo-rites. When a ritual is reduced to a ceremony it becomes much more symbolic than substantive. Yet in responding to this need and to this truth, we need to ensure that whatever rites we might adopt have a solid Biblical and Judeo-Christian orientation. Here are five aspects of the current Men's Movement that I feel are worth adopting into men's ministries in the church.

1. The Men's Movement appears to be addressing the deep psychic pain of twentieth century men. Men's image has gone through a radical transformation in the last fifty years. The insensitive, macho man is the brunt of much humor these days, and middle-aged man bashing has become quite a sport. You may have noticed how middle-aged white men are currently the target of much humor on television these days, and the recent movie. *"Thelma and Louise"* portrays only one man in the entire cast as sensitive to women. The image of men that is repulsive not only to women and to children but to men as well is of the hard-driving, hard-drinking male, driven by power, money, fame, and sex. He exploits the environment and sucks dry the people in his orbit. Out of touch with his feelings, out of touch with his body, he is insensitive to the needs of the people around him and is more interested in genital sex than in love. He engages in win/lose battles with all who oppose his objectives. He is the blight and the curse of all that is decent, civilized, and wholistic for individuals and for the world. The Terminator might be nice to have by your side if you ever found yourself in a bar room brawl, but these days that need may only arise once every twenty years. As a house guest at a dinner party, he might be an embarrassment. This type of man is constantly driven by the fear that in all circumstances he won't be a real man.

Given our revulsion toward that image of men, what is the alternative? Hordes of men have swung to an opposite pole and have adopted a feminine spirituality. They have tried to become sensitive to women's needs, to become more feeling oriented, to become more introspective, gentle, kind, and considerate. But woman's spirituality will not work for men. As Robert Bly, author of Iron John, has discovered, there remains a deep sadness in men as though their lives have lost something essential. These men carry their pain deep within, feeling strange and alone.

This is the core of men's pain today. What does it mean to be a real man among the many conflicting images of men? Where is there a balm in Gilead for men? The evidence of this pain is obvious.

- Women outlive men by eight to ten years.
- The suicide rate among men is four times that of women.
- The alcoholism rate among men is five times that of women.
- The crime rate among men is twelve to fourteen times that of women.
- Childhood emotional disorders are twice as common in men as in women.

These are all symptoms of the conflicting messages society gives to young boys. From early childhood, girls are cuddled and kissed by their parents—boys are wrestled with and tossed in the air. When little girls are hurt they are told that it's all right to cry, it will make them feel better—when little boys are hurt they are told that it's not all right to cry and they should be brave. These mixed messages combine with the absence of any initiation into manhood by older men and the lack of collegiality among men. The Men's Movement is finally taking these symptoms seriously. And the church cannot afford to be any less caring of men.

2. The Men's Movement is not anti-feminist. I believe the Movement was prodded by the Feminist Movement, which challenged males to "get it together." This is no longer the case. Men are joining the movement to address their own pain; they are not joining to please their women. And the movement is not into female bashing. Men are not learning to discover who they really are a the expense of women.

Initially, some pans of the Men's Movement will appear threatening to women. All change, at first, is perceived as a threat. Men are changing, sometimes dramatically. In the way they relate to themselves, to their families. and to the women in their lives. The old way may have been oppressive, but at least it was predictable. As men free themselves from their own oppression, they become more unpredictable.

Robert Bly, sometimes seen as a cult hero for the Men's Movement, encourages men to get in touch with the wild man within. Bly relates the wild man in every man to the myth of "Iron John," one of Grimm's Fairy Tales. When the wild man is buried within, like in the swamp in the King's forest, he is much more destructive than when he is connected to the conscious mind.

Yet all these stories about the wild man must be quite unsettling to women today. It is the challenge of most mothers to tame the wild man in their sons. Men can become mamma's boys, but, as the women in their lives will attest, mama's boys often are passive, dull, and boring to be around. Ultimately, the Men's Movement is a gift to women. What woman would be unhappy with a whole man? Someone who can be strong and tough when that is what is needed, but also tender, loving, and empathic when that is what is needed.

Robert Moore and Douglas Gillette in their book, *King, Warrior, Magician Lover,* go so far as to say that the patriarchy and patriarchal systems are immature manifestations of the deep masculine. Those menwho desperately cling to the power of patriarchal systems are manifesting their insecurity. Such males exploit not only women and minorities, but other males as well. Picture such a man at the top of a pyramid, rigid in his ways, hardfast in his macho self-image. He is afraid to come down off his pinnacle and he won't let anyone up there with him.

3. The Men's Movement helps men connect with other men in positive ways. Men are notorious for keeping their distance from one another. Research on child development indicates that girls experience intimacy by getting together and telling secrets. Boys experience intimacy by doing something together, like building a tree house. No surprisingly, women score high on relational skills, while men score high on project/accomplishment-oriented tasks.

Traditionally, men relate by telling jokes or stories. We have a more difficult time carrying on a "here and now" conversation. Men will readily tell you about the time they went on a hunting trip, got drunk, and got their jeep stuck in the mud, but ask them to share their gut feelings or to reveal their pain, and the conversation quickly comes to a halt.

As a result many men experience a powerful loneliness. It is common for women to complain about how their husbands are emotionally dependent on them. Those men may share their fears and insecurities with women who are important to them but rarely with another man. Unlike women, men will rarely call one another just to talk.

The Men's Movement supports intentional relationships among men. Men's colleague groups appear to be multiplying. It is here that the church can engage men at deeper levels by going beyond the traditional church men's club.

4. The Men's Movement is forging a pathway for men's journey into wholeness. Rather than leaving men to wallow in confusion about what it means to be a man, the movement provides a kind of roadmap for moving from brokenness and alienation to integrity and peace. The plethora of books and audio cassettes available on the Men's Movement indicate that:

- the journey is not easy;
- the pain is one of the clear markers that you are on the path;
- men need to leave the world of objective accomplishments as a way to fulfillment and, for a time, connect with energies trapped deep in their unconscious;
- the journey is not a rational process; and
- we need to connect with archetypes of the mature masculine; these archetypes are in the "hard wiring of our system," and we either manage them well or we manage them poorly.

For example, men will manage poorly the archetype of being warriors by either becoming crazed killers or by being so frightened of this aspect of themselves that they become wimps. Or men will manage this archetype well by making appropriate sacrifices for causes important to their value systems.

In short, we need to take much more seriously what is happening in our dreams, in our fantasies, and with our feelings, intuitions, and instincts. For many men this feels like entering the abyss, yet the movement supports and encourages men to get on with the difficult tasks related to being whole persons.

The movement also encourages men to look into their woundedness. The old ways of behaving lead men toward denying their wounds yet being inextricably controlled by them. What follows is only a partial list of some of the more profound wounds men carry:

- Guilt over disappointing their mothers;
- A sense of betrayal or abandonment by their fathers;
- A naive dependence on special relationships
- An unreadiness to deal with the human side of the special people in their lives;
- The idolatry of work and its false sense of identity (witness how many men die within months of their retirement);
- The pain of seeing sex as performance (fear of not being able to get it on, not being able to satisfy, not being big enough).

5. The Men's Movement calls forth a more dynamic relationship between fathers and sons. Implied in this is a need to mentor boys, especially those without fathers at home. Also implied is the need for models of rites of passage from boyhood to manhood.

The movement talks about the difference between initiated men and those who are uninitiated—those who are left to wander painfully, trying to find their way into the promised land of the mature man. Because of the lack of initiation rites in our churches or in our culture, many men spend small fortunes in therapy trying to get it right. In short, when we aren't initiated into manhood by the significant males in our lives, we have to pay a therapist to try (who, by the way, is distinctly disadvantaged in attempting this task).

Many African or primitive tribes have rites of passage for boys. Mothers raise their sons until a certain age when the men come and take the boys away for a period of initiation. This is usually a frightening time for the boys and often involves some hardship and pain. A test of endurance or survival is part of the initiation. In some tribes a vision quest is pan of this transition process from boyhood to manhood. During this time the wisdom of the elders is shared with the youths, and the boys are told what is expected of them now that they are men.

Nowadays, how is a boy to know when he has become a man? Some say the only people initiating boys into manhood are the leaders of street gangs. Others claim manhood happens for some boys when they serve time in prison or enter into military service. Yet all of these initiation rites introduce boys into an immature masculine archetype which focuses on suppression and violence.

It is my conviction that today's drug scene is fueled by the fact that many young boys don't have a mature man in their households—many young boys have never even met such a man. In such a situation, how do I know when I have become a man? When I have the courage to ingest a powerful drug that takes me on a mystical yet frightening journey. If I return without dying, then I am a man.

We in the church need to reclaim our duty to provide meaningful rites of passage for boys. Ours is the realm of the symbolic. Ours is the realm of myths and stories. Yet we first need to become initiated men ourselves before we can provide a passageway for younger men. We also need to care enough to leave Wall Street and to pick up our responsibility to the next generation of boys. We are so busy trying to make it in the market place that we are abandoning our boys—most harmful to them at their important life transition points.

In a three-day conference I led with clergy and laymen on the subject of Men's Ministries, I challenged the group to think of some meaningful rituals that could engage both older and younger men in a rite of passage. The group struggled with the complexity of the task, given the cultural expectations of today. We couldn't think of an activity that men do together that boys would even aspire to join. We also became painfully aware of how difficult it would be to get a group of men to sacrifice time and energy for this effort. We noted how we constantly try to make it easy for the people who belong to our congregations, and that this activity would require much from a group of men.

I am sorry to report that this group of approximately forty men could not come up with even a few creative suggestions. It seems so right that this activity should take place in our congregations today, yet we fumble along with empty ceremony instead. I don't intend to give up easily, and I hope to keep on challenging the men in our congregations to care enough about the young males in the congregation to reach out in significant ways.

I think that the Men's Movement is one way of addressing a genuine need that more and more men experience today. If we can come to understand even a fraction of the complexities, the movement can become part of our outreach to a hurting world. I hope that it will be a way to reengage the men in our congregations and to encourage them to invite their male colleagues to our churches. I will be sad if the church continues to ignore the men's pain, sending them back to secular movements to have their needs met.

The good news is that America is no more in a moral crisis than it ever has been; it's just that leaders are now forced to admit the crisis

—Gloria Steinem

9

On Family Values: If Moral Decay Is the Question, Is a Feminist Ethic the Answer?

by Gloria Steinem

- Thirteen cases of insider trading on Wall Street
- A major TV evangelist in disgrace for using his position to extort both sex and money.
- A Presidential candidate forced to withdraw through his own arrogance, sexual and otherwise.
- An Attorney General of the United States who invests in a "blind trust" that was not approved and who thus stands to profit from a business whose officers are now indicated for ripping off government funds intended for minorities.
- A Marine war hero and other White House aides who are secretly immersed in the international arms trade, and who lie to Americans about facts that even the Soviets know.
- A former Miss America forced to resign her current city post for influencing a judge against the interests of her lover's ex-wife and children.
- More Presidential appointees and staff who have been forced to resign in disgrace during Reagan's Administration than any other in history.
- A President who publicly encourages the conduct of a private war against the expressed will of Congress, and then fails to take responsibility when his own aides privately pursue that goal.

I am sure each of us could add more examples of high level hypocrisy from our own part of the country and our own reading of the media. Perhaps the only kind of story that has become more frequent than an expose of scandal is the moral hand wringing of media commentators over the prevalence of scandal. America must go back, they insist, to the values of its past.

But there is one shared characteristic of these examples of moral decay: they all involve people in high places. On that ground alone, I would argue that our knowledge of them—

especially while those leaders are still in power and accountable—is itself a step forward. So is our growing expectation that these leaders be held to the same ethical standards as a lowly employee who steals from the cash box, or a neighbor who sexually exploits a teenage baby-sitter. (Indeed, those are direct comparisons to greed on Wall Street, or evangelist Jim Bakker's sexual use of the worshipful young woman who had once helped to care for a colleague's children.) Thanks to a combination of the media revolution, which has made more information available to more people, and social revolutions, which have made those who are not influential and powerful feel confident enough to judge whose who are, a lot of dirty linen is being brought into public view. Not only are we refusing to wash it anymore, but we're holding leaders personally responsible for their own decisions to get dirty.

If that sounds too optimistic, let me explain one of the two major reasons I am suspicious of all that moral handwringing from media pundits. It assumes that there was a higher ethical standard in the past.

Would these commentators suggest that we go back to the time of the Founding Fathers? Children are taught in school about George Washington's honesty, but other realities have surfaced. For instance: we now know that Thomas Jefferson secretly fathered children by his black slave mistress at the same time that he was publicly refusing to oppose slavery and refusing all rights of citizenship to any American women, black or white. (Here is Jeffersonian morality: "Were our state a pure democracy, there would still be excluded from our deliberations…women who, to prevent deprivation of morals and ambiguity of issues, should not mix promiscuously in gatherings of men.") Yes, Gary Hart badly damaged the sexual dignity of women, his wife and others, but he didn't deny their legal and economic rights at the same time. And whatever our judgment of Hart's character, we can assess its impact now, not 200 years later.

After Gary Hart's disgrace, for instance their flight to the past was often betrayed by truculent questions: What would have happened if the same moral standard had been applied to Presidents Roosevelt or Kennedy? To Eisenhower or even Martin Luther King, Jr.? Wouldn't we have lost good leaders?

Well, what *would* have happened? It's true there was a different standard of sexuality but it's also true that Gary Hart's behavior was different from that of those past leaders. His cover-up of a relationship with Donna Rice and other women seemed to confirm a pattern of pretense and arrogance—from changing his name and age to denying affairs and daring reporters follow him—that certainly wasn't limited to his sexual life. In 1983, when he was among the Presidential candidates speaking before a convention of the Nation Women's Political Caucus, he could have won approval on issues; yet he lost his audience by his arrogance in being the only candidate to defy a simple time limit. An even larger turning point came when arrogance helped him to lose the Illinois primary. It also seemed to have ended his marital separation for reasons of political ambition (Indeed, a case could be made that his problem began, not with an affair, but with pretending to have a viable marriage.) The public perceived the Donna Rice affair as only the last straw.

On the other hand, Franklin Roosevelt's long-term friendship with Lucy Mercer, whom he seemed to love while still loving and treating Eleanor as a partner, was both committed and never denied by him. If it had been revealed in the press, and if Eleanor had defended him

248

with even half the force that Lee Hart defended her husband, the public might have gone along with Eleanor's attitude; especially given respect for her as a moral force. President Eisenhower also had a long-term and committed relationship outside his marriage. He was open enough about Irish Kay Summersby, who had been his driver in Europe, to commission her as a WAC even though she was not a U.S. citizen.

Even Jack Kennedy, whose sexual pattern seemed to differ from Gary Hart's only in that he was said to have treated women better the morning after, was not hypocritical enough to dare reporters to "Follow me." He was fairly honest about his exploits in the belief that the press would then protect him—and it did. Given Reverend Martin Luther King, Jr.'s religious profession, he certainly would have had the worst time with sexual revelations.

On the other hand, Congressman and Reverend Adam Clayton Powell pursued sexual exploits in New York and Bimini that seemed to be tolerated by the black community with such support that he was insulated against his white critics.

Even in those days, the lesson was that a lack of hypocrisy in personal relationships was often valued over the simple question of sex versus no sex. That is more true today. When the homosexual affairs of Maryland Congressman Robert Bauman were revealed in 1980, he was rejected by his own constituency. Bauman had been virulently antihomosexual in his public policy, and so had left himself open to blackmail as an influence on his actions in Congress. When Massachusetts Congressman Gerry Studds's affair with a young male working in Congress was revealed in 1983, he was reelected by his constituency. Studds had not been hypocritically punitive toward homosexuality in his public attitudes, and he was liked and trusted as an honest representative. So is Massachusetts Congressman Barney Frank, who has talked about his homosexuality to the press in what may be an example of the kind of honesty that most benefits idealism and pragmatism at the same time.

Setting aside the 10 percent to 25 percent of the American public that opinion polls show to believe in inflexible morals, often imposed by religion, the majority of Americans seem willing and able to make judgments that are based on the ethical content of a particular act, not just on its form. Reporters who ask candidates about their attitudes toward "adultery"—toward any sex versus no sex outside marriage—are missing that point. So are those pollsters who asked only whether Oliver North was telling the truth, and not about public opinion or his actions in setting up a secret government.

Indeed, ethics *are* the evaluation of human behavior in the light of moral intuition. Morality implies the easy immutability of a simple code, but ethics have to do with the effect, intent, and content of everything we say and do.

Which brings me to the second major reason to be suspicious of the current nostalgia for virtues of the past. While calling for a return to traditional values, business ethics, and the teaching of ethics to school children, there is nothing but attention to generality and form: not one word about content.

For instance, a lively national debate is focused on whether ethics should be taught as a separate academic course, or integrated into every field of study. Interesting comparisons are made to Sunday religion versus one that is an integrated part of our lives. A former head of the Securities and Exchange Commission has given a whopping $20 million to Harvard Business School for an ethics program. An institute for the advancement of ethics is being set up by a millionaire in California. But so far, not one of these discussions or announcements has mentioned what is going to be taught. Like the media's reporting and editorializing, they all mourn America's moral illness without describing what health might look like—or how to get there.

Since most women are now more optimistic and more willing to take risks than most men (see "How Optimistic Are American Women?" *Ms.*, July/August 1987), and since feminists are responsible for some of the new standards that are tripping up old leaders, perhaps we should make some suggestions.

After all, we've learned a lot from being forced to live on the seamy underside "the old legalistic, public/private versions of morality. We've also learned to practice the flexible ethics of fairness that keep families together without sacrificing individual differences.

Finally, feminists have spent the last 15 or 20 years asking for—and trying to gain experience in practicing—the ethic of empathy. We've built a national movement of thousands of large and small organizations on the principle of bringing consensus out of inclusiveness and diversity. In fact, we may be so trained by both family and feminist culture to think ourselves into the other person's shoes that we fail to fully occupy our own—but we are definitely the empathy experts. We should be able to teach it.

These are suggestions for the ethics of the future. They are not inflexible, but they are guidelines that should be constantly kept in mind:

1. Whatever means you use will become part of the ends you achieve. From Machiavelli to Marx, authoritarians have been arguing that the end justifies the means. From Moses to the Ayatollah, absolutists have been insisting that there is only one moral means to each moral end. The first belief defers judgment on the morality of an act into the future, and creates constant revisionism. The second belief takes moral responsibility even further away from the individual, and gives it to an external system. Ethical judgments are so simplified that they might just as well be made by computer.

In the sensitive-seismic system of the family, however, women have learned that the end result always reflects the character of the actions taken to achieve it. A child disciplined by violence is likely to be violent toward others. A child given too much will remain too weak to use those gifts. A parent who doesn't spend time with a child gives up her or his power to have influence. Each act is a microcosm of what will result from it. Process is all.

Given this kind of ethical guideline, Oliver North and others involved in the Iran/contra affair might have questioned whether democracy *could* be protected through such very undemocratic means: whether lying to Congress about funding a private war and setting up a secret non-elected group of decision-makers, might not bring this country closer to the authoritarian secrecy that the war was supposed to be fighting against.

Or, with this kind of ethical insight, New York's Mayor Ed Koch and others might have thought twice before elevating Bess Myerson, an intelligent but inexperienced former Miss America, into high civic and corporate board positions. Since part of her appeal was her willingness not to rock the corporate or political boat and to value male approval above all, she was also vulnerable to private male blandishments to the detriment of her public job. She who lives by male approval can also die by male approval, so to speak.

Many men in families could also learn from this guideline. For instance: a dominating father produces the very weakness in his children that he despises. And many women could learn, too. For instance: you can't fulfill yourself by sacrificing yourself.

To cite two final examples, Gary Hart and Jim Bakker misused their positions of power to entice women into sex. Now that those positions are gone, their unrealistic egos may have to survive the fact that women just aren't as interested in going to bed with them anymore.

2. *No ethical decision is exactly transferable from one situation to the next.* Yes, laws have precedents, and the spirit of a law is transferable. But if laws were inflexible, they could be applied by numbers, not by judges. Taken out of the context in which it was made, an ethical system may become very unethical.

For instance, Robert Bork, the Reagan Administration nominee for the U.S. Supreme Court vacancy, does not believe that the U.S. Constitution should guarantee rights unless they are specifically mentioned within it.

Thus, abortion is not part of the constitutionally guaranteed right of privacy because neither the word "abortion" nor "privacy" is mentioned, and therefore the legality of abortion should be left up to any legislative vote in each of the 50 states.

But that Constitution was an ethical system created without reference to or inclusion of women. Men interpreted their private space as heir homes but thought less about the internal private space of their bodies. It was an era when a man's home was his castle, but a woman's body was literally not her own.

Given the real genius of the Constitution—that is, its provision for change through amendment and interpretation—women's inclusion as citizens also has extended the right of privacy to women's bodies. Our ability to give birth makes us more sensitive to bodily integrity, though that legal concept is also proving beneficial to men.

Would ethics be served by applying to women a literal version of a Constitution that wasn't written by, for, or about women or even with women in mind?

3. *The people with the most ethical right and responsibility to make a decision are the people who will be affected by it.* The best judgment in the world is less likely to be accepted if it has been imposed from above. Furthermore, people who have experienced a thing are more expert in it than the experts.

This is a guideline that both enforces and rewards democracy. Laws to be obeyed by a wide variety of people have to be made by representatives of that same variety. Process is still all.

When this principle can't be followed literally—for instance, when decisions for lawbreakers must be made by police officers and judges—there is still the possibility of empathy and putting oneself in the position of those affected. This could be exact: part of police and judicial training should be a few days or weeks spent in jail. (Think of the healthy impact on prison guards who are not sure if the guy in their cell block is really a prisoner, or a police cadet or a guard in training.) It could also be a required exercise of mind: What would rehabilitate us and keep us from breaking the law again if we were the prisoner?

4. *There is a human and humane principle called simple fairness.* Surveys show that the overwhelming majority of Americans are willing to sacrifice for the good of the community, or the environment, or the country, but only if that sacrifice is equally spread in the long term. The glue that holds society together, and keeps us willing to maintain any ethical system as a standard of behavior, is our sense that we are not the only ones who are trying.

Furthermore, fairness can begin at any point in an unfair history. Even children understand that mistakes can be made, and that no situation stands alone. If we must be badly treated on one day, it can still be made up to us the next. What breeds resentment and festers anger is the long-term unrelieved sense that our acts are not being rewarded or punished in the same way as the acts of those around us. Compensatory action. Affirmative action. All can restore our faith in fundamental fairness.

It's also fair to distribute blame for a destructive act according to the responsibility for it. Those with more authority accrue more of the blame. Thus, President Reagan's public statement that the contras were "freedom fighters...the moral equal of our Founding Fathers" was a very strong call to their support. Significantly, public opinion polls show majority belief in Oliver North's truthfulness, but not majority support for what he did; in other words, North acted in the belief that he was doing what Reagan said was good for the country. Therefore, whether or not Reagan knew in detail of the Iranian arms payments and other contributions being made by Americans and by foreign governments influenced by his aides, he is ethically responsible. Whether or not the Boland Amendment makes those arms and contributions to the contras technically illegal, the fact that they were made against the expressed will of Congress makes them unethical.

5. *Do unto others as you would have others do unto you.* Empathy is still the most democratic and therefore revolutionary of emotions. I don't mean to be corny about this, but the most radical injunction is still this Golden Rule. It requires reflection as careful as one would apply to oneself. It turns healthy self-interest into equally healthy altruism—and vice versa. Probably, it works for everybody with the exception of masochists, and if we actually put it into practice, the number of those would be severely reduced.

If we considered how we would like to be judged as political candidates, for instance, we might not make some of them feel they have to lie about their private lives, a pressure toward hypocrisy that the public must take responsibility for. We would stop missing the talents of those potential candidates who are divorced or never married, gay, lesbian, or otherwise beyond a stereotype that fits only a minority of Americans. We certainly need all the talent we can get.

If greedy stockbrokers attended to other people's money as they would want someone else to attend to their own, their ethical behavior might turn inside out.

If State Department and other U.S. officials who refused Jews entry at the start of World War II had thought what they themselves would feel if they were *Jews,* they would have had a much more realistic political forecast on the seriousness of National Socialism. And they would now be remembered with gratitude instead of outrage.

If Jefferson had been capable of empathy with his black slave mistress, we might have had a different country. We might have spent much less time on simple equality—and more on solving conflicts without violence, or improving the quality of life, or figuring out what we were doing to nature, or looking outward for friends instead of enemies.

Ethics are their own reward.

The good news is that America is no more in a moral crisis than it ever has been; it's just that leaders are now forced to admit the crisis. The better news is that ethical judgments are beginning to come from below, from women and others with a clear view from the bottom. We haven't spent all this time down here for nothing.

Having paid more of a price for past mistakes has given us wisdom. The country's admission of an ethical crisis now gives us a historic chance to use it.

Discussion Questions
Part V: Prognosis for the Future:
Religion and Health

1. Describe a sexually transmitted disease, as well as any steps that can be taken to prevent the spread of this disease.

_____

_____

_____

_____

_____

_____

_____

2. Discuss how a specific religion may perpetuate racism.

_____

_____

_____

_____

_____

_____

_____

...of this class of women, I am constrained to say...that their education is miserably deficient; that they are taught to regard marriage as the one thing needful, the only avenue of distinction.

—Sara Grimke

Part VI

Working Out the Differences: Communication and Core Curriculum Issues

Since the writer-activist Sara Grimke wrote those words in 1838, much has been written of how the American educational system discriminates against females. But other categories of Americans have been discriminated against in this regard as well, certainly including minorities and gays.

Education is yet another area in which race, class, and gender intersect. The selections in Part IV examine some of the many problems afflicting communication and our schools today. In the 1960s and early 1970s, Black and Latino/a students and professors fought for the establishment of academic programs which would both raise their consciousness as members of minority groups and better prepare them for future social and political challenges.

In recent years, many of these programs have come under attack. Witness "Civil Rights Issues Facing Asian-Americans in the 1990s." This examines the popular view that all Asian-Americans are "success stories." The reality is that many Asian-Americans and Asian immigrants face severe discrimination, and their supposed "success" is in reality a myth that is used to disguise the inequality that is often their daily lot.

Communication and language play key roles in the activity of any society. Unfortunately, many kinds of barriers often create significant communication difficulties between the races, classes and gender. PART VI examines some of these barriers, and discusses ways of overcoming these difficulties.

There are many biases in the way that language is used. "Ebonics: Echoes of the Drum" presents an unusual perspective on how racism in language limits flexibility and creativity in the roles of black Americans, as well as promoting unhealthy stereotypes.

"Ebonics: Echoes of the Drum," recounts the international incident of a California school system attempting to improve the writing and reading ability of its minority students.

Many of these students are also active in sports, which is not only racist, but also sexist and heterosexist. Witness, "Gender Stereotyping in Televised Sports."

"Gender Stereotyping in Televised Sports" finds that women's sports events are underreported compared to men's events, and that the coverage of women's events is often biased and stereotyped.

To look at Ebonics
fairly means
examining the
history of slavery
and racism in America.
As we study the
subject, we see why
the comments of
most White people
are not to be taken
at face value.

1
Ebonics:
Echoes of the Drum

"Language is the first stage of Liberation or Subjugation" Professor William Mackey

To look at Ebonics fairly means examining the history of slavery and racism in America. As we study the subject, we see why the comments of most White people are not to be taken at face value. African Americans must follow their best instincts and listen to the voices of African American linguists who have studied the question of Ebonics over the years. First of all, Ebonics is the African American's linguistic memory of Africa applied to English words. Ernie A. Smith, PhD. is a Professor of Linguistics, Ethnology and Gerontology at the Charles R. Drew University of Medicine & Science. Professor Smith says that in the same way that you hear any accent, whether Chinese, Russian, Italian or Hispanic, you are listening to our African accent when you hear things like "mo" instead of "more" or "ax" instead of "ask". Dr. Smith explains that grammar exists not just in the syntax (how we use words), but also in the deep phonology and phonetics (how words are formed and sound). He goes on to inform us that language rests on its grammar, not its vocabulary. Our language base remained in Africa even as we adopted the local vocabulary. The speaking patterns we hear in our home or remember from our past, are not a matter of stupidity or "lazy tongues," as some white folks would have you believe, but the simple sound of African accents on English words. It is an accent that has stayed with us long after the original vocabulary has been forgotten. It is an accent that is strong in some and weak in others—set aside for the workday world, but held on to in private moments with ourselves or our friends, and there is no wrong with that.

As any other nationalities, when the Africans came to this hemisphere, they came carrying their many languages and their learning. But unlike any other nationality, the Africans who came in the slave trade had everything else taken from them. They were delivered physically decimated and naked on these shores. Those who survived the 240 years of that Middle Passage (1619–1859), found themselves to be Africans-in-America, held captive by a people who viewed them as property to be bought, sold, used and raped. Forbidden their own languages, and separated so that it was difficult to speak even amongst themselves, the Africans began to use local words to identify objects and their environment. They standardized on the local vocabulary, whether it was French, Portuguese, or English. For the Africans, this learning process had to be done in an atmosphere of terror, where killings and beatings were only an upward glance away.

As the centuries passed, many Africans escaped and joined others in the tribes of the Indigenous People, or went into Canada, and later into Northern American cities. By the 1800's, the Africans had positioned themselves to build schools and large churches.

They built the schools because they knew the importance of learning, and they built the churches because they needed God's strength. While this was going on in northern settlements, legal slavery was the reality for the vast majority of Africans in the United States. Through all of this time, African Americans, wherever they were, lived in virtual social isolation. There was no radio or television to bring the voices of others into their lives. The only speakers of English they heard were each other and whites giving orders. In this environment of isolation, the African accents and rules of grammar stayed with us.

PROFESSOR ERNIE A. SMITH EXPLAINS EBONICS

"Ebonics is the linguistic continuation of Africa in Black America. It is a relexified Niger-Congo system." Thus declared Dr. Ernie Smith at a recent meeting of the United African Movement, headed by Alton Maddox. Professor Smith went on to explain Ebonics in depth. "The labels used for the language spoken by the descendants of black slaves has varied over the years. Black English, Negro Non-Standard English, the Black Dialect, Black Vernacular English, Vernacular Black English….all of these labels assumed that there was a break with the linguistic tradition of Africa, this has never been proved….The argument "Is it a language or a dialect?" is a White supremacist argument. All dialects belong to some language. Either it is a dialect of English, or the Niger-Congo languages in Diaspora. At the base of the historical process is the differences that came from Africa. And it is the difference that remain that is the evidence they're not the same." "The history of segregation and social isolation served to preserve Africanisms in the deep structure of the way you think and talk. The reason we don't sound like the brothers and sisters in the Caribbean is that they have more Africanisms in their speech. One of the first scholars that did the seminal work establishing the linguistic continuity of Africa in the Americas as Lorenzo Turner. In his book, "Africanisms in the Gullah Dialect", Turner tells you the ethnic-specific roots that we brought from the mother country. "The slaves brought to South Carolina and Georgia direct from Africa came principally from a section along the west coast, extending from Senegal to Angola. The important areas involved were Senegal, Gambia, Sierra Leone, Liberia, the Gold Coast, Togo, Dahomey, Nigeria, and Angola. Today the vocabulary of Gullah contains words found in the following languages, all of which were spoken in the above mentioned areas: Wolof, Malinki, Mandinka, Bambara, Fula, Mende, Vai, Twi, Fante, Ga, Ewe, Fon Yoruba, Bini, Hausa, Ibo, Ibibio, Efik, Kongo, Umbundu, Kimbundu, and a few others." These are the ethno-specific languages that we were speaking. These are basically Niger-Congo languages geographically, and they are various dialects of the same system. So don't think of these as different languages, think of them as languages that belong to the Niger-Congo language group. Since in many Niger-Congo languages, consonant do not occur in the final position at all, or do so with considerable restriction. Therefore in Ebonics, when you learn their words, but you don't know their grammar, what you're going to find slave descendants of African origin doing, is modifying their words according to the grammar of the Niger-Congo African languages. So first if you just look at isolated words that end in certain kinds of consonant blends, or consonant clusters, take the "st.." configuration, the "ld" configuration, the "Nd", the "ft", the "pt", those consonant blends will not occur. So instead of "best", "west" "test", "last" "fast" you get "wess" "tess", "lass", and "fass." "Build, "Bold" "Hold" you get "Bill", "Bole", and "Hole." You won't find doubly articulated stops in the language of a slave, because their grammar is based on the African root. The differences that remain are proof that they are not the same." "Professor Smith goes on to say, "So because some slaves have had the fortune of being up in the Big House, with old massa and Miss Anne, and learned how to mimic old Miss Anne, and "Papa" Charlie, that doesn't change what's going on for the 99% of the slaves that were living out here in the fields. So I'm not talking about the house slaves who will tell you straight up, "They're my color, but they're not my kind. I'm an individual, I swam along side the slave ship, I didn't come with them." So we're not talking about the "Betcha by golly wow." House Negroes, we're here talking about the masses of slaves, who speak Ebonics, and who are comfortable with their African heritage, not them that are ashamed, that put the Yard Negroes and Field Negroes, down. So clearly understand, that just because all of us don't talk this way, don't make what I am talking about untrue. When we their words, we don't use them the way they use them. In the syntax of their grammar. So even though we are people who have learned the vocabulary of English, our thought process is not the same." "Now, there are a lot of words that people will find offensive. As far as linguists are concerned, there's no such thing as a bad word. There are words that annoy people because they associate them with things which offends their values. And you can get yourself hurt, using the wrong word at the wrong time to the wrong people. Much of what they're trying to claim is Ebonics in rap music, if it is obscene, if it is garbage, if it is profane, if there are curse words, they're not African. All of that is from their language stock. They're not African. So it's their filth if it's anybody's filth, because none of those words are African."

"Re-Lexification of a language is when you borrow the words of a language but not its grammar. If you say "The Bionic Man" using Spanish words, you might say, "El Bionico Hombre." But just because you are using Spanish words, it does not mean you are speaking Spanish. For that you must use Spanish grammar. In Spanish, the sentence would be "El Hombre Bionico." Just because you know Spanish words don't make you a speaker of Spanish. You must learn the grammar of the language you want to speak. "Where yo momma at?" Those are English words but that is not English. First of all, you don't put prepositions at the end. It is not grammatical in English to end a sentence with a preposition. Take the "at" out the mix, "Where yo momma?" Still not plugged in, where is your verb? "Where" is a pronoun, "your" is a pronoun, "momma" is a common noun, you're not speaking English, "Where yo momma?" "Ah man, she gon." "She gon", that means "She's not here." What's the difference between "she gon", and "She been gon." A long time. You know when I say "She been gon", that is a different amount of time, than just, "She is not here." We simply use English words differently," "Carter G. Woodson, in his book "The Mis-Education of the Negro" writes, "In the study of language in school, pupils were made to scoff at the Negro dialect, as some peculiar possession of the Negro, which they should despise, rather than direct the study of the background of this language as a broken down African tongue. In short, to understand their own linguistic history, which is certainly more important to them, than the study of French phonetics or historical Spanish grammar. To the African language as such, no attention was given except in the case of preparation of traders, missionaries, and public functionaries, to exploit the natives." I believe with Dr. Woodson, that we must study our own linguistic history." And it is from an understanding of our own linguistic history that the Oakland School Board drew its conclusions. "The Oakland Unified School district is saying that the African language systems are, linguistically speaking, genetically based. They meant that the term "genetically based" refers to the genesis, or origin and the genetic characteristics that are inherited by one generation of speaker from another, as opposed to those that are acquired from other sources. So if African language systems are "genetically based" then we knew our language first, and our language can never be dialect of German. That's what that Black school district had the nerve to say. That's what Brooklyn needs to say. Declare your humanity and stand on it. The archeological evidence is irrefutable. That's what they said in Oakland, and that's what rocked their world."

(The phrase "genetically based" has greatly upset a lot of people who are either not aware of its linguistic application or else choose to ignore it. This includes Brent Staples, writing in the New York Times, and that excretion from Rupert Murdoch that passes for the editorial page of the New York Post. And If you read their editorial "The Ebonics hustle," you know we're being kind here.) Professor Smith goes on. "From the American Heritage Dictionary, "The Indo-European family of languages, of which English is a member, is descended from a pre-historic language, proto-Indo-European, spoken in a region that has not yet been identified, probably in the fifth millennium, B.C. The chart shows the principle languages of the family, arranged in diagrammatic form that explains their genetic relationship." See what it says right there? "genetic relationship". The not talking about DNA and RNA, their talking about what the term genetic means in linguistics. "It displays the genetic relationships, and loosely suggests their geographic distribution." English comes off of the German line. Languages are not classified according to their vocabulary but by their grammatical structure. A language retains its grammatical structure even though it has been swamped by foreign borrowing." What we had was a theory put forth, by a White supremacist culture, that claimed that when the African and non-African languages came into contact, the result was a hybrid of the White European languages and the African languages, but this hybrid was not based on African retentions, but rather that the Europeans simplified their language and borrowed a few Africanisms into the simplified form of their language, and taught the Africans this language. "In other words, they did not even want to acknowledge that the Africans had languages in the first place. This "Pidgin Creole Theory", says this simplified form of the European language is a Pidgin, and this Pidgin language is basically a European invention, a baby-talk, and that the Europeans were the sole creators of Pidgin. So where the Portuguese had contact with Africans they developed a Portuguese Pidgin, where the Spanish had contact with Africans, they developed a Spanish Pidgin, where the French had contact, they developed a French Pidgin, where the Dutch had contact with Africans, they developed a Dutch Pidgin, and where the English had contact, they developed a English Pidgin.

This whole premise is that the Africans broke with their linguistic tradition, if they had one at all, and adopted a baby-talk, a simplified form of the European language as their mother tongue. After years of living in the colonial diaspora, exposed only to the hybrid or Pidgin languages, the Africans began to learn these hybrids as their mother tongue. By learning a Pidgin as your mother tongue, you are by definition speaking Creole. The difference between a Pidgin and a Creole, is that a Pidgin has no native speakers. If you're speaking a Pidgin, you're speaking a hybrid of one language that has come into contact with another. This hybrid serves as a Lingua Franca, a common language used between two people who cannot communicate with each other in their mother tongue. For example, if I speak Arabic and you speak Chinese, we cannot communicate with each other. But if we both speak French, then we can use French as a Lingua Franca and speak to each other. If instead we develop a synthesis, a hybrid of Chinese and Arabic, then that hybrid is a Pidgin. All pidgins are Lingua Francas. English is a today's diplomatic and commercial Lingua Franca." "The task given to school districts throughout the country, including the Oakland School District, is to teach the English language. Ebonics is not taught in the classroom, the child learns Ebonics in the home environment, and it is a barrier to the acquisition of English because it is structurally different. The task is to teach English to an Ebonics speaking child. The best person to teach a child English is someone who knows that child's language, so they can transition the child from Ebonics to English."

While the report does offer some cause for optimism regarding the status of women's sports on television, the weight of the evidence clearly suggests that women's sports is underreported and that what coverage does exist is inferior to that afforded men's sports.

—Anita L. De Frantz

2

Gender Stereotyping in Televised Sports *

INTRODUCTION

Television both shapes and reflects the attitudes of our society. National networks and local stations broadcast thousands of hours of sports coverage each year to millions of viewers. The way in which television covers, or fails to cover, women engaged in athletics affects the way in which female athletes are perceived and also tells us something about the status of women in our society.

The Amateur Athletic Foundation of Los Angeles has sponsored research on the topic of television coverage of women's sports with the hope that it will lead to a more informed discussion of the issues.

The study presented here analyzes the quantity and quality of women's sports coverage and compares it to the coverage of men's sports. It examines six weeks of local sports coverage on a Los Angeles television station during summer 1989; the "Final Four" of the 1989 NCAA women's and men's basketball tournaments; and the women's and men's singles, women's and men's doubles, and the mixed doubles of the 1989 U.S. Open tennis tournament.

Our major findings are summarized at the beginning of the report and are followed by several policy recommendations. An explanation of methodology, a more detailed discussion of each finding and an interpretive essay appear later in the report.

While the report does offer some cause for optimism regarding the status of women's sports on television, the weight of the evidence clearly suggests that women's sports is under-reported and that what coverage does exist is inferior to that afforded men's sports.

Sport is an important part of the human experience. Television is a powerful medium. Women and girls comprise a majority of our population. Their experience in sports should be reported and reported accurately. Broadcasters who fail to do so fail in their professional responsibility.

---

*Co-Investigators: Margaret Carlisle Duncan, Ph.D., University of Wisconsin, Milwaukee; Michael A. Messner, Ph.D., University of Southern California; Linda Williams, Ph.D.; Kerry Jensen, Research Assistant, University of Southern California. Edited by Wayne Wilson, Ph.D., Amateur Athletic Foundation of Los Angeles. Sponsored by The Amateur Athletic Foundation of Los Angeles, August 1990.

This report, "Gender Stereotyping in Televised Sports," identifies problems with the way that the broadcasters we studied treated women's sports and it suggests solutions. Although this study did not examine every national network, all of the networks and their local affiliates we can learn from it. We may debate the solutions, but there is no denying the fundamental finding of the study: The television programs that we examined did not cover women's sports as well as they covered men's sports. This inequity is unfair. It is wrong. It can be changed and it must be changed.

Anita L. DeFrantz, President, Amateur Athletic Foundation of Los Angeles

1. SUMMARY OF FINDINGS

A. Televised Sports News: Women Are Humorous Sex Objects in the Stands, but Missing as Athletes

Women's sports were underreported and underrepresented in the six weeks of television sports news sampled in the study. Men's sports received 92% of the air time, women's sports 5%, and gender neutral topics 3%.

The television sports news did focus regularly on women, but rarely on women athletes. More common were portrayals of women as comical targets of the newscasters' jokes and/or as sexual objects (e.g., women spectators in bikinis).

B. Women's and Men's Basketball: Significant Differences in the Quality of Technical Production Tend to Trivialize the Women's Games, While Framing Men's Games as Dramatic Spectacles of Historic Significance

The quality of production, camera work, editing and sound in men's basketball were superior to that of women's games.

Slow-motion instant replays were utilized more often in men's basketball games (18/game) than in women's games (12.7/ game). Replays in men's games were more likely to be shown from more than one angle and to be accompanied by on-screen graphics.

Viewers of men's basketball games were more often informed of relevant statistics than in women's games. In men's games, there was an average of 24.3 on-screen graphic statistics and 33.3 verbal statistics, for a total average of 57.6 statistics per game. In the women's games, there was an average of 9.3 graphic on-screen statistics, 29 verbal statistics, for a total average of 38.3 statistics per game.

The network-produced openings which introduce events, often revealed a marked difference in how men's and women's events were framed. Men's basketball contests were framed as dramatic spectacles of historic import. By contrast, women's basketball contests were given the feel of neighborhood pickup games.

C. Tennis and Basketball: Women Players Constantly Are "Marked" Verbally and Visually, and Are Verbally Infantilized. Male Athletes of Color Share Some of this Infantilization

Gender was verbally, visually and graphically marked (e.g., "Women's National Championship") an average of nearly 60 times per game in women's basketball, and never was marked in men's games (which would be referred to, for instance, as "The National Championship Game").

Women athletes frequently were referred to as "girls" and "young ladies." Men athletes, never referred to as "boys," usually were called "men," "young men" and "young fellas."

In the tennis commentary, women athletes were called by only their first names 52.7% of the time, while men were referred to by only their first names 7.8% of the time.

In basketball, first name only descriptions by commentators were patterned along lines of race as well as gender. Women athletes were referred to by first name 31 times, men 19 times. Among the men, all 19 instances of first-name use occurred in discussing men of color. First names only never were used in discussions of white male basketball players.

Commentators' use of martial metaphors and power descriptors was more frequent in men's basketball (82 descriptors) than in women's basketball (28 descriptors), and more frequent in men's tennis (34) than women's tennis (17).

Commentators' verbal attributions of strength and weakness for men and women athletes contrasted sharply. In discussing men tennis players, commentators used a total of 146 descriptors suggesting strength, and 38 descriptors suggesting weakness (a strength/weakness ratio of 3.84/1). Attributions of strength and weakness for women tennis players totaled 95 and 103 (for a ratio of 0.92/1). In basketball, there was a similar pattern. Men's attributions of strength and weakness totaled 59 and 10 (5.9/1 ratio), while women's totaled 51 and 24 (2.1/1 ratio).

D. Less Overt Gender Stereotyping Exists in Basketball and Tennis Commentary, When Compared with Past Studies

Through the televised sports news was clearly biased against women, in basketball and tennis coverage there was very little of the overtly sexist language, sexualization and/or devaluation of women athletes that existed in the recent past. In fact, there appeared to be conscious efforts by some commentators to move toward non-sexist reporting of women's sports.

II. POLICY RECOMMENDATIONS IMPLIED BY FINDINGS

Televised sports news should provide more coverage of existing women's sports.

Televised sports news coverage of women's sports should include visual as well as verbal coverage in proportions that are roughly equivalent to the coverage of men's sports. Viewers should be able to hear about and see women's sports on the news.

Sports broadcasters should cease the sexist practice of focusing on female spectators as sexualized comic relief.

Television networks should commit themselves to more equal amounts of coverage of women's events such as college basketball. Regular season games should be aired regularly.

Television networks should commit themselves to equal quality of coverage of women's athletic events. The amount of resources and technical and production quality should be equivalent in the coverage of men's and women's sports.

Women athletes should be called "women" or "young women," just as men athletes are called "men" and "young men." Announcers should stop referring to adult female athletes as "girls" just as they avoid referring to adult male athletes as "boys."

Commentators should consciously adopt a standard usage of first and last names and it should be applied equally to men and women athletes and athletes of all races.

When gender marking is necessary for clarity, it should be done in ways that are symmetrical and equivalent for women's and men's events. If announcers use phrases such as "women's game" and "women's national championship," then they also should refer to gender when discussing men's sport (e.g., men's NCAA final, smartest player in men's tennis, etc.). The same symmetry should apply to the use of graphics.

Commentators should increase their use of strength descriptors when announcing women's sports. They should reduce the use of descriptors implying weakness in women's sports.

I realize now that my parents did not understand racism any better than we did. My siblings and I were constantly asked, "What color are you?" and "What do you consider yourself?"

—Ana Class-Rivera

3

Through Boricua Eyes

by Ana Class-Rivera

There is a lifetime of memories intertwined in my head, positive juxtaposed with negative, island attached to mainland, Puerto Rican interfaced with North American, Spanish laced with English, blended to Spanglish and so on.

For me it all began on the island, a lush tropical haven of childhood pranks and dreams. We lived on a small farm which lay nestled within the hills of Morovis. It was a place of safety, warmth, family and community. It was, also, a place of racial equality, although that realization came much later. As I reminisce about my childhood, I always remember those cherished friends with faces that come in all different colors. Yet there was no significance attached to that difference. We were all "Boricuas."

Indeed, our survival in our beloved paradise was not predicated on racial concerns but on finances. We had none. My father and mother had each obtained only a fourth grade education. Although they both loved learning, education for them was unattainable. Therefore, they were condemned to the meager existence of those without privilege and access. My father cut sugar cane. He labored in the treacherous heat from dawn to dusk, garnering minimal wages for his heroic efforts. My mother cared for the six children, who were born on the island without any modern conveniences. It seemed the harder they both worked, the less money they had.

Eventually, they both began to believe the stories which permeated our village about the vast wealth and opportunity in the land of the skyscrapers. In a classic leapfrog effect, my paternal grandparents and some uncles and aunts came first. My father followed. He worked as a laborer and saved enough money to send for my mother and all six children. I still remember the plane trip here. It was filled with turbulence, perhaps a portent of things to come.

We settled in Jersey City, New Jersey simply because our paternal relatives had settled there. Of course, their selection was based on availability of employment. Those lacking access to education clearly lack economic power and, ultimately, power of choice. The ability to plan and prepare adequately is, also, nonexistent (as we soon realized).

Our first winter on the mainland, the winter of 1960, was brutal. Our tropical clothing offered minimal protection against the cold and snow. It was difficult enough having to actually learn to walk up and down the stairs since all of the homes in our village were on ground level. Walking on snow and ice required abilities which took me several years to master. Our collective immune systems were unprepared to face drastic climatic changes. Our home was fraught with illness. Indeed, I spent my first Christmas season at the hospital. Kind neighbors and desperate resilience enabled us to survive.

A factor which proved more destructive than illness was the racism in the Catholic schools we attended. My mother insisted on availing us of the best possible education. (To obtain the necessary money, she would babysit up to five children, in addition to her own—which now numbered nine.) However, our private schooling came at a price—racism. The prejudice was particularly virulent, coming from children. I did not know it was racism then. I only knew we were somehow different. The most hurtful was the absence of touch, as if we were somehow repulsive. There were two sisters who would rub saliva on their arms if African American children or we Puerto Ricans touched them. How painfully frightening this level of hatred! I was only eight years old, but I knew then that there was something intensely flawed in our new country.

The inability to speak English, to understand and be understood, exacerbated the frustration. Moreover, Spanish was openly discouraged at school. My siblings and I cried every day. We tormented our mother by begging her to return to the island. She placated us gently, knowing well that returning was economically impossible. Almost instinctively, we resolved to learn the language and culture as we clung to our own reality. Ironically, I remember being constantly told "you are in America now, so speak English!", yet there was no one who would take the time to teach us English. The message implied that somehow we knew English, but blatantly were refusing to speak it. Also, we were born American citizens. Thus, the notion of "being in America now" suggested that our citizenship was of a second-class nature.

I realize now that my parents did not understand racism any better than we did. My siblings and I were constantly asked "what color are you?" and "what do you consider yourself?". We would go home and ask our mother what this meant. She always replied "that sounds like foolishness, don't respond...". It was actually years later, while in high school, that I began to realize the magnitude of the racial schism existing in this society. Although my complexion is fair, the harsh rejection which my siblings and I initially faced prevented me from defining myself within the parameters of this society. Rather, my siblings and I vehemently clung to our self-definition as Puerto Rican.

By the seventh grade, I had acquired some mastery of the English language. I had spent countless hours in the Jersey City Public Library, reading books ad infinitum. This had enhanced my vocabulary and expanded my natural curiosity. My progress was reflected in my schoolwork. However, I soon learned that even when I excelled, I could be invalidated and humiliated. My teacher accused me of cheating on a test, although my seat was directly in front of her desk and the other students sat behind me. I was offended because I took genuine pride in my own accomplishments and never cheated. The teacher held fast to her views and never apologized to me.

Perhaps more profound is the impact that these experiences have had on how we view others. We have not been encouraged to attempt assimilation and engage in disparaging the immigrants that have arrived after we did. Nor have we engaged in treating persons endowed with high levels of melanin as pariahs.

At long last, the time for high school arrived. This educational experience was more humane. Although the environment was certainly not bias-free, I was able to navigate it with some support. My guidance counselor took a special interest in me. She provided me with the opportunity to join the Upward Bound Program and to work part time for an insurance company. Some of my teachers were encouraging, as well. My English teacher, Mrs. Pinkham, helped me with my pronunciation, although I never did perfect the American English accent. I was inducted into the National Honor Society and ranked second in my high school graduating class.

Despite my academic success, college was not in my plans. Our family's economic situation was still tenuous. My oldest sister had gotten married and I had been catapulted to the role of eldest sibling. I felt it was my duty to work and contribute financially. In sync with the times, I aspired to employment as a secretary. However, our formidable principal, Dr. Margaret Finn, had other ideas. She literally locked me in her office until I completed a college application. Apparently, she found fear to be an excellent motivator. It worked. It was the only college application which I completed. I was accepted to St. Peter's College through the newly created Educational Opportunity Fund Program.

My parents were proud and supportive. I was the first in my immediate family and my paternal family to attend college. Eventually, other siblings, cousins and even neighbors followed in my footsteps. I went on to obtain a Masters degree and I now work in an Educational Opportunity Fund Program at a New Jersey University. Providing assistance and opportunities to youngsters with backgrounds parallel to mine strengthens my sense of purpose.

While the causes and solutions to juvenile crime are many, they all begin with adults. Each of us has the responsibility to do something to prevent our children from doing harm to themselves and to others.

—Hillary Rodham Clinton

4

Adults Can Combat Juvenile Crime

by Hillary R. Clinton

A few Sundays ago, a friend and I were walking through one of Washington's residential neighborhoods when we happened upon a little girl selling lemonade from a homemade stand in front of her house. We bought two cups—for 5 cents apiece.

"How's business?" I asked the little girl.

"It's great," she said. "You're my first customers ever."

The girl couldn't have been more than 5 or 6, but there she was, renewing that time-honored (and vanishing) tradition of American children: spending a hot summer afternoon peddling lemonade to thirsty adults and taking pride in doing something all by herself. My visit with the little girl brought back memories of the ways my brothers and I spent summer days while we were growing up.

We were blessed to live in a community that provided lots of summer activities for children. School cafeterias and playgrounds were open in the morning for arts and crafts projects and vigorous games of scatterball and kickball. Teen-agers hired by the recreational district ran these programs, and all during grade school, I dreamed of becoming one of those supervisors and having a whistle of my own.

Finally, when I turned 13, I was eligible to apply for a position. It was my first real job besides baby-sitting. I had to be interviewed by Mr. O.K. Wilson, a former coach, who ran the summer activities. I can still remember his questions about whether I would take good care of the equipment I'd be given. I swore to guard those bats, balls and board games with my life.

So I was hired. The only trouble with my assignment was that the school was about 2 miles from my home. My mother didn't drive at the time, which meant I had to get to and from work by bike. Worse, I had to carry my equipment with me.

First, I tried balancing the bag on my bike. That was a no go. Then, I put the bag in our old red wagon and tied the handle to my bike seat. I quickly discovered that I couldn't steer. So I ended up walking and pulling the wagon behind me. Finally, I arrived at the playground, which was filled with kids who wanted to climb on my lap, challenge me to endless rounds of jacks or checkers, or beg me to join in games of volleyball. (In these games, the ball rarely cleared the net.)

After lunch, my brothers and I headed for the local swimming pool. I hung out there with my friends for hours, swimming, gossiping and trying to catch the lifeguards' attention. The pool emptied out by closing time because we all had to be home for dinner. I had to set the table and help my mom. After dinner, we were out the door again to play until dark.

Thinking back on those summers past, I realize that our days were filled with activities organized by a whole community of caring adults and teenagers. Too many kids today don't have that help. Instead, they have too much free time and too little supervision. It's a situation that often leads to trouble.

That's why I'm heartened to see efforts in some of our communities that provide our children with productive and safe outlets for their energies.

Under Mayor Bob Lanier, the city of Houston has started soccer leagues and golf instruction for kids, built parks and playgrounds, and supported a variety of youth programs.

Curfews can also be an effective tool for keeping our children safe, especially when they are part of a larger strategy of programs for young people. Two years ago in New Orleans, Mayor Marc Morial declared a dusk-to-dawn curfew for children under 17. Curfew violators are sent to centers staffed by counselors, law enforcement officers, and religious and medical professionals. There, the children and their parents (who are required to meet their children at the center) are counseled about the curfew violation. The counselors help get parents and children to talk to each other more directly about their problems.

After the first year of the curfew—part of a comprehensive effort to combat juvenile crime that included more summer recreation programs and new summer jobs for young people—youth crime dropped by 27 percent during the hours it was in effect.

While the causes and solutions to juvenile crime are many, they all begin with adults. Each of us has the responsibility to do something to prevent our children from doing harm to themselves and to others.

With hot summer days now upon us, maybe we can come up with some new ways to recreate the secure, fun and creative environment my brothers and I and so many of our peers enjoyed during our childhood. Our kids deserve nothing less.

As with the criminal justice system, Special Education appears to be "a dumping ground" for minorities.

—Steven Agbenyega and
Joseph Jiggetts

5

Minority Over-Enrollment and Special Education

by Steven Agbenyega and Joseph Jiggetts

THE CONTINUING DISPROPORTIONATE MINORITY ENROLLMENT IN SPECIAL EDUCATION

Minority children, especially African-American children, (boys in particular) continue to be enrolled in disproportionate numbers in Special Education programs. Census projections of public school enrollments show that, by the year 2000, minority enrollments in the United States will be between 40% and 60% of the public school population. African-American students alone will represent the majority in over 80% of the schools. As with the criminal justice system, Special Education appears to be "a dumping ground" for minorities. Minority children are often labeled as "trouble-makers and disrupters of classroom decorum."

Children from minority groups often attend poor schools. Their medical, psychological, and social dysfunctions are not properly diagnosed or evaluated. They are frequently placed into Special Education programs because of culturally-biased IQ tests or testing criteria which have no immediate validity to ecological and intervening environmental experiences among minority children.

US News & World Report (13 December 1993, p. 48) characterizes IQ scores and testing criteria in this way:

> Subjective testing criteria, that rely on funding formulas and identification procedures that funnel ever greater numbers of children into special programs each year and that, in state after state, include disproportionately high numbers of black school children. The system has ballooned into more than a $30 billion-a-year industry, and the costs are climbing. More troubling, nearly 40 years after *Brown v. Topeka (Kansas) Board of Education*…Americans continue to pay for and send their children to classrooms that are often separate and unequal.

There are many reasons why so many minority children (particularly African-American and Latino children) are enrolled in Special Education:

- Ineffective oversight and lax enforcement by the Office of Civil Rights of the Department of Education. There has been only one enforcement success out of 10,147 cases which have gone before this office since 1987—a success rate of 0.000098551296% (*US News & World Report*, 13 December 1993, p. 46)

279

- The immigrant influx into high density urban environments where placements into Special Education are already a problem.
- High fertility ratios of immigrant women, African-American and Latino women.
- The balanced budget movement in Congress, however attractive to taxpayers, has tended to freeze or dismantle important social service programs.
- Self-perpetuating Special Education bureaucracies which seek to maintain their own politico-economic interests and which show an inclination to support increasing placements of African-American, Latin-American and immigrant children into Special Education because it benefits their economic interests; and, finally,
- The absence of strong children's and minority parents' advocacy institutions to educate parents about alternatives to Special Education in placement, re-assessment, and "de-placement."

To be able to deal with these problems effectively, Congressional funding and oversight may have to assume all children's services as fixed costs just as Social Security services and entitlement for our senior citizens are guaranteed by the federal government. In the intermediate period of finding long-term solutions for this crisis, a national commission may have to evaluate the necessity of using present IQ tests as basis for placement in our public schools, weighing ecological, cultural, social, historic, and environmental factors against so-called "innate abilities" of children.

Kindergarten facilities and resources should be increased in urban areas to deal with the education of children from deficit-ridden economic and social environments, and to provide such children with educable/cultural reinforcers within their socio-cultural ecology, while relating these goals progressively with higher expectations into the larger society.

Teacher-training programs should be encouraged and funded with a focus on early intervention (birth to 3 years of age) and should address issues of poverty, bilingual education, multiculturalism, and problems related to drug-exposed young children having disabilities in order to prepare them for an inclusive school environment.

Above all, the Federal Freedom of Information ACT (FFOIA) should be applied rigorously to the Special Education bureaucracy, and to the US Department of Education, Office of Schools Survey and Office of Civil Rights. There must be a Congressionally-appointed non-partisan national body from universities and elsewhere to annually monitor the activities of the Office of Civil Rights (US Department of Education) and to assess compliance successes and failures, and to enable public discourse to correctly engage the problems of Special Education. Ultimately, in a free society an informed and engaged public is our guarantor to the resolution of Special Education problems. It is only then that minority school children can ever hope to believe that a system constructed for white children can benefit them too.

Some even believe that Asian Americans receive "too many special advantages."

6
Civil Rights Issues Facing Asian Americans

INTRODUCTION

In the spring of 1991 the *Wall Street Journal* and NBC News conducted a national poll of voters' opinions about a variety of social and economics issues. The poll revealed that the majority of American voters believe that Asian Americans[1] are not discriminated against in the United States. Some even believe that Asian Americans receive "too many special advantages."[2] The poll shows plainly that the general public is largely unaware of the problems Asian Americans confront. Considering the widely held image of Asian Americans as the "model minority," this is hardly surprising. Yet participants at the Civil Rights Commission's Roundtable Conferences in Houston, San Francisco, and New York[3] recounted numerous incidents of anti-Asian prejudice and discrimination. Their statements made evident that, contrary to the widespread belief captured in the *Wall Street Journal*/NBC News poll, Asian Americans encounter many discriminatory barriers to equal opportunity and full participation in our society.

Asian Americans do face widespread prejudice, discrimination, and barriers to equal opportunity. Asian Americans are frequently victims of racially motivated bigotry and violence; they face significant barriers to equal opportunity in education and employment; and they do not have equal access to a number of public services, including police protection, health care, and the court system.

ASIANS IN THE UNITED STATES: A BRIEF HISTORY

The first Asians to arrive in the United States in large numbers were the Chinese, who came to work on Hawaiian plantations by the 1840s and to the West Coast of the mainland start-

---

[1]The term Asian American is used in this report to refer to persons of Asian descent who are either citizens or intending citizens of the United States, or who plan to spend the rest of their lives in the United States.
[2]Michel McQueen, "Voters' Responses to Poll Disclose Huge Chasm Between Social Attitudes of Blacks and Whites," *Wall Street Journal,* May 17, 1991, p. A16.
[3]The Commission's Roundtable Conferences on Asian American Civil Rights Issues for the 1990s were held in Houston, TX, on May 27, 1989; in New York, NY, on June 23, 1989; and in San Francisco, CA, on July 29, 1989.

ing in the early 1850s to work in gold mines and later to help build the cross-country railroads. The Chinese were followed in the late 19th and early 20th centuries by Japanese and Filipinos and, in smaller numbers, by Koreans and Asian Indians. Restrictive immigration laws produced a 40-year hiatus in Asian immigration starting in the 1920s, but in 1965, when anti-Asian immigration restrictions were liberalized, a new wave of immigration began bringing people from Southeast Asia, China, Korea, the Philippines, and other Asian countries to the United States.

The history of Asian Americans in this country is replete with incidents of discrimination against them. Asian Americans experienced, at one time or another, discriminatory immigration and naturalization policies; discriminatory Federal, State, and local laws; discriminatory governmental treatment; considerable prejudice on the part of the general public; and outright violence. Not only was today's Asian American community shaped by historical forces, but today's civil rights issues need to be viewed in the context of past discrimination against Asian Americans.

NATURALIZATION AND IMMIGRATION LAWS

Throughout most of their history in this country Asians have been victimized by discriminatory naturalization and immigration laws. These laws have had the legacy of making Asian American newcomers feel unwelcome in their adopted country and have also been important in shaping the Asian American community as it exists today.

As this country became a nation, its founders sough to restrict eligibility for citizenship. In 1790 Congress passed a law limiting naturalization to "free white persons."[5] The law was modified in 1870, after the adoption of the 14th amendment, to include "aliens of African nativity and persons of African descent." At that time Congress considered and rejected extending naturalization rights to Asians,[6] thus making Asian immigrants the only racial group barred from naturalization.[7] Because the 14th amendment granted citizenship to all

---

[4]Asian American groups considered in this report are persons having origins in the Far East, Southeast Asia, and the Indian subcontinent. At times, the report also includes information about Pacific Islanders, but limited resources precluded a systematic investigation of the civil rights issues facing Pacific Islanders.

[5]U.S. Commission on Civil Rights, *The Tarnished Golden Door: Civil Rights Issues in Immigrations* (September 1980), p. 10 (hereafter cited as *The Tarnished Golden Door*).

[6]Roger Daniels, *Asian America: Chinese and Japanese in the United States Since 1850* (Seattle, WA: University of Washington Press, 1988), p. 43 (hereafter cited as *Asian America*).

[7]These laws were widely held to bar the naturalization of the Chinese. In 1922 the Supreme Court held that the naturalization bar applied to Japanese (Ozawa v. United States, 260 U.S. 178 (1922)). The following year, the Supreme Court held that East Indians were also barred from naturalization, because the term "white" did not include all Caucasians (United States v. Thind, 261 U.S. 204 (1923)).

[8]*The Tarnished Golden Door,* p. 10.

[9]Pub. L. No. 82–414, 66 Stat. 163 (1952).

[10]Don Teruo Hata, Jr., and Nadine Ishitani Hata, "Run Out and Ripped Off: A Legacy of Discrimination," *Civil Rights Digest,* vol.9, no.1 (Fall 1976), p. 10 (hereafter cited as "Run Out and Ripped Off").

persons born in the United States, however, the American-born children of Asian immigrants were citizens. Filipinos and Asian Indians were granted eligibility for naturalization in 1946,[8] but it was not until 1952, with the McCarran-Walter Act,[9] that naturalization eligibility was extended to all races.[10] Thus, through most of this country's history, immigrant Asians were ineligible to become citizens.

SOME SOLUTIONS AND RECOMMENDATIONS

This report presents the results of an investigation into the civil rights issues facing Asian Americans that was undertaken as followup to the commision's 1989 Asian Roundtable Conferences. Contrary to the popular perception that Asian Americans have overcome discriminatory barriers, Asian Americans still face widespread prejudice, discrimination, and denials of equal opportunity. In addition, many Asian Americans, particularly those who are immigrants, are deprived of equal access to public services, including police protection, education, health care, and judicial system.

Several factors contribute to the civil rights problems facing today's Asian Americans. First, Asian Americans are the victims of stereotypes that are widely held among the general public. These stereotypes deprive Asian Americans of their individuality and humanity in the public's perception and often foster prejudice against Asian Americans. The "model minority" stereotype, the often-repeated contention that Asian Americans have overcome all barriers facing them and they are a singularly successful minority group, is perhaps the most damaging of these stereotypes. This stereotype leads Federal, State, and local agencies to overlook the problems facing Asian Americans, and it often causes resentment of Asian Americans within the general public.

Second, many Asian Americans, particularly immigrants, face significant cultural and linguistic barriers that prevent them from receiving equal access to public services and from participating fully in the American political process. Many Asian American immigrants arrive in the United States with minimal facility in the English language and with little familiarity with American culture and the workings of American society. There has been a widespread failure of government at all levels and of the Nation's public schools to provide for the needs of immigrant Asian Americans. Such basic needs as interpretive services to help limited-English-proficient Asian Americans in their dealings with government agencies, culturally appropriate medical care, bilingual/English as a Second Language education, and information about available public services are largely unmet.

A third, but equally important, problem confronting Asian Americans today is a lack of political representation and an inability to use the political process effectively. Asian Americans face many barriers to participation in the political process, in addition to the simple fact that many Asian Americans are not yet citizens and hence ineligible to vote. Although some Asian Americans are politically active, the large majority have very little access to political power. This lack of political empowerment leads the political leadership of the United States to overlook and sometimes ignore the needs and concerns of Asian Americans. It also leads to a failure of the political leadership to make addressing Asian American issues a national priority.

This chapter lays out specific conclusions and recommendations. Many of the civil rights issues facing Asian Americans also confront other minority groups. For example, issues related to the rights of language minorities are equally important for other language-minority groups. Thus, many of our conclusions with respect to violations of Asian Americans' civil rights and our recommendations for enhancing the protection of their civil rights are applicable to other minority groups as well.

Discussion Questions
Part VI: Communication and Core Curriculum Issues

1. Discuss the role of racism in communication, i.e., print, radio, or television media.

2. In the remaining blank pages of the textbook, choose an article from your local newspaper and then analyze it as it relates to issues of race, class, or gender.

References

Adair, Margot & Howell, Sharon. To Equalize Power Among Us. Adapted from the pamphlet, *Breaking Old Patterns Weaving New Ties: Alliance Building*, @ Tools for Change, PO # 1414 S, San Francisco, Calif. 94114. Permission granted by the authors.

Adair, Margot. Common Behavioral Patterns that Perpetuate Relations of Domination. Permission granted by the author.

Adam, Barry. *The Survival of Domination: Inferiorization and Everyday Life*. Permission granted by the author.

Agbenyega, Steven, Jiggetts, Joseph. Black Boys and Special Education. Permission granted by the authors.

Barnes-Schwartz, Arnie. Black Daughter, White Father. Permission granted by the author.

Bowman, Meg. Why We Burn: Sexism Exorcised. Originally printed in *Dramatic Readings on Feminist Issues*, Vol. I, Hot Flash Press, 64–69, 1988 and *Women without Superstition*, Annie Laurie Gaylor, ed., FFRE, 525–530, 1997. Permission granted by the author.

Connel, Bob, Masculinity, Violence and War. Permission granted by Smyrna Press.

Class-Rivera, Ana. Through Boricua Eyes. Permission granted by the author.

Clinton, Hillary Rodham. Reprinted by permission of Creators Syndicate, 5777 W. Century Blvd., Suite 700, Los Angeles, Calif. 90045.

Cohen, Lawrence. © 1993 by Lawrence Cohen. Reprinted by permission of the author.

DeFrantz, Anita L. Gender Stereotyping in Televised Sports, August 1990, 1–5. © 1990 by AAFLA. Reprinted by permission of The Amateur Athletic Foundation of Los Angeles.

Ehrenreich, Barbara. Welfare is Not a Lap of Luxury. Reprinted by permission of the author.

Flournoy, Craig. Federally Subsidized Housing in America: Still Separate and Unequal. U.S. Commission on Civil Rights.

Galvin, Maryanne and Read, Donald D. Combatting Racism and Sexism in Health Education. This article is reprinted with permission of *The Journal of Health Education,* March/April 1983, 10–14. *Journal of Health Education* is a publication of the American Alliance for Health, Physical Education, Recreation and Dance, 1900 Association Drive, Reston, Virginia 22091.

Gilkeson, Dean. Daddy, Why is Your Penis Different from Mine?. Mentor Magazine, Fall 1992, 11–14.

Greaves, David Mark. Ebonics: Echoes of the Drum. Reprinted by permission of *For Our Times*, February 1997.

Grune, Joy Anne. Pay Equity is a Necessary REmed for Wage Discrimination. From *Comparable Worth: Issue for the 80's. A Consultation of the U.S. Commission on Civil Rights*, June 6–7, 1984, Vol. 1, 165–173. Reprinted by permission of the U.S. Commission on Civil Rights, Washington, D.C. 20425.

Heasley, Robert. Some Effects of Sexims on Men. Reprinted by permission of the author. Material was adapted from an article written by John Irwin entitled "The Liberation of Males," published by Rational Island Publishers, Seattle Washington.

Keen, Sam. The Rite of Work: The Economic Man. Reprinted by permission of the author.

Lee, Charles. "Evidence of Environmental Racism. Reprinted by permission of *Sojourners,* 2401 Fifteenth St., N.W., Washington, D.C. 20009.

MacKinnon, Catharine A. Sex and Violence: A Perspective. Reprinted by permission of the author.

McClean, Vernon. Black Past, Black Present. Copyright 1997 by the New York Times Company. Reprinted by Permission.

McClean, Vernon. No More "Jewels in the Crown." Copyright 1995 by The New York Times Company. Reprinted by Permission.

McClean, Vernon. "Take our Daughters"? Always Have. Copyright 1996 by The New York Times Company. Reprinted by Permission.

McQuaide, Sharon and Ehrenreich, John. IDS: The Shameful Disease. Reprinted by permission of the authors from The Social Casework: *The Journal of Contemporary Social Work*, April 1985, pp. 247–249.

Mollenkott, Virginia Ramey. Coping with Biblical Fundamentalism: An Interpersonal Approach. *Clergy and Laity Concerned Report,* November 1987, 62–70. Reprinted by permission of the author.

NAAFA. Size Discrimination: Its Links to Other 'Isms' as a Civil Rights Issue and Myths about Fat People. Reprinted by permission of the National Association to Advance Fat Acceptance.

National Black Women's Health Project. Taking the Home Out of Homophobia: Black Lesbian Health. Permission granted by NBWHP.

Oswald, Roy M. The Men's Movement: Challenge to the Church's Ministry, from Congregations, September–October 1992, 7–10. Reprinted by permission of the Alban Institute, Washington, D.C.

Pharr, Suzanne. Why Rightwing Christians Should Fear Lesbians and Gay Men. *Transformation,* July/August 1991. Reprinted by permission from the author.

Polish American Congress. Things to do During National Polish American Heritage Month. Reprinted from the 1992 Convention Resolution Committee Report of the Polish American Congress.

Polish American Congress. The 1992 Convention Resolution Committee Report of the Polish American Congress.

Rochlin, M. The Heterosexual Questionnaire. *Changing Men*, Spring 1982.

Rockwell, Paul. Angry White guys for Affirmative Action. Reprinted by permission of the Oakland Men's Project. Copyright, Paul Rockwell, 1996.

Steinem, Gloria. On Family Values: If Moral Decay is the Question, is a Feminist Ethnic the Answer? From the Ms Magazine, September 1987, 57–58, 62–63. Reprinted by permission of the author.

Suaree, Octovio de la. Cubans in the United States. Permission granted by the author.

U.S. Commission on Civil Rights. Civil Rights Issues Facing Asian Americans in the 1990's. Washington, DC 20425

Wallerstein, Edward. Circumcision: An American Health Fallacy? © 1980. Reprinted by permission of Springer Publishing Company, Inc., New York 10012. Used by permission.

Wiley III, Ed. & Conciatore, Jacqueline. Solutions to Black Male Prison Crisis: Elusive and Difficult. Reprinted by permission from Black Issues in Higher Education. September 28, 1989.

About the Editor

Dr. Vernon McClean, the editor of Solutions for the Millennium, is Professor of African-American and Caribbean Studies at the William Paterson University of New Jersey, where he was the founder of that department and its chairperson for over a decade.

An activist as well as scholar, Dr. McClean has sought to integrate African-American Studies and Women's Studies, helping to propose and develop the very popular course "Racism and Sexism in the United States," now required of all students at the University.

As a pioneer in educating students and others about the problems of, and solutions to, racism and sexism for the new millennium, Dr. McClean has also served as a consultant to area school districts regarding curricula changes pertaining to issues of race, class, and gender.

Dr. McClean is the author of numerous articles and has contributed chapters to several books. He has written for *The New York Times, The Chronicle of Higher Education, The Activist Men's Journal, The Western Journal of Black Studies, The Society for the Psychological Study of Men and Masculinity*, and many other publications. He is also a guest columnist or contributing columnist for several regional and local newspapers in the Northeast.

A Fulbright Scholar, Dr. McClean has done post-graduate work at Yale University, Johns Hopkins University, and the University of Michigan.